Argentina and the Failure of Democracy

Argentina and the Failure of Democracy

Conflict among Political Elites

1904–1955

Peter H. Smith

The University of Wisconsin Press

Published 1974
The University of Wisconsin Press
Box 1379, Madison, Wisconsin 53701

The University of Wisconsin Press, Ltd.
70 Great Russell Street, London

First printing

Printed in the United States of America

For LC CIP information see the colophon
ISBN 0-299-06600-2

for Mary

Contents

List of Figures

List of Tables

Acknowledgments

The writing of this book has left me with countless personal and professional obligations, which I can only begin to acknowledge here. Grants for the research have come from varied sources: the American Philosophical Society, the Graduate School of the University of Wisconsin at Madison, and the Ibero-American Studies Program at the same institution. The Center for Latin American Studies at the University of California, Berkeley, provided office space and other facilities during the summer of 1969. At the Institute for Advanced Study in Princeton, where I was a Visiting Member in 1972-73, I was able to compose a manuscript under optimal working conditions.

Courteous assistance has been rendered by many librarians, especially the staffs at the Biblioteca del Congreso Nacional, the Jockey Club, and the Sociedad Rural Argentina, all in Buenos Aires; the Bancroft Library, at the University of California; and the Memorial Library, at the University of Wisconsin.

I am profoundly grateful to the student assistants at Wisconsin who have collaborated on this project at one time or another. Gary Linn, Valerie Poellnitz, Joette Reuter, and Margaret Schwertfeger helped compile some of the data. James Bauknecht and Jeanne Schroeder worked on various phases of the study, especially the data coding. Natalie Aikins did the keypunching, and David R. Olson handled technical aspects of the computer programming. Geraldine Booth assisted with proofreading and indexing.

I am indebted to the University of Wisconsin Cartographic Laboratory for drafting the figures in my book.

Professional colleagues in Argentina and this country, too numerous to mention *in toto*, have given invaluable advice and encouragement. Richard Hartwig and Joseph Tulchin let me use some data from their own research. Samuel L. Baily, Atilio Borón, Lee C. Fennell, Tulio Halperín Donghi, Peter G. Snow, Carl Solberg, Richard J. Walter, and Peter Winn have been kind enough to read through early drafts, and their thoughtful critiques have prompted me to make numerous and extensive revisions in the manuscript—although I have not been able to incorporate all of their suggestions, and on some points we have agreed to disagree. The errors that remain are mine alone.

P. H. S.

Madison, Wisconsin
May 1974

Introduction

Argentina underwent a fundamental, and in some ways perplexing, process of political transition during the first half of the twentieth century. A genteel, landed aristocracy monopolized power until 1912, when electoral reform—put through by the aristocracy itself—brought forth an era of relatively open competition. This experiment in democracy lasted until 1930,[1] when the army perpetrated a coup and installed itself as a dominant factor in Argentine politics. In the early 1940s started yet another development: the emergence of Juan D. Perón, himself a military man, as supreme leader of a populist authoritarian mass movement. Since his overthrow in 1955 the armed forces have, with interruptions, continued their political hegemony.

This pattern of change has baffled many observers because it contradicts some cherished precepts in contemporary social science. Whereas most theories envision democratic government as the culmination of political development, Argentina passed through a democratic period and then moved on to dictatorial forms. Furthermore, this took place despite the country's compliance with many of the alleged socioeconomic requisites for democratic growth.[2] These anomalies, in one way or another, have shaped the basic

1. Throughout this study I shall follow Juan J. Linz's definition of *democracy* as a government which "supplies regular constitutional opportunities for peaceful competition for political power (and not just a share of it) to different groups without excluding any significant sector of the population by force." By contrast *authoritarianism* refers to "political systems with limited, not responsible, political pluralism; without elaborate and guiding ideology (but with distinctive mentalities); without intensive nor extensive political mobilization (except at some points in their development); and in which a leader (or occasionally a small group) exercises power within formally ill-defined limits but actually quite predictable ones." Linz, "An Authoritarian Regime: Spain," in Erik Allardt and Stein Rokkan, eds., *Mass Politics: Studies in Political Sociology* (New York, 1970), pp. 254-55. I do not think that Argentina has ever experienced *totalitarianism* in any strict sense of the term, not even during the late Perón regime (discussed below, especially in Chapter 6), so I shall make no reference to that concept.

2. Consult Seymour Martin Lipset, *Political Man: The Social Bases of Politics* (Gar-

question which has pervaded so much writing on the history and politics of this society: What happened to politics in Argentina? What could have gone wrong?

One standard line of reasoning argues that profound and rapid socioeconomic transformation created pressures which, by their intensity and incompatibility, simply overwhelmed the political system. In modern argot, societal demands outstripped institutional capacity to moderate and channel conflict. According to this view, large-scale immigration, sudden growth, urbanization, and the onset of industrialization gave rise to social forces which have necessarily been locked in permanent struggle. It was not so much that politics failed; confronted by these massive problems, the system never really had a chance.

Another kind of argument focuses upon the military as an institution. The creation of professional armed forces, it is held, imbued officers with such militaristic and antidemocratic values that, almost inevitably, they used their growing power to overthrow civilian governments in 1930, 1943, 1955, 1962, and 1966. Logically enough, this proposition has helped stimulate a vast body of literature on the history and organization of Argentina's military.

Without denying the significance of rapid societal change and military professionalization, however, I find these interpretations a bit deterministic. Other polities have managed to withstand great social pressures and survive. As for the armed forces, I agree with Samuel P. Huntington: "The most important causes of military intervention in politics are not military but political and reflect not the social and organizational characteristics of the military establishment but the political and institutional structures of the society. Military explanations do not explain military interventions."[3]

In order to comprehend processes of change in Argentina, we therefore need to understand the sources of political weakness, particularly in the country's constitutional system—and it is to this end that I address this book. This perspective leads me to examine the neglected side of several coins. Instead of concentrating on the victors, as historians commonly do, I quite self-consciously deal with the losers. My primary concern is not with the gaining of power or success; it lies with the dynamics of failure and decay. My research also encroaches on the area of civil-military relations, but fastens

den City, N.Y., 1963), Ch. 2, "Economic Development and Democracy"; and Robert A. Dahl, *Polyarchy: Participation and Opposition* (New Haven and London, 1971), Ch. 5, and citations therein.

3. Samuel P. Huntington, *Political Order in Changing Societies* (New Haven and London, 1968), p. 194. K. H. Silvert has also stated that, in Argentina, military hegemony "is not so much a demonstration of military might as it is of civilian weakness." Silvert, "The Costs of Anti-Nationalism: Argentina," in Silvert, ed., *Expectant Peoples: Nationalism and Development* (New York, 1963), p. 354.

upon the civilian side of that relationship—and the sorts of situations which may have invited intervention.

Generally speaking, I intend to explore the conduct and character of elected leadership in Argentina. By this I do not mean the personal qualities of famous men and presidents, though such factors obviously have importance of their own. Rather, I am referring to regularities (and irregularities) in behavior among the leaders of a polity's constituent groups. Modes of interaction between elites comprise a basic characteristic of any political system, and they bear a direct connection to the means and capabilities for mediating and resolving social conflict.

These thoughts are not particularly original. Nor have they escaped the attention of specialists on Argentina.[4] In general, however, literature in this area has been impressionistic or polemical.[5] And much of the most rigorous work has focused on the social background of elites, rather than upon their interaction and behavior.[6]

As a means of confronting such issues, this book undertakes to analyze some basic developments in the Argentine Chamber of Deputies from 1904 through 1955. The time span, almost exactly half a century, provides extensive perspective on the overall sequences of political transition. As stated above, my central thematic concern stresses the formation, duration, and decay of democratic rule. Accordingly, the chronological coverage reaches back to the predemocratic era, in order to show how traditional political practices conditioned the establishment of Argentine democracy; it focuses upon the period of democratic government from 1916 to 1930; it includes the 1930s, when democratic precepts were distorted and adapted for nondemocratic goals; and to analyze the consequences of these trends, it stretches through the Peronist era, when populist authoritarianism brought the cycle of change to an end. In short, I view the transition from aristocracy through democracy to populism as a coherent and unified process which came to a climax in 1955—and which has significantly shaped the course of

4. Significantly enough, survey research has revealed a broad attitudinal consensus within the Argentine populace, leading Jeane Kirkpatrick to surmise that "the divisions that split parties, legislatures, cabinets, armed forces, unions, and related groups largely reflect elite rivalries and interpersonal conflict rather than mass opinion . . . . Argentina's most important problems are problems of political organization, problems deriving from the failure of institutions . . . to reflect and implement the agreement on goals that exists at the base of the society." Kirkpatrick, *Leader and Vanguard in Mass Society: A Study of Peronist Argentina* (Cambridge, Mass., and London, 1971), p. 231.

5. Notable exceptions to this rule are the passages in Dahl, *Polyarchy*, pp. 132-40; and the remarkable study by Guillermo A. O'Donnell, *Modernization and Bureaucratic-Authoritarianism: Studies in South American Politics* (Berkeley, Cal., 1973).

6. See José Luis de Imaz, *Los que mandan* (Buenos Aires, 1964); and Darío Cantón, *El parlamento argentino en épocas de cambio: 1889, 1916 y 1946* (Buenos Aires, 1966).

subsequent events. Moreover, I shall attempt to argue that this pattern of change is understandable: both the decline of democracy and the rise of Peronism bear logical relationships to their respective historical contexts. To deal with politics in Argentina, we need not search for villains, heroes, or apocalyptic explanations.

Throughout this formative half century, I shall confront three sets of questions relating to the Chamber of Deputies: (1) Who were the deputies? What were the common elements in social background and careers? (2) What issues did they fight about? What were the substantive dimensions of parliamentary conflict? (3) What were the predominant types of alignment? To what degree, for instance, did deputies vote on party lines—and what were the prevailing coalitions? By also seeing how elite interaction within the Chamber may or may not have stimulated responses from outside organizations, such as labor unions and the military, I hope to elucidate some fundamental aspects of the crucial problem of political transition.

This analytical strategy does not rest upon any assumptions about the role or importance of the Argentine Congress in making policy decisions. There is little doubt in my mind that ultimate power has, for the most part, resided in the Executive branch. At some times the Argentine Congress has exerted considerable influence on the uses of power, in a negative sort of way, but it has rarely initiated and approved legislation over strong presidential opposition.[7]

For the purposes of this study, the significance of the Chamber of Deputies lies precisely in its status as an intermediate institution. Being a representative assembly, elected by the voting populace, it permits the observation of a wide (if not complete) spectrum of the country's constituent groups. Almost by definition, deputies tend to be activists: as spokesmen and opinion-makers, they articulate the interests of their real and would-be followers and may in so doing offer policy alternatives. It is in this sense, not as omnipotent wielders of power, that Argentine deputies qualify for membership among the national political elites.[8]

In another sense, Congress offers some clues to the behavior and attitudes of people in high executive positions. Of the ten men who became constitutional presidents between 1904 and 1955, seven had previously served in the

7. See Lee C. Fennell, "Congress in the Argentine Political System: An Appraisal," and Peter Ranis, "Profile Variables among Argentine Legislators," both in Weston H. Agor, ed., *Latin American Legislatures: Their Role and Influence* (New York, 1971), pp. 139-71 and 173-257.

8. In abstract terms, I conceive of a political elite as a leadership group which controls at least a significant share of predominant political power. Despite their obvious lack of supreme authority, deputies constitute one of Argentina's national elites because of their important role within the (increasingly fragmented) power structure. Ranis, "Profile Variables," pp. 173-76.

Chamber of Deputies; two others had been in the Senate. As illustrated in Chapter 1, many members of the Cabinet were former congressmen too. The point is that a high proportion of the country's truly powerful political leaders passed through the Congress, particularly the Chamber of Deputies, and their attitudes and actions were bound to be affected by this experience.

Despite its weakness as a policy-maker, the Argentine Congress therefore possesses great significance in three respects: as a microcosmic representation of effectively competing forces in the national community, as an arena for the articulation of policy alternatives, and as a stepping-stone for men who went on to make executive decisions. Of course, these and other functions varied greatly over time (a subject to be taken up in Chapter 1). In general, however, the Chamber of Deputies offers an excellent opportunity for concentration on a crucial theme: the interaction of political elites.

There are methodological advantages too. Alignments on the 1,712 roll calls taken in the Chamber between 1904 and 1955 yield objective signs of individual and collective reaction to a wide variety of issues. They are subject to statistical manipulation. And most important of all, from a historical view, they permit the detection and analysis of behavioral trends over time. Accordingly, focus on the sequences and rates of change—as well as the type of change—will be a basic part of my approach.

The organization of this study bears straightforward correspondence to its character and purpose. Setting a context for the subsequent analysis, Chapter 1 traces general patterns of change in twentieth-century Argentine politics, with special reference to the Congress. Chapter 2 uses data on social background and career patterns to construct a typology of Argentine legislators and examine the composition of the Chamber over time. Chapter 3 concentrates on the variety and content of dimensions of roll-call voting. Utilizing the results of this analysis, Chapter 4 compares the explanatory power of four conceivable determinants of voting alignments: political party, social status, regional constituencies, and age. Chapter 5 proceeds to deal with party behavior and interparty coalitions. A concluding chapter then attempts to integrate these empirical findings on the Chamber of Deputies into a far-ranging, sometimes speculative interpretation of cleavages and crises in Argentine politics.

Methodological questions receive extensive treatment in two discursive appendices. Appendix A derives a dichotomous variable indicating whether or not individual deputies belonged to Argentina's aristocracy. Appendix B discusses procedures, decisions, and technical problems involved in handling the roll-call voting data, particularly in connection with my efforts to measure quantitative changes over time.[9]

9. Partly because of the vexing methodological problems, time-series analysis of legislative voting is relatively rare. One important study of this sort is Thomas B.

In order to support my own interpretations, and also to make the information available to other scholars, Appendix C gives the documentary location, the subject matter, and the mutual relationships of all the roll calls studied (through their respective loadings in rotated factor matrices).

As a result, this book has varied facets—it is part history, part methodology, part reference work. But my fundamental purpose is interpretive and should be so understood. Moreover, my conceptual focus is extremely general, and readers will see that the figures and tables in the text contain many subtleties, implications, and paradoxes which I have not taken the time or space to explore. I have been painting with a broad analytical brush.

Throughout my labors on this project, in fact, I have viewed it as complementary to my already published work on *Politics and Beef in Argentina*.[10] Covering much the same chronological period, my previous book attempts to mold generalizations about political transition in twentieth-century Argentina from detailed examination of conflicts connected with a single major issue—control of the beef industry. By contrast, this study approaches the same basic problem from a very different angle, seeking substantial conclusions from a simplified analysis of votes in many varied issue areas. Neither kind of book can be conclusive by itself; but between the two, I hope that some persistent trends in Argentina's politics have been uncovered.

I also hope that other scholars will take up where I leave off. There are many important questions about the Argentine Congress which I have touched barely or not at all. Some social scientists, such as Lee C. Fennell, have done much good and valuable research on these matters; but many further possibilities remain. For this reason I have deposited my computer cards and code books with the Data and Program Library Service at the University of Wisconsin—Madison, where they may be obtained upon request. No doubt my assistants and I have made some errors in tracing and coding approximately 330,000 bits of information, but having used and checked and double-checked the material, I believe such instances are very few. The data await further use.

Alexander, *Sectional Stress and Party Strength: A Study of Roll-Call Voting Patterns in the United States House of Representatives, 1836-1860* (Nashville, Tenn., 1967). See also Duncan MacRae, Jr., *Parliament, Parties, and Society in France, 1946-1958* (New York and London, 1967).

10. Peter H. Smith, *Politics and Beef in Argentina: Patterns of Conflict and Change* (New York and London, 1969).

Argentina and the Failure of Democracy

1
Society and Politics in Argentina

Political processes derive their ultimate importance from their impact upon, and place within, society at large. In some communities, politics commands a central role in the allocation of power, wealth, and prestige; in others, it performs a relatively marginal function. To gain perspective on the significance of politics in Argentina, this chapter offers a sketch of some patterns and changes in the relationship between the political system and its social context from the mid-nineteenth century to approximately 1955. Because of the specific purpose of this study, I shall also devote particular attention to the roles and functions of the national Chamber of Deputies.[1]

STRUGGLES OVER DEVELOPMENT

A full half century after the declaration of political independence from Spain, Argentina was a divided—and largely undeveloped—society. In 1869, the first national census found only 1.7 million people in a land of more than a million square miles.[2] Small-scale industries and trading communities continued to exist in the central and northwestern interior (La Rioja, Salta, Tucumán, and surrounding provinces) which had once provided commercial and other services for Spanish mining cities in what is now Bolivia. The coastal areas, in and around the province of Buenos Aires, had no such artisan base. Some ranchers produced hides and salted meat for export, and the city of Buenos Aires was growing into an active seaside port. But in general, the vast, rich pampas in the countryside were still unexploited. Largely inhabited

1. Some of the material in this chapter has been presented, from a somewhat different perspective, in my chapter on "Argentina: The Process of Modernization," in *Politics and Beef in Argentina: Patterns of Conflict and Change* (New York and London, 1969).
2. Gino Germani, *Estructura social de la Argentina: análisis estadístico* (Buenos Aires, 1955), p. [21].

by hostile Indians, these fertile lands would soon provide the resource for rapid agricultural expansion.

These regional economic disparities furnished the basis for the bitter political struggles which dominated nineteenth-century Argentina. At stake was control over the direction of national development. One faction in this conflict consisted of "unitarians," mainly from the province of Buenos Aires, who wanted to nationalize the city of Buenos Aires (then part of the province), extend political control over the rest of the country from the port city, break down internal barriers and open the doors to international trade. Another group was composed of "federalists" from the interior, who agreed on the desirability of nationalizing the city of Buenos Aires but who staunchly supported provincial sovereignty and wanted tariffs to protect their local industries. Third were "federalists" from the province of Buenos Aires who vigorously opposed nationalization of the city—since that would take away the province's monopoly on customs revenues—and who also advocated free trade in economics.[3]

The conflict took many years to resolve. In 1829 Juan Manuel de Rosas—a tough and energetic cattle rancher who could outride, outfight and outcurse his rugged gaucho followers—became the governor of Buenos Aires Province and began spreading autocratic rule over the whole of Argentina. Assisted by efficient spies and an ambitious wife, he appealed to popular masses with his charisma and favored *estancieros* (ranch owners) with his economic policies, thus furthering the formation of a landed aristocracy. Himself an ardent Buenos Aires federalist, Rosas laid the groundwork for eventual unification by his military campaigns against regional *caudillos*, his xenophobic nationalism, and his concentration of authority.

After Rosas fell in 1852, Justo José de Urquiza, an interior federalist, took the reins of power. One of his first acts was to call a convention which, in 1853, promulgated the country's constitution. Deeply influenced by the United States example and by the writings of Juan Bautista Alberdi, the document provided for a federal system of representative government. Presidents would be named for six-year terms by an electoral college, whose members would be chosen by popular vote. A bicameral Congress was set up, the lower house, the Chamber of Deputies, elected by direct vote and the upper house, the Senate, elected by provincial legislatures. In deference to federalist demands the provinces were given the right to establish their own governments, and all powers not specifically accorded to the national state were conceded to the local administrations—though this rule was sharply qualified by a pro-unitarian provision allowing the central government to

3. Miron Burgin, *The Economic Aspects of Argentine Federalism, 1820-1852* (Cambridge, Mass., 1946).

intervene in the provinces whenever such action seemed necessary.[4] Because of another unitarian stipulation about nationalizing the city of Buenos Aires, the province of Buenos Aires refused to join the new confederation, but later capitulated after a military defeat in 1859. In 1861 the tables turned: under Bartolomé Mitre the province revolted again and this time captured the confederation.

Upon his inauguration as president in 1862, Mitre began to accelerate the process of national unification. The trend was continued through the 1860s and 70s by Domingo Sarmiento, author of *Facundo*, the classic analysis of "civilization" and "barbarity" in Argentine life, and by Nicolás Avellaneda. The government was at last able to nationalize the city of Buenos Aires in 1880, making it the country's capital. A central bank was set up in 1891, giving the state exclusive control over the issuance of currency. In 1893, consolidation of the national debt further weakened provincial autonomy and struck, in H. S. Ferns's words, "the last blow at the federal structure of Argentine politics: more deadly than the interventions and military thrusts of the past."[5] Ultimately, unitarians achieved decisive victory.

Thus Argentina entered the era of the well-bred and talented "Generation of 1880"—landed aristocrats, mainly from the coastal and central areas, who held the keys to social, political, and economic power and who guided national development during and after the decade of the eighties. Led by Julio A. Roca, hero of the Conquest of the Desert from the Indians, they justified their hegemony through an eclectic blend of nineteenth-century liberal doctrines. Drawing upon the pseudoscience of Herbert Spencer as well as the theories of Adam Smith, they firmly maintained that competition was the ruling principle of life: if an aristocracy governed Argentina, that was a consequence of natural selection. Under the combined influence of laissez-faire economics and positivist philosophy, Argentina's leaders eagerly pursued the materialistic goal of economic growth—in accordance with unitarian prescriptions.[6]

4. Texts of the constitution of 1853 and its amended form of 1860 can be found in Faustino Legón and Samuel W. Medrano, *Las constituciones de la República Argentina* (Madrid, 1953), pp. [409]-64.

5. H. S. Ferns, *Britain and Argentina in the Nineteenth Century* (London, 1960), p. 477.

6. See Thomas F. McGann, *Argentina, the United States and the Inter-American System, 1880-1914* (Cambridge, Mass., 1957); and Oscar E. Cornblit, Ezequiel Gallo, and Arturo A. O'Connell, "La generación del 80 y su proyecto: antecedentes y consecuencias," in Torcuato S. di Tella, Gino Germani, and Jorge Graciarena, eds., *Argentina, sociedad de masas* (Buenos Aires, 1965), pp. 18-58.

ECONOMIC GROWTH AND TRANSFORMATION

The appearance and accessibility of consumer markets in Europe during the late nineteenth century created strong international demand for raw materials, such as meat and grain, that could be easily produced in Argentina.[7] Anxious to exploit this opportunity, the Generation of 1880 undertook a program to realize the country's agricultural potential. Not only would this policy result in economic growth; it would also strengthen the landowners' political position. The country consequently developed an export-import economic structure: Argentina sent raw materials to Europe, mainly Great Britain, and purchased manufactured goods abroad.

As Alberdi had urged in a famous aphorism, "to govern is to populate," the government encouraged immigration. Colonization began in the 1850s, a law of 1876 held out the promise of land distribution, and by 1880 Roca's campaign against the Indians cleared the pampas for cultivation. Attracted by the lure of economic opportunity, immigrants flocked to Argentina in great numbers. Some were discouraged by the practical obstacles to upward mobility, especially the constraints on land acquisition, and made their way back to Europe; others came as migrant workers, like the Italian *golondrinas* (swallows) who would harvest one crop per year in Argentina and then another one at home. Even so, net immigration was immense. Coming to a country with only 1.7 million inhabitants in 1869, foreigners added more than 2.6 million residents within the following four decades!

Another major aspect of liberal economic strategy involved the attraction of foreign capital, especially for building railroads. Exploitation of the pampas required communications, and ranchers and farmers needed transportation for their goods and access to the ports. A series of extravagant concessions to foreign entrepreneurs eventually yielded tangible results. In 1880 there were only 2,300 kilometers of track in the country; by 1910 there were nearly 25,000.[8] Demonstrating the privileged position of the coastal regions (and the differential implications of unitarian policy), the lines all radiated from the city of Buenos Aires—the nation's leading port—and most of them ran through agricultural and pastoral production zones in the provinces of Buenos Aires, Sante Fe, Entre Ríos, and Córdoba.[9]

With rising demand abroad, increasing manpower at home, and new

7. Recent studies of the Argentine economy include Aldo Ferrer, *The Argentine Economy*, trans. Marjory M. Urquidi (Berkeley and Los Angeles, 1967); Guido di Tella and Manuel Zymelman, *Las etapas del desarrollo económico argentino* (Buenos Aires, 1967); and Carlos F. Díaz Alejandro, *Essays on the Economic History of the Argentine Republic* (New Haven and London, 1970).

8. Juan A. Alsina, *La inmigración en el primer siglo de la independencia* (Buenos Aires, 1910), p. 59.

9. See the map in James R. Scobie, *Revolution on the Pampas: A Social History of Argentine Wheat, 1860-1910* (Austin, Tex., 1964), p. 41.

facilities for transportation, Argentine exports became the most dynamic element in a rapidly growing economy.[10] Available statistics indicate that the gross national product climbed by roughly 4.5 percent a year between 1900 and 1930; and despite the population growth, GNP per capita increased at an annual average rate of 1.2 percent. Up until the mid-1940s agriculture and livestock contributed a larger share of the GNP than did manufacturing.[11] During this entire period, Argentina's economic modernization was based upon commercial agriculture, rather than upon industrialization.

Admittedly, the gradual expansion of the manufacturing sector posed an implicit threat to the export-import economic structure, as industrialists consistently clamored for tariff protection. Yet this antagonism was softened by the symbiotic relationship between industry and agriculture. During the first few decades of this century, most manufacturers in Argentina processed products from the countryside (such as wool and beef) and therefore shared some common interests with the landowners. As late as 1935, foodstuffs still accounted for 47 percent of all industrial production, while textiles contributed another 20 percent.[12] Sectoral conflicts over structural priorities did not appear until the 1940s.[13]

Despite its evident success, the dependence on exports, imports, and foreign capital entailed some fundamental weaknesses. First, Argentina was extremely vulnerable to economic influence from abroad. Stimulated by official policy, foreign capital came to control a high proportion of the country's total fixed investments—from 1900 to 1929, between 30 and 40 percent. Perhaps more important, the concentration on exports and imports left Argentina at the mercy of the international market. Up to the 1930s exports contributed about one-quarter of the GNP; imports were equally large.[14] As time would eventually tell, reductions in overseas trade could have catastrophic effects on the national economy.

Second, this pattern of development produced startling inequities. One

10. The value of Argentine exports increased at the average annual rate of approximately 7 percent between 1880 and 1920, according to data in Dirección General de Estadística, *Anuario de la Dirección General de Estadística correspondiente al año 1912* (Buenos Aires, 1914), II, 44; and the *Anuario de la Sociedad Rural Argentina* (Buenos Aires, 1928), p. 72.

11. Economic Commission for Latin America (United Nations), *El desarrollo económico de la Argentina* (Mexico, 1959), I, 15.

12. Computed from data in Adolfo Dorfman, *Evolución industrial argentina* (Buenos Aires, 1942), p. 67.

13. Carl Solberg has convincingly documented the struggle over tariffs in the 1916-30 period, but I do not believe these debates involved genuine structural priorities over the direction of development. Solberg, "The Tariff and Politics in Argentina, 1916-1930," *Hispanic American Historical Review*, 53, no. 2 (May 1973), 260-84.

14. ECLA, *El desarrollo económico*, I, 18, 26, 28. Most of the foreign investments were British, as shown in Dorfman, *Evolución industrial*, p. 289.

dimension of this imbalance was regional. While economic expansion proceeded on the pampas and in Buenos Aires, the old interior fell into a state of stagnation. Mendoza and Tucumán escaped this sorry fate, because of their wine and sugar production, but the other central and northwestern provinces—notably Jujuy, La Rioja, Santiago del Estero, Salta—underwent severe economic and social decay. The interior had lost the battle of the nineteenth century, and the price of that defeat was poverty.[15]

Another aspect of maldistribution followed horizontal lines. Within the booming coastal economy, wealth was highly skewed: the rich were very rich, the poor were very poor. In the rural zones cattle-rich *estancieros* built elegant chalets, while foreign-born tenant farmers and displaced native migrants eked out harsh existences amid ignorance and isolation.[16] In the cities, aristocrats lounged in elite clubs while workers struggled to keep up with inflation on their modest wages.[17] Economic growth provided considerable opportunity for upward mobility, but still the discrepancies remained.

Despite these latent tensions, the export-import pattern of economic growth established by the Generation of 1880 continued throughout the 1930s. Agricultural production and international trade were the defining features of the Argentine economy. Industrial growth did not begin to gain importance until the 1930s, and concentrated mainly on traditional consumer goods; it was not until mid-century that the production of new and intermediate and capital goods came to dominate the industrial process. How these facts affected the country's politics will be one concern of this book.

THE SOCIAL STRUCTURE: GROUPS AND CLASSES

Argentina's economic transformation was matched by far-reaching changes in the country's social structure, originally consisting of a landed elite on the top and gauchos and wage labor on the bottom. Spurred by the immigration from abroad as well as by natural increase, the national population swelled from 1.7 million people in 1869 to 7.9 million in 1914 and then to 15.9 million by 1947.[18] This demographic growth helped provide the skill, expertise, and manpower that were essential to economic development. Many

15. See James R. Scobie, *Argentina: A City and a Nation*, 2nd ed. (New York, 1971), esp. Ch. 6, aptly entitled "Two Worlds."

16. Scobie, *Revolution on the Pampas*, esp. Ch. iv; and Carl Solberg, "Decline into Peonage: The Fate of Argentina's Gaucho Population, 1860-1930" (unpublished manuscript).

17. James R. Scobie, "Buenos Aires as a Commercial-Bureaucratic City, 1880-1910: Characteristics of a City's Orientation," *American Historical Review*, 77, no. 4 (October 1972), 1035-73; and Hobart Spalding, ed., *La clase trabajadora argentina* (*documentos para su historia—1890/1912*) (Buenos Aires, 1970), pp. 36-43.

18. Germani, *Estructura social*, p. [21].

immigrants moved into the agricultural areas of Entre Ríos, Santa Fe, and Córdoba as colonists, tenant farmers, and rural laborers. As the rural sectors stepped up production for export, other groups appeared in the cities to fulfill complementary roles: export houses, transportation companies, processing industries, and the professions acquired increasing importance. Exploitation of the pampa region thus created an intricate network of economic interests and also contributed to the formation of primarily urban middle-class groups.[19]

The attractions of urban life, combined with an eventual shortage of available land and rural job opportunities, led to the growth of Argentina's cities. Much of this expansion took place in Greater Buenos Aires, which contained 28 percent of the national population by 1947; an additional 19 percent lived in other urban communities.[20]

One result of this trend was the appearance of an urban working class, mainly composed of manual laborers. According to one estimate, this category may have included nearly 60 percent of the population in the city of Buenos Aires in the early twentieth century. But its character was as important as its size. By the 1940s, the lower class in Buenos Aires was about 90 percent literate; it was mobile, as many of its members had recently migrated from the countryside; and because of this process, it consisted increasingly of native Argentines rather than European immigrants.[21] As urban workers found it difficult to locate jobs, especially during the Depression,[22] their economic interests came to call for industrialization. Coupled with their mounting political resources, their tacit opposition to the export-import economic structure eventually presented a serious challenge to Argentine leadership.

For the purposes of this analysis, class stratification can be construed as involving two separate dimensions: economic power and social prestige. Applied to Argentina, this perspective yields four general categories: (1) the upper class, or "aristocracy," high in both prestige and economic strength, typically associated with land ownership; (2) the upper middle class, prosperous but not prestigious; (3) the lower middle class, with moderate economic means and virtually no social prestige, but which had at least some chance of

19. Scobie, *Revolution on the Pampas, passim*; and Gino Germani, *Política y sociedad en una época de transición: de la sociedad tradicional a la sociedad de masas* (Buenos Aires, 1963), esp. p. 195.

20. In this context, I have considered population centers of 20,000 or more inhabitants as urban while the official records (and Gino Germani) put the minimum at 2,000. See Germani, *Estructura social*, p. 69.

21. Germani, *Estructura social*, pp. 210, 219, 232; Germani, *Política y sociedad*, p. 230.

22. Between 1910-14 and 1940-44 the economically active population dropped from 42.2 percent to 37.7 percent: ECLA, *El desarrollo económico*, I, 37.

upward ascent; (4) the lower class, standing at the bottom of both ladders and confronted by major obstacles to upward mobility. Actually the lower class contained two elements: a proletariat or working class, and a lumpen-proletariat of displaced marginals. Large segments of the middle and lower classes lived in urban centers, and many members of these strata had been born abroad.[23]

For lack of better information, it seems fair to use the presumed socio-economic attributes of occupations in order to gauge the relative size of the different classes (although, as explained in Appendix A, I shall also stress family background and social prominence in dealing with specific historical actors). On the basis of census materials, Table 1-1 sets forth the results.

Table 1-1. Class Structure in Argentina, 1914-47

	1914 (%)	1947 (%)
Upper class	1	1
Middle classes	32	39
(Upper)	(8)	(7)
(Lower)	(24)	(32)
Lower class	67	60
Total	100	100

Source: Reprinted by permission of the publisher from Peter H. Smith, *Politics and Beef in Argentina: Patterns of Conflict and Change* (New York: Columbia University Press, 1969), p. 20; adapted from Germani, *Estructura social*, pp. 198, 220-22, with methodological problems and techniques discussed on pp. 139-51.

The likelihood of conflict between these classes would depend largely upon the attitudes, aspirations, and self-identification of the people involved. But whether or not class struggles took place, Argentina's social development was eventually bound to exert pressures on the political system as expanding parts of the population sought active parts in politics.

THE POLITICAL SYSTEM: CENTRALIZATION AND EXPANSION

Under the Generation of 1880, Argentina was ruled by unitarian aristocrats whose political strength came from several sources. They controlled the army, they controlled elections (through fraud if necessary), they controlled the only genuine political party—the Partido Autonomista Nacional (PAN)—and they confined the decision-making process to their own exclusive circles. Congress did not provide much of a national forum, and most significant decisions were made by *acuerdo*—literally by informal "agreement" with members of the Executive branch—not by public contestation and debate.

As these aristocrats continued to consolidate their power, the centraliza-

23. For a different categorization, see Scobie, "Buenos Aires," 1056-64.

tion of authority gave paradoxical emphasis to the fundamentally passive relationship between politics and Argentine society at large. By the late nineteenth century, the distribution of political power had become essentially dependent upon, and derivative from, the distribution of social and economic power. Mobility was unidirectional: socioeconomic prominence was a necessary, and sometimes sufficient, precondition for the attainment of political influence. And though aristocrats built up the strength of the state, and used it for promoting economic policies, the political system did not provide—nor was it intended to be—an autonomous power resource.

But in time, other pressures forced aristocrats to broaden the base of the political system and relinquish part of their monopoly. As noted above, Argentina's economic modernization spread rapidly into the pampa and engaged important new groups, from landowners to merchants, in the production and export of raw material goods. Yet this redistribution of economic power, without corresponding changes in the social and political arenas, provoked discontent among three major factions: (1) newly prosperous landowners of the upper Littoral; (2) descendants of old aristocratic families, often from the distant interior, who were unable to profit from the export-import pattern of growth; and (3) middle-class people who took part in the economic expansion but who were excluded from the strongholds of power.

As Ezequiel Gallo and Silvia Sigal have shown, these three social elements combined to form the Radical party.[24] In 1890, as the country plunged into a short but severe economic crisis, an organization called the Civic Union tried to overthrow the ruling aristocracy. The revolt was ended by *acuerdo*, when Bartolomé Mitre reached an agreement with the government, but two years later the movement's dissident faction established the Radical Civic Union (UCR). Led first by Leandro Alem and then by Hipólito Yrigoyen, the Radicals boycotted elections in protest against the fraud and attempted two more abortive coups. Although they failed both times, the UCR and its supporters continued their steadfast pursuit of political power. Intimately connected to the country's export-import development, they did not want to alter the existing political and economic structure as much as they wanted to control it.

While the Radicals persisted in their opposition, President Roque Saenz Peña promoted an electoral reform in 1911-12 which called for universal male suffrage, the secret ballot, and compulsory voting. Despite its apparently democratic implications, the plan was clearly meant to strengthen and perpetuate the prevailing oligarchic system. Alarmed by labor agitation and concurrent threats of violence, Saenz Peña and his colleagues wanted to

24. Ezequel Gallo and Silvia Sigal, "La formación de los partidos políticos contemporáneos: la U.C.R. (1890-1916)," in Di Tella et al., eds., *Argentina, sociedad de masas*, pp. 124-76.

assure stability. Cooptation of the Radicals seemed to be an appropriate tactic, for Saenz Peña appears to have understood the underlying commitment of the middle classes to the existing political and economic structure and did not regard their Radical spokesmen (many of whom were from the aristocracy) as a threat to it.[25] In a way, the Saenz Peña reform was a tacit *acuerdo*; as such, it complied with time-honored tradition.

With the application of the voting law in 1912, the Argentine political system retained its constitutional form but underwent some fundamental alterations. First, the popular base expanded. As under previous law, all Argentine males over eighteen years old were allowed to vote; nearly 1 million people could claim this right in 1912, and, as revealed by Figure 1-1, the number climbed to 3.4 million by 1946. Because of the mandatory voting clause and the reduction in fraud, participation was moreover high. Usually around 70 percent of eligible voters, and sometimes over 80 percent, cast

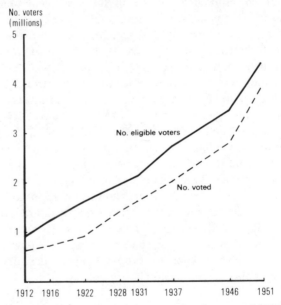

Figure 1-1. Growth and participation of the Argentine electorate, 1912-51. To maintain comparability data for 1951 refer to men only, though suffrage had already been extended to women. Data from Darío Cantón, *Materiales para el estudio de la sociología política en la Argentina* (Buenos Aires, 1968), I, 81-148.

25. See his comment in Ministerio del Interior, *Las fuerzas armadas restituyen el imperio de la soberanía popular* (Buenos Aires, 1946), I, 9. Besides, most proponents of the electoral reform believed that Radicals would come to form a loyal opposition, with Conservatives maintaining a majority. On this and related points consult Darío Cantón, *Elecciones y partidos políticos en la Argentina. Historia, interpretación y balance: 1910-1966* (Buenos Aires, 1973), Ch. 4.

ballots in presidential elections. Second, as both cause and effect of these developments, Argentine elections were, in the main, closely contested; winners rarely emerged with more than 60 percent of the vote. As Saenz Peña had apparently foreseen, these changes greatly strengthened the legitimacy of the existing governmental structure.

There were other consequences too. As I shall argue in more detail below, the national Congress gained importance both as a forum for the expression of group interests and as a critic of presidential policy. Given the necessities of electoral competition, political parties, almost nonexistent under the Generation of 1880, became primary vehicles for the organized pursuit of power. In turn, trends of this kind produced a new kind of political elite: a cadre of professionals, mainly middle-class in origin, who made politics into a viable career.

Notwithstanding such far-reaching changes, intended and unintended, the Saenz Peña reform opened the political system in a limited, restrictive fashion. In view of the large number of unnaturalized immigrants, the electoral law actually offered voting rights to only 40 or 45 percent of the adult male population around the date of its first application.[26] Since immigrants comprised approximately one-half of the expanding middle class and an even greater share of Argentina's working class (around 60 percent in urban areas),[27] this meant that suffrage was effectively extended *from the upper class to selected segments of the middle class, to the distinct disadvantage of the lower class, especially the urban working class.*

In addition, the mechanics of the electoral system severely circumscribed the range of actual representation in the national Congress. Under the so-called incomplete list (*lista incompleta*), which prevailed from 1912 through 1949, each party put forth candidates for two-thirds of the deputy seats available, and each voter could cast ballots for two-thirds of the seats; the leading candidates filled the two-thirds majority position, and the next ones filled the minority posts. Though some ticket-splitting occurred, the first-place party in each provincial election normally won two-thirds of the province's seats in the Chamber of Deputies; the second-place party got the

26. This estimate is based on a comparison between the number of eligible voters in 1912-14 and the number of adult males over 20 years of age in 1914. See Darío Cantón, *Materiales para el estudio de la sociología política en la Argentina* (Buenos Aires, 1968), I, 81, 83; and Díaz Alejandro, *Essays*, p. 423. For detailed data on selected districts, see Ezequiel Gallo and Roberto Cortés Conde, *Argentina: la república conservadora* (Buenos Aires, 1972), p. 232.

27. See Germani, *Política y sociedad*, p. 195; Carl Solberg, *Immigration and Nationalism: Argentina and Chile, 1890-1914* (Austin, Tex., 1970), p. 44; Gustavo Beyhaut, Roberto Cortés Conde, Haydée Gorostegui, and Susana Torrado, "Los inmigrantes en el sistema ocupacional argentino," in Di Tella et al., *Argentina, sociedad de masas*, pp. 85-123; and Scobie, "Buenos Aires," p. 1058.

remaining third; and all other parties were shut out entirely. These regulations discriminated sharply against small parties, discouraged the formation of new movements, favored the established interests, and created a paradoxical principle: the greater the degree of competition, particularly multi-party competition, the less representative the delegation. In practice the incomplete list usually meant that less than two-thirds of Argentina's voters, and sometimes little more than one-half, had spokesmen of their own within the Chamber.[28] Taken with the high percentage of ineligible adult males, the Saenz Peña law therefore gave effective political representation to something like *30 percent* of the adult male population, mainly in the middle and upper classes. This was a limited democracy indeed.

In fact, one might well wonder if this was democracy at all. One could reasonably describe Argentina's political system after 1912 as a form of electoral authoritarianism, in which pluralism was limited to a small segment of the population and regulated by elections which were still marred by frequent fraud. Yet I still prefer to view the system as democratic, in a strict sense of the term: up until 1930, at least, Argentine politics supplied "regular constitutional opportunities for peaceful competition for political power (and not just a share of it) to different groups without excluding any significant sector of the population by force."[29] Obviously this phraseology presents democracy as a relative concept, susceptible to multiple gradations, rather than an absolute condition of personal liberty and universal equality. And my analytical concern accordingly focuses, not upon the system's fall from a state of perfection, but upon its evident inability to transform itself into a more democratic polity and respond effectively to the changing challenges of Argentine society.

While the Saenz Peña law's partial accommodation of middle-class interests helped sustain the stability of constitutional government, other developments gave rise to power groups which eventually threatened the survival of the system. One, the conscious creation of national leaders, was the formation of a professional military. The other, resulting from the processes of economic growth, was the appearance of a vital labor movement.

28. According to my own computations, based on election returns for selected years from 1912 through 1946. In 1912, to take the most extreme example, approximately 53 percent of the voters cast ballots for Deputies who won seats in the Chamber. But this was still an improvement over the previous system, the *lista completa*, under which the party with a plurality got *all* the seats in the Chamber.

29. The definition is taken from Juan J. Linz, "An Authoritarian Regime: Spain," most easily consulted in Erik Allardt and Stein Rokkan, eds., *Mass Politics: Studies in Political Sociology* (New York, 1970), pp. 254-55. Robert A. Dahl also writes of Argentina in this period as a polyarchy, or relatively democratized regime. *Polyarchy: Participation and Opposition* (New Haven and London, 1971), esp. pp. 132-140.

EMERGING POWER GROUPS

The post-Rosas liberals regarded a professional army as an essential part of national development in nineteenth-century Argentina. Only a well-trained military establishment, they reasoned, could crush provincial *caudillos,* maintain order, and thus provide conditions for the kind of economic growth they sought.[30]

Acting on this perception, Sarmiento began the trend towards professionalization[31] by founding the Colegio Militar (1870) and the Escuela Naval (1872), still the basic training schools for officers in present-day Argentina. A few years later Julio Roca, himself a general, greatly encouraged the trend. During the 1890s his colleague and protégé, General Pablo R. Riccheri, negotiated large-scale purchases of new German weaponry. In 1899 Roca and Riccheri engaged a German mission to train staff officers in modern methods and military technology, thereby inaugurating a forty-year period of service collaboration between the two nations. In 1900 the Escuela Superior de Guerra was created by the Ministry of War.

This emphasis on expertise precipitated fundamental alterations in the structure and outlook of Argentina's officer corps. By 1910 the criteria for promotion had changed from political favoritism to seniority and, more particularly, to the mastery of modern warfare. Related to this was a shift in control of promotions from the presidency to an all-military committee composed of commanders of army divisions and headed by the highest-ranking general. As the army thus developed a common esprit, based partly on a sense of its own efficiency, it also acquired substantial institutional autonomy.

In time the possibilities for advancement by merit opened careers to members of the middle class. Specifically, as various studies have revealed, many of the newly promoted generals were sons of immigrants, most notably from Italy.[32] For a considerable portion of Argentina's top-echelon officers, military careers provided avenues to upward social mobility. Gratified by

30. Important studies of Argentine military history can be found in Marvin Goldwert, "The Rise of Modern Militarism in Argentina," *Hispanic American Historical Review,* 48, no. 2 (May 1968), 184-205; Robert A. Potash, *The Army and Politics in Argentina, 1928-1945* (Stanford, 1969); Darío Cantón, *La política de los militares argentinos, 1900-1971* (Buenos Aires, 1971); and Goldwert, *Democracy, Militarism, and Nationalism in Argentina, 1930-1966: An Interpretation* (Austin, Tex., 1972).

31. By professionalization I mean the development of career situations wherein (a) the command of particular skills, in this case military ones, provides grounds for personal advancement, and (b) the application of these skills receives enough remuneration to constitute a full-time occupation.

32. Potash, *Army,* p. 20; and José Luis de Imaz, *Los que mandan* (Buenos Aires, 1964), pp. 56-57.

such an opportunity, they forged strong allegiance to the institution as a whole—and a jealous regard for its independence, honor, and professional reputation. Deeply resentful of intrusions by outsiders, especially by politicians, they often beheld civilian officials with a mixture of scorn and apprehension.

Throughout the twentieth century the Argentine armed forces, particularly the army, steadily gained in importance. By 1930 the armed forces consisted of around 50,000 men; by 1943 this number had doubled, and by 1955 it had doubled again.[33] In the meantime the military share of the national budget climbed from around 20 percent in the 1920s to approximately 50 percent in 1945.[34]

In short, the process of professionalization gradually turned the Argentine military, especially the army, into a formidable political force—quite apart from, and sometimes antagonistic to, the country's constitutional apparatus. To one degree or another, there was constant tension between military and civilian authorities. In 1930, 1943, and 1955, pressure broke out in the form of *coups d'etat*.

Just as the military was accumulating and expanding its institutional power, another force emerged on the political scene: organized labor. As indicated above, lower-class groups, largely immigrant in origin, obtained limited participation under the Saenz Peña law. Unable to articulate their grievances through the ballot alone, workers took to various forms of self-organization.[35]

The roots of the Argentine labor movement run back to 1857, when the printers of Buenos Aires established the Sociedad Tipográfica Bonaerense. In the 1870s and 1880s a number of European labor leaders, anarchists and socialists, sought refuge in Argentina, and by 1890 their efforts had led to the formation of a short-lived Federación de Trabajadores de la Región Argentina (FTRA).

In 1895 some other worker representatives, led by Juan B. Justo, created the Socialist party. Committed to evolutionary parliamentary techniques, Argentine Socialists encouraged the naturalization of immigrants, electoral participation, and the use of political power in order to achieve socioeconomic goals. Eventually the party forged a significant base among the working class of urban Buenos Aires. Despite able leadership and a consistent clamor for social reform, however, the Socialists failed in their attempts to

33. Peter G. Snow, *Political Forces in Argentina* (Boston, 1971), p. 53.
34. Potash, *Army*, pp. 8, 34, 99; and George I. Blanksten, *Perón's Argentina* (Chicago, 1953), p. 311.
35. On the history of the labor movement, see Samuel L. Baily, *Labor, Nationalism, and Politics in Argentina* (New Brunswick, N.J., 1967), esp. Chs. I-IV; Sebastián Marotta, *El movimiento sindical argentino*, 2 vols. (Buenos Aires, 1961); and Spalding, *La clase trabajadora*, plus the works cited on p. 17 therein.

assimilate immigrants and, as a result, never acquired a predominant hold on national politics. In a way the fate of the party circumscribed the outer limits of effective working-class representation through constitutional means.

Most workers preferred to employ other methods. A Federación Obrera Regional Argentina (FORA), dominated by anarchists, appeared soon after the turn of the century. Propounding the need for direct action, FORA's directorate initiated a wave of local and general strikes. In the most successful of these, in May 1909, between 200,000 and 300,000 laborers halted work in Buenos Aires. As a result of such efforts, workers obtained substantial increases in real wages between 1904 and 1909.[36]

In retaliation against the strikes, the Argentine government, still led by aristocrats, adopted harsh measures. One, the so-called Ley de Residencia, passed in 1904, permitted the state to deport all foreigners whose conduct "compromised national security or disturbed public order"—by, for instance, taking part in strikes. The second measure, the Ley de Defensa Social of 1910, achieved the specific purpose of crushing the anarchist movement.[37]

Despite these and other setbacks, organized labor continued to grow, and also changed its coloration. In addition to the traditional craft unions, syndicates sprang up among new groups as well: transportation workers, dockworkers and, most important of all, railroad men; white-collar workers and government employees; meat packers, textile and metal workers, and the sugar workers of the north. In 1920 the nation's leading labor organization, then the FORA, had 200,000 members. By the early 1940s—after setbacks in the 1920s and 30s—the number of unionized workers had climbed to 547,000, of whom 331,000 belonged to the Confederación General del Trabajo (CGT), and in 1947 the CGT could claim 1.5 million members.[38]

And yet, with some exceptions, these developments took place outside the framework of Argentina's national political structure. Under varying leadership—socialist, anarchist, syndicalist, communist—labor's major weapon remained the strike. To illustrate the point, Figure 1-2 depicts the annual number of strikes and strikers in the city of Buenos Aires from 1907 through 1954. Through the many oscillations, highly suggestive in themselves, a simple fact comes forth: despite frequent political repression, strikes were a common feature of urban life in Argentina.

With the passage of time, Argentina's working class started to confront the country's political process. By the 1930s the lower class came to consist not so much of immigrants as of native Argentines, often second-generation, and this demographic tendency steadily swelled the ranks of eligible voters. In 1946, as shown in Figure 1-1 above, over 3.4 million Argentines possessed the

36. Baily, *Labor*, pp. 21, 23.
37. Ibid., pp. 23-26.
38. Ibid., pp. 35, 70; and Spalding, *La clase trabajadora*, pp. 22, 25.

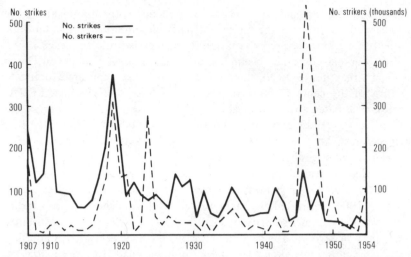

Figure 1-2. Industrial strikes and strikers in the city of Buenos Aires, 1907-54. Data from Dirección Nacional de Investigaciones, Estadística y Censos, *Síntesis estadística mensual de la República Argentina*, 1, no. 1 (January 1947), 7; Guido di Tella and Manuel Zymelman, *Las etapas del desarrollo económico argenino* (Buenos Aires, 1967), pp. 537-38.

right to vote. More to the point, this number accounted for approximately 70 percent of the entire adult male population, compared to the 40-45 percent eligibility of 1912.[39] Eventually, this gradual enfranchisement of the lower class presented a major challenge to Argentina's constitutional form of government.

The political system's ability to cope with this situation would depend upon many factors, including the role and viability of the Chamber of Deputies. As the most explicitly representative institution in the country, the Chamber bore fundamental responsibility for reflecting and articulating the needs and cares of the constituent public. An assessment of the system's responsive capability therefore requires careful scrutiny of the Chamber itself.

CHANGING ROLES OF CONGRESS

According to changes in circumstances, the Argentine Congress performed a wide variety of political functions. In many respects it did not, of course, bear much resemblance to its counterpart in the United States. Because it made so few laws by itself, in fact, one might properly conceive of the Argentine Congress as a public assembly or parliament rather than as a legislature (and I shall use both terms in this book). But this does not mean

39. See note 26.

that the Congress had no significance at all. An understanding of its diverse roles demands the adoption of multiple categories for evaluating institutional performance. To explore this matter I shall first deal with the Chamber of Deputies and then turn briefly to the Senate.[40]

As demonstrated above, the composition of the Chamber was far from wholly representative. Deputies spoke for just a fraction of the adult male population. Even after 1912 they sometimes won their seats illegally; during the 1930s, in fact, "patriotic fraud" was widely recognized as standard policy. And deputies frequently obtained nominations for legislative office through negotiation and arrangement rather than by demonstrating popular support. In the pre-Saenz Peña era candidacies were launched informally, frequently by cliques of personal friends; then party conventions, dominated by the leaders and committees, controlled most nominations; and throughout the 1904-55 period, and especially in the late Perón years, there was the process of *digitación* (fingering), or outright appointment by a top leader or inner circle.[41]

Despite these restrictions in representation, however, the most important

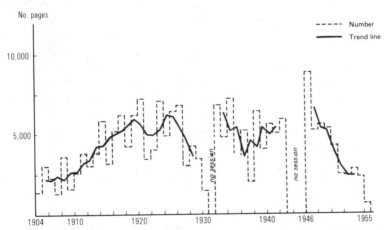

Figure 1-3. General levels of congressional activity, 1904-55, as measured by the number of pages in transcripts of annual sessions. Trend line is based on three-year moving averages. Truncated sessions of 1930 and 1955 are excluded from the averages.

40. This section draws heavily upon Lee C. Fennell, "Congress in the Argentine Political System: An Appraisal," in Weston H. Agor, ed., *Latin American Legislatures: Their Role and Influence* (New York, 1971), pp. 139-71.

41. These are impressionistic statements. To test these generalizations, there is great need for historical studies to complement the work by Richard Robert Strout, *The Recruitment of Candidates in Mendoza Province, Argentina* (Chapel Hill, N.C., 1968). One exception should be noted: the Socialist party, which chose candidates by a vote among all members.

function of the Chamber was to provide a national forum for the expression of constituent interests, however limited their scope. Once in the Chamber, deputies presented, according to their lights, the needs and demands of their supporters (or their sponsors). The size of provincial delegations was in proportion to the distribution of the population. Aside from its other implications, the *lista incompleta* prevented any single party from gaining more than two-thirds of the seats between 1912 and 1949 and thereby assured some competition in the Chamber. As a result there was a good deal of public discussion, argumentation, and debate. To measure this phenomenon, albeit crudely, Figure 1-3 traces the number of pages in the *Diario de Sesiones* for annual proceedings of the Chamber from 1904 through 1955. The trend line shows a steep rise in activity from the early years to the mid-1920s, a generally high level through the 1940s (barring periods of military rule), and then a sudden decline. As a national forum, the Chamber appears to have been relatively muted before 1912 and after 1950; but at other times, it performed this function fairly well.[42]

Yet the fulfillment of the Chamber's role as forum came at the expense of its role as lawmaker. Though charged with some specific legislative responsibilities, the Chamber seems to have initiated and promulgated very few laws of its own.[43] One reason for this weakness was simply the historic preeminence of the presidency, and the wide-ranging authority of executive decrees. Another problem, which worsened over time, was the inadequacy of relevant resources—particularly staff support and office space.[44]

Thus hampered in the making of laws, the Chamber of Deputies could still offer public criticism of presidential policies. Chief instruments for this purpose were the right of interpellation, which allowed deputies to interrogate cabinet members on specific issues; and the investigating committee, formed on an *ad hoc* basis to explore a wide variety of areas. In this fashion, indirect and even negative, Congress could sometimes exert a substantial impact on practical policy.

It is extremely difficult, and maybe impossible, to gauge the intensity of congressional criticism of the executive branch. But a tentative measure of parliamentary resistance to presidential demands, in a general sense of the term, might be taken from the dates that budget bills were passed, since Congress could hamstring (or at least embarrass) the president by refusing to grant him a budget. Passage of the bill by September 30, when ordinary sessions ended, would suggest a compliant spirit within the legislature; passage

42. This was true despite the electoral abstention of most Radicals from 1931 to 1935, since other opposition parties in the legislative sessions from 1932 to 1936 were vigorous enough to help the Congress retain its role as national forum.

43. For one case study of this situation, see my *Politics and Beef*, esp. pp. 94-103.

44. Fennell, "Congress," pp. 154-57.

after that, particularly after January 1, would imply varying degrees of resistance.[45]

According to this logic, Figure 1-4 reveals important changes over time. Prior to Yrigoyen's inauguration in 1916, Congress demonstrated a notable, but moderate, level of resistance. Between 1916 and the late 1920s parliamentary resistance climbed to extremely high levels, then dropped sharply

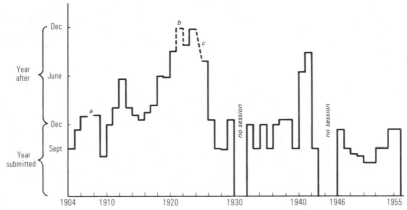

Figure 1-4. Congressional resistance to the Executive, 1904-55, as reflected in the calendar dates of budget bill passage. *a*, budget for 1908 established by presidential decree; *b*, no general budget for 1922 ever passed, budget for 1921 extended on a monthly basis; *c*, data for 1925 budget unavailable.

after the one-sided elections of 1928 and 1930. After the coup of 1930 and resumption of the legislature in 1932, Congress was generally compliant—and then, for a couple of years at the end of the decade, sturdily resistant. Under Perón, from 1946 through 1955, compliance consistently prevailed.

Autonomous or not, the Argentine Congress also served as a training ground for top executive officials. Historically, experience in the Chamber of Deputies formed an essential part of the political *cursus honorum*.[46] Of the ten individuals who gained the presidency through constitutional means between 1904 and 1955, seven had been deputies at one time or another. And out of 27 appointments to the critical and sensitive Ministry of the Interior, 16—nearly 60 percent—went to former deputies.[47]

This pattern, however, varied sharply over time. To illustrate this fact,

45. One problem with this index is that the Socialists—a minority party—often bore a disproportionate share of the responsibility for delaying passage of the budget. Another useful technique would be to evaluate budget changes, particularly cutbacks, attempted or made by the Congress.

46. See the quotes in Darío Cantón, *El parlamento argentino en épocas de cambio: 1889, 1916 y 1946* (Buenos Aires, 1966), pp. 67-69.

47. See also Fennell, "Congress," pp. 159-62.

Figure 1-5 traces the percentage of top executive officials (presidents, vice-presidents, and cabinet ministers) during successive administrations who had served in the Chamber of Deputies.[48] Prior to the inauguration of the Radicals, the Chamber clearly occupied a central role in political careers, as roughly two-thirds of the officials tended to be former deputies. The curve shows a temporary decline in 1916-22, when the Radical party came into

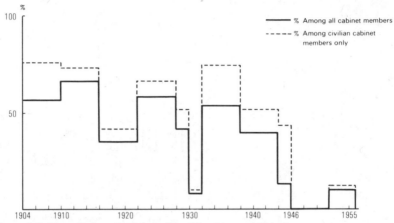

Figure 1-5. Former deputies in presidential cabinets, 1904-55, as percent among presidents, vice-presidents, and ministers.

power for the first time, then resumes the previous level. The precipitous drop for 1930-32, during the provisional military government, underscores a basic thrust of the regime: abhorrence and disdain for professional politicians. Restoration of constitutional procedures brought the politicians back, however, and some former deputies (known as the "collaborationists") even received cabinet posts in the military dictatorship of 1943-46. A startling shift took place under Perón: not one of his first-term ministers had been a deputy, and only one ex-deputy held a portfolio between 1952 and 1955. Perón, it is plain, was forging his own political elite.

Thus the Argentine Chamber of Deputies performed various functions, in various degrees, during the era covered by this study. To summarize the argument, Table 1-2 approximates degrees of role fulfillment during four major time periods; (1) 1904-15, when the traditional aristocracy reigned supreme, though the electoral reform of 1912 started to erode the situation; (2) 1916-30, when political processes were dominated by the Radical party;

48. I am indebted to Richard Hartwig for a list of cabinet members from 1904 through 1966. The names of deputies can be found in the *Diario de Sesiones* for each annual session of the Chamber; and, in alphabetical order up through 1951, in Cámara de Diputados, *El parlamento argentino, 1854-1951*, 2nd ed. (Buenos Aires, 1951), pp. 340-465.

(3) 1932-42, the so-called Infamous Decade, when constitutional practices were compromised by fraud and overt military tutelage; (4) 1946-55, when Juan Perón asserted his authoritarian control. Of course, the boundaries between these periods are artificial, and there are internal breaks within each period, but for analytical convenience I shall also employ these periods in other portions of this book.

Table 1-2. Degrees of Role Fulfillment by the Argentine Chamber of Deputies, 1904-55

Role	1904-15	1916-30	1932-42	1946-55
Forum	Low, but rising	High	High and moderate	Declining
Lawmaker	Low	Low	Low	Low
Critic	Moderate	Moderate to high	Generally low	Low
Training ground	High	Moderate to high	High to moderate	Low

For the sake of contrast, it should be noted that the national Senate performed these same functions—although in differing degrees. With the security of nine-year terms, senators could fulfill the roles of critic and lawmaker somewhat more effectively than deputies. The upper house also provided a training ground for high officials, especially prior to 1916, but it then came to be eclipsed by the Chamber in this regard.[49] By far the Senate's weakest role was as a forum. Elected by provincial legislatures,[50] senators spoke for dominant groups and parties within each province, rather than the voting populace; the result was a pervasive bias in favor of the status quo. And since each province had two senators, the geographical balance of power in the upper house was highly skewed. It is largely because of the Senate's inadequacy as a forum that this study focuses exclusively upon the Chamber of Deputies. The study of interaction among elites requires a broad selection of elites—and this could be found within the Chamber, however unrepresentative it may have been in other ways.[51]

All in all, the material in this chapter refines the purpose and scope of this study in two fundamental respects. First, the Argentine Chamber of Deputies possesses analytical and historical significance primarily for its role as a national forum, particularly between 1912 and 1950, and also (to a lesser degree) for its role as a critic of presidential policy. As a training ground for top executive officials, prior to Perón (except in 1930-32), the Chamber of Deputies can moreover furnish insight into the political experience of men who came to make decisions. It was an arena of conflict and contention, not an institution of great autonomous power.

49. Fennell, "Congress," p. 162.

50. In the Federal Capital, voters selected an electoral college which chose senators in the same manner as president and vice-president.

51. Furthermore, the relative infrequency of roll-call votes and the small number of senators (30) present additional methodological problems.

Second, deputies—and government officials at large—eventually formed only a segment in the circle of national decision-makers. In 1930 the armed forces emerged as an arbiter of the political process. By the 1940s labor leaders, at the head of a surging workers' movement, had begun to accumulate vast reserves of strength. Power was building up outside the electoral system, a fact which makes it necessary to approach conflict among political elites from two different perspectives: first by looking at conflict *within* the elected leadership, and then by examining struggles *between* elected politicians and the military-labor power centers. Such a bifocal view will, it is hoped, yield a reasonably clear picture of the role and responsiveness of electoral politics in Argentina, and help lead to understanding of the reasons for its ultimate demise.

2
A Typology of Deputies

One of the most fundamental characteristics of any political institution concerns the composition of its membership. What kind of people gained access to the Chamber of Deputies? Did they constitute identifiable social types? If so, did their relative weight in the Chamber vary over time? Such inquiries not only bear substantial intrinsic interest. Directly and indirectly, they cast light upon patterns of behavior within the institution and also upon the relationship between the institution (or the political system in general) and the society at large.

One pioneering approach to these questions, by Darío Cantón, has made an intensive study of the social origins and career patterns of Argentine congressmen at three single points in time: 1889, 1916, and 1946.[1] In an attempt to complement that analysis, this chapter seeks to elucidate key characteristics of *all* the 1,571 deputies who served between 1904 and 1955. My sample therefore differs from Cantón's; so do my data, techniques, and interpretive emphasis.[2]

My specific goal is to elaborate a general typology of deputies, and then to measure the relative incidence of each type over time. The following categorization attempts to focus on both the *direction of social mobility* involved in gaining access to the Chamber and the *degree of commitment to political activism*. In quite a straightforward way, this orientation helps elucidate the connection between the legislature and the structure of Argentine society. And as I shall argue in subsequent chapters, it can enhance our understanding of elite conduct and interaction.

1. Darío Cantón, *El parlamento argentino en épocas de cambio: 1889, 1916 y 1946* (Buenos Aires, 1966).
2. Sources for my data are described in the Bibliography at the end of this book. One major difference between Cantón's study and this effort lies in my construction of a rather explicit typology, whereas his approach is somewhat open-ended. Unfortunately, and despite his personal cooperation, I was unable to gain access to his data while in Buenos Aires in August-September 1969.

The typology partakes of two operational dimensions, the first of which is *social status*. The defining characteristic of this commodity, as I shall speak of it, is social prestige; a standard accompanying characteristic, at least in Argentina, is economic influence. Analysis of this concept rests upon a single composite variable which divides the deputies into two groups: aristocrats (people of great social prominence and, usually, personal wealth) and non-aristocrats. This dichotomy ignores many of the realities and subtleties of social stratification, and to this extent its meaning must be modified, but it still points to a sharp and salient cleavage in Argentine society. In practice, as spelled out in Appendix A, I identify individual aristocrats by (a) reputation of the family name, according to a panel of qualified judges, and (b) membership in exclusive social clubs.

With reference to political commitment, the second dimension of the typology concerns *political professionalism*. By professionalism, in this context, I mean persistent personal dedication to the accumulation of political skills. Professionalization, the social process which gives rise to professionalism, necessarily entails (a) the extended or even full-time pursuit of such skills and (b) the assumption that skill, rather than family background or some other ascriptive feature, provides the basis for individual advancement. Whether politics in Argentina gained widespread recognition as a legitimate profession or had a formalized ethical code is not germane to this particular, albeit limited, usage of the term.[3]

Even in the best of all methodolological worlds it is difficult to measure professionalism (however conceived), and in this case, given the paucity of data, I shall rely upon a dubious criterion; the number of terms served in the Chamber of Deputies over the course of a lifetime, on the ground that repeated elections to the Chamber imply commitment, success, and mastery of necessary skills. Deputies elected for three or more terms, to take an empirical threshold, shall be viewed as "hard-core professionals." Those elected for only one term shall be called "amateurs." And in a kind of residual category, two-time winners can be thought of as "semiprofessionals"—men who probably, but only probably, had an abiding interest in the acquisition of political office and skills.

Such distinctions are naturally subject to error and exaggeration. Many one-time deputies undoubtedly regarded and pursued politics as a full-time career and held numerous positions aside from their term in the Chamber.[4]

3. Problems in the conceptualization and definition of professionalization have produced a large literature, as exemplified in Harold L. Wilensky, "The Professionalization of Everyone?," *American Journal of Sociology*, 70, no. 2 (September 1964), 137-58; and Howard M. Vollmer and Donald L. Mills, eds., *Professionalization* (Englewood Cliffs, N.J., 1967).

4. By taking on a smaller group of deputies, Cantón has been able to include nonlegislative offices in his treatment of what he calls the intensity of political careers.

Able and ambitious men might pass quickly through the legislature on their way to a governorship or cabinet post, and faithful party bureaucrats might receive a nomination in return for years of loyal service: both are political professionals in my sense of the word. For these reasons the number-of-terms criterion has a definite tendency to overestimate the number of amateurs and to underestimate the number of professionals, particularly of the hard-core type. Assuming that the degree of distortion holds constant over time, however, I think it is reasonable and fair to use this standard in order to identify some elementary trends.

In brief, I propose to locate legislative types in Argentina along two separate dimensions: the direction of social mobility, as implied by class origin, and the commitment to political activism, as reflected by experience and presumed skill. As put into operation here, the two basic variables—social status and political professionalism—yield a sixfold classification of deputies. Table 2-1 presents the possibilities.

Table 2-1. A Typology of Argentine Deputies

Political professionalism		Social Status	
No. terms served	Category	Aristocrat	Nonaristocrat
1	Amateur		
2	Semiprofessional		
3 or more	Hard-core professional		

Needless to say these categories represent empirical approximations of ideal types, and genuinely precise measurement of their relative importance in the Chamber is virtually impossible. There are weaknesses in my information (as "Unknown" entries in some of the tables will show), and available variables do not lend themselves to unequivocal circumscription of the differing types.

What follows, then, is crude—but it is also fundamental for a comprehension of legislative elites in twentieth-century Argentina. To provide a focus for this inquiry, and also to anticipate some later findings, let me offer some preliminary observations and hypotheses.

For men of aristocratic status, the acquisition of political prominence constituted an essentially lateral move. Admission to the Chamber of Deputies tended to confirm their place in Argentine society, rather than open new channels of social mobility. Moreover, many aristocrats regarded public office as a matter of *noblesse oblige* and, despite long periods of service, they considered politics an avocation. They believed that political power was their birthright, they did not enjoy the hurly-burly of electoral struggle, and they

Cantón, *El parlamento*, esp. pp. 79-82. It is encouraging that, despite differences in data and approach, most of our findings on professionalization reinforce each other.

did not feel deep commitments to party loyalty.

For nonaristocrats the case was just the opposite. Politics could offer a means of social elevation and it could constitute an economically rewarding occupation. Nonaristocrats could achieve this mobility either by being coopted, or by working their way up through a party machinery. In the latter case, they owed great allegiance to the party apparatus. I therefore surmise that as the incidence of nonaristocratic professionals increased, so did the degree of partisan conflict, *regardless of the particular parties involved.*

Amateurs, especially nonaristocratic ones, showed relatively little behavioral autonomy. As novices, acknowledging their inexperience, they tended to respond to the dictates of congressional leaders. Where leadership was decisive and strong, the amateurs were quick to follow. Where leadership was weak or contradictory, amateurs could show a helter-skelter pattern of behavior, each individual pursuing personal preferences rather than organizational imperatives.

GENERAL TRENDS

For the sake of broad perspective it would first be useful to establish basic dimensions of change between the four time periods employed in this study: 1904-15, 1916-30, 1932-42, and 1946-55. Accordingly, this section will concentrate on chronological patterns in the distribution of social status and the duration of parliamentary careers. Subsequent portions of the chapter will then go on to analyze relationships between these variables and party affiliation within each of the separate time periods.

To begin, Figure 2-1 displays the percentage of deputies in each legislative session who can be classified as aristocrats (again, see Appendix A for the derivation of this categorization). However gross the data, the trends are unmistakable. Throughout the years from 1904 through 1915 over 60 percent of the deputies fell in the aristocratic group. The figure steadily declined between 1916 and the mid-1920s, levelling off around 30 or 35 percent. The one-third ratio continued, with minor fluctuations, during the Infamous Decade of 1932-42. Under Perón, from 1946 through 1951, aristocrats accounted for only about 15 percent of all the deputies; after that, the rate was down to 5 percent.

Changes of this direction and magnitude suggest some fundamental alterations in the relationship between the Chamber of Deputies—and, by implication, the political system as a whole—and the structures of socioeconomic power. Prior to 1916, the socioeconomic elite was also the political elite; in Robert Dahl's formulation, it was an era of "cumulative inequalities."[5] From

5. Robert A. Dahl, *Who Governs? Democracy and Power in an American City* (New Haven and London, 1961).

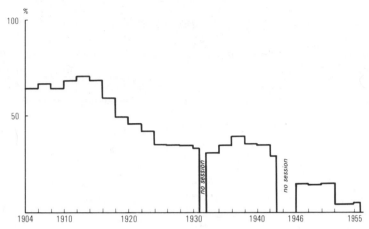

Figure 2-1. Aristocrats in the Chamber of Deputies, 1904-55, as percent of total in each legislative session.

1916 to 1930, and even to 1942, the situation became fairly fluid. Aristocrats had access to but did not dominate the Chamber, so inequalities were becoming somewhat dispersed. By 1946-55, however, aristocrats were almost completely shut out of the Chamber. Thus the tables had turned. Within a half century the correlation between individual social status and political office, and probably political power as well, had gone from strongly positive to negative.[6]

In contrast to the gradual displacement of aristocrats, the overall incidence of professionalism showed great stability—followed by sudden decline. The percentage of deputies belonging to the hard-core category, always a fairly low number, held steady at 22.8 percent in 1904-15, 21.9 percent in 1916-30, and 19.5 percent in 1932-42; then came a precipitous drop to 2.9 percent in 1946-55. The figures for all professionals, semiprofessionals as well as hard-core types, followed a roughly similar path: 47.5 percent, 44.1 percent, 45.1 percent and, under Perón, 19.5 percent. From the turn of the century through the 1930s, it appears, professionals occupied a constant proportion of seats in the Argentine Chamber of Deputies, and in many ways they tended to dominate the actual workings of the institution.[7] In the Peronist era, professionals were most conspicuous by scarcity.

Even during its ascendancy, however, parliamentary professionalism under-

6. Although aristocrats had lost their near-monopoly of economic power by the 1940s, which they shared with new industrialists and others, they still possessed a great deal of economic influence.

7. This is an impressionistic statement, one which could be subjected to empirical verification by an analysis of committee assignments and other indicators of internal influence. On this point, consult Weston H. Agor, *The Chilean Senate: Internal Distribution of Influence* (Austin, Tex., 1971).

went a fundamental transition, passing largely from aristocrats to nonaristo-crats. Figure 2-2, which depicts the general composition of the Chamber during each time period according to the sixfold typology, demonstrates the nature of this change. In 1904-15 the number of aristocratic hard-core professionals accounted for 15.6 percent of all the deputies; for subsequent

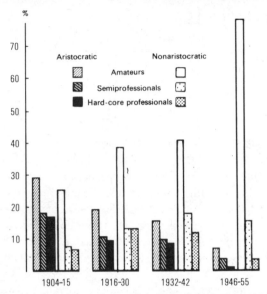

Figure 2-2. General composition of the Chamber of Deputies, 1904-55; percent of legislative types in each period.

periods the figures decreased to 10.0 percent, 8.0 percent, and finally 0.5 percent. Meanwhile the proportion of hard-core nonaristocrats rose from 7.2 percent in 1904-15 to 11.9 percent in 1916-30, held at 11.5 percent in 1932-42, then dropped to 2.4 percent under Perón. To make the point another way: of all hard-core professionals in the Chamber of Deputies, 68.4 percent came from aristocratic ranks in 1904-15; 45.8 percent, less than half, came from such backgrounds in 1916-30; 41.0 percent did so in 1932-42, and only one-sixth (16.7 percent) did so in 1946-55. As time progressed aristo-crats not only declined in number. They also declined in experience and, by implication, expertise and influence.

In general, these data suggest a steady process of disengagement from politics by Argentina's aristocracy. Under the oligarchic system inherited from the nineteenth century, aristocrats took a direct, active part in running the country's affairs. After 1916 they retreated a bit, giving way to nonaristo-crats and, in particular, to upwardly mobile political professionals. This partial phase-out probably reflects the organizational response of national parties to the implications of the Saenz Peña law, which tended to make politics a full-time task. And by the late 1940s, of course, aristocrats had no choice: after a brief and abortive rapprochement, Perón shut them out almost entirely.

But Perón did not create a professional cadre of his own. As Figure 2-2 makes clear, by far the largest single category in 1946-55 consisted of nonaristocratic amateurs, one-time deputies of modest social background, who accounted for nearly three-quarters (74.3 percent) of all the individuals who served throughout the period. One of the most striking trends during the entire half century, in fact, is the steady growth in the relative size of this category, which comprised the biggest single group in 1916-30 and 1932-42 as well as in 1946-55. But it is my strong impression that one-term winners in the pre-Peronist periods were much more likely to be professional aspirants with sustained career commitments than were their Peronist counterparts. The difference was one of quality as well as quantity.[8] Perón's elite was new, it was rather young,[9] and it consisted of inexperienced politicians, most of whom held office only briefly. One reason for such high turnover is that Perón viewed political office as a form of patronage, and wanted to spread out the benefits as far and wide as possible. Another, as we shall see in Chapter 6, is that political professionals of the traditional type had little place in his governmental scheme.[10]

To summarize, this analysis reveals fundamental transitions in the balance between various sociopolitical types in the Chamber of Deputies. The first time period, 1904-15, saw the political hegemony of the aristocrats. In 1916-30 and 1932-42 nonaristocratic professionals assumed a major role, though not to the exclusion of the other types. And ambiguities of measurement aside, 1946-55 was dominated by the nonaristocratic amateurs. Keeping these general trends in mind, now let us explore the relationships between the types of deputies and party affiliation during each of the time periods.

PARTIES AND ARISTOCRATS

One of the most obvious, and most salient, sets of questions about Argentine history deals with the connection between social status and political party. Were differences in partisan allegiance drawn along, or reinforced

8. It should be remembered, however, that the ideological commitment of Peronist deputies may well have been greater than that of other legislators.

9. Substantial (but incomplete) data show that Peronist deputies were slightly younger than their opponents, but the difference did not begin to constitute a generation gap. For example, about 15 percent of the Peronists entered the Chamber by the age of 35, compared to 10 percent of the opposition delegates; and roughly 60 percent of the Peronists became deputies no later than the age of 45, compared to 50 percent for the opposition.

10. This is the only substantive point on which I disagree with Cantón, who presents

by, social distinctions on the elite level? Which parties tended to recruit their leaders from the aristocracy? And how did the association between class and party change over time?

As an approach to these matters, Table 2-2 displays the relationship between social status, with its dichotomous categorization for aristocrats and nonaristocrats, and party affiliation for all deputies who sat in the Chamber at any time between 1904 and 1915.[11] Parties are listed in rank order, from the most aristocratic to the least aristocratic; the "Other" category refers to 24 small factions (with fewer than 10 deputies each) lumped together merely for convenience.

Table 2-2. Social Status and Political Party, 1904-15

Party	No. deputies	No. aristocrats[a]	% aristocrats[a]
Unión Nacional	11	10	90.9
Unido	26	23	88.5
Autonomista	13	11	84.6
PAN	29	20	70.0
Conservatives[b]	19	13	68.4
UCR	36	23	63.9
Oficial	69	34	49.3
Unión Popular	15	7	46.7
Popular	10	3	30.0
Other[c]	74	44	59.5
Unknown	31	18	58.1
Total	333	206	61.9

[a]As defined in Appendix A.
[b]National Conservative party (name varies over time).
[c]Parties with less than 10 deputies each.

The data clearly demonstrate the absence of any powerful link between social status and party affiliation in the 1904-15 period. Aristocrats dominated the Chamber at large and accounted for over half the deputies from most of the parties. There were differences, as the percentage figures show, but only the Popular party—a small party at that—stood far apart from the other groups. Particularly striking is the formerly rebellious UCR, which bore a remarkable social resemblance to its partisan foes. Nearly two-thirds of all Radical deputies (63.9 percent) came from aristocratic backgrounds, com-

the Peronist era as one of continuing professionalization. Cantón, *El parlamento*, pp. 96-101. In my view, prelegislative experience in the Laborista party could not indicate substantial professionalization since the party did not exist prior to 1945.

11. In this and subsequent tables, the few deputies representing more than one party during any time period are identified as members of the party first involved. Incidentally, the total number of observations for Tables 2-2 through 2-5 is greater than the total number of individual deputies, since some served in more than one time period.

pared to 70.0 percent for the archestablishmentarian PAN, 68.4 percent for the Conservatives, and 49.3 percent for the Partido Oficial. At this time, partisan affiliation was almost entirely independent of social status. Politics was controlled by the aristocracy, and on the elite level political conflict—even the challenge by the UCR—took place essentially *within* the upper class.

This situation underwent little change in 1916-30, the era of Radical rule. To demonstrate the point, Table 2-3 tabulates social status for eight parties or party groupings, some of which have been collapsed for the sake of coherence and convenience. (See Appendix B, Table B-3, for a summary of this procedure.) Again the parties are listed in rank order of aristocratic composition.

Table 2-3. Social Status and Political Party, 1916-30

Party[a]	No. deputies	No. aristocrats[b]	% aristocrats[b]
UCRAP	4	3	75.0
Conservatives	48	35	72.9
PDP	34	18	52.9
Local Radicals	50	24	48.0
Local Conservatives	50	22	44.0
UCR	266	83	31.2
Independent Socialists	8	2	25.0
Socialists	24	2	8.3
Unknown	4	2	50.0
Total	488	191	39.1

[a]On party groupings see Appendix B, Table B-3.
[b]As defined in Appendix A.

As in the previous period, the overall relationship between party and status was low. Nevertheless, important differences also began to appear. In 1916-30 aristocrats found their most consistent representation in the national Conservative party, which recruited more than 70 percent of its deputies from upper-class ranks; Local Conservatives and the Progressive Democrat party (PDP) also counted a substantial number of aristocrats among their leaders. But the Radicals, particulary the UCR, the core of the party, had begun to change their coloration. Less than one-third of the UCR deputies—compared to almost two-thirds in 1904-15—came from aristocratic backgrounds. Coupled with the almost completely nonaristocratic character of the Socialist party, this shift within the UCR lent a genuine, but by no means overwhelming, tone of social differentiation to political alignment.

Equally important is the composition of the Local and Antipersonalist Radicals (UCRAP), many of whom broke away from the UCR in the mid-1920s. Fully one-half of the deputies from these two groups (combined) came from the upper class. The implication, to be explored in Chapter 5, is that the schism within the Radical party bore some social overtones.

After the coup of 1930 and two years of military government, the relationship between social background and political party tended to increase. According to Table 2-4, which gives data from 1932-42, the Conservatives, local and national, provided the most aristocratic deputation in the Chamber (50.0 percent and 44.6 percent); less than one-quarter of the UCR group (24.0 percent) came from the aristocracy, along with virtually none of the Socialists. In testimony to the continuing process of dearistocratization, too, the PDP, UCRAP, and Local Radicals now also drew most of their deputies from outside the aristocracy.

Table 2-4. Social Status and Political Party, 1932-42

Party[a]	No. deputies	No. aristocrats[b]	% aristocrats[b]
Local Conservatives	14	7	50.0
Conservatives	138	75	44.6
Independent Socialists	10	4	40.0
Local Radicals	28	7	25.0
UCR	125	30	24.0
PDP	22	4	18.2
UCRAP	25	3	12.0
Socialists	58	1	1.7
Unknown	6	3	50.0
Total	426	134	31.5

[a]On party groupings see Appendix B, Table B-3.
[b]As defined in Appendix A.

It was under Perón, in 1946-55, that the aristocrats came to a thorough political demise. Less than 10 percent of all the deputies came from the traditional upper class, and according to Table 2-5 a disproportionate share of the aristocrats were in the opposition (17.6 percent for the UCR, against 7.1 percent for the Peronist groups). As implied by Figure 2-1, above, the social dimensions of political conflict intensified during the course of the Perón regime: from 1950 onward there were practically no aristocrats in the Chamber at all, as Perón apparently gave up his efforts to establish some sort of *modus vivendi* with aristocrats—or even with their black-sheep sons.

Thus the connection between social status and party allegiance gradually sharpened over time. In illustration of the trend, the statistical association

Table 2-5. Social Status and Political Party, 1946-55

Party[a]	No. deputies	No. aristocrats[b]	% aristocrats[b]
Conservatives	1	1	100.0
UCR	74	13	17.6
Peronists	339	24	7.1
UCRAP	1	0	0.0
PDP	1	0	0.0
Total	416	38	9.1

[a]On party groupings see Appendix B, Table B-3.
[b]As defined in Appendix A.

between class and party (on a scale from 0 to approximately 1.0) increased from 0.29 for 1904-15 to .31 for 1916-30 to .37 for 1932-42. Paradoxically, a low value of .19 for 1946-55 confirms the general tendency; it is partly due to Perón's early efforts to coopt the upper class, but it mostly reflects the negligible number of aristocrats in the Chamber at large.[12]

So much for aristocrats. The next step is to combine the information on social background and political professionalism in order to produce the sixfold classification, and then see whether and to what degree differing parties tended to recruit differing legislative types at changing points in time.

PARTIES, STATUS, AND PROFESSIONALISM

In a sense the relationship between party affiliation and political professionalism, operationally defined by the number-of-terms criterion, is tautological. Almost by definition, strong parties win a lot of elections and are more likely to have more two- and three-time deputies than are weaker parties. But the connection is not necessary: collective triumph for a party is one thing, and repeated election for individuals is quite another. It is to this latter problem, rich in implications for the organizational structure of parties as well as the Chamber itself, that we now turn.

For the 1904-15 period, Table 2-6 offers data on the relationship between party affiliation and the legislative typology.[13] The information includes, from left to right, the total number of deputies representing each party and the proportional composition of each party delegation. Accordingly the six percentage figures in each row add up horizontally to or near 100, with allowance made for rounding. As in previous tables, and for the sake of uniformity, parties are ranked according to the incidence of aristocratic membership. (I shall employ the same basic format in dealing with subsequent periods too.)[14]

12. This is the contingency coefficient C, which expresses the overall relationship between party affiliation and social status (when the latter is treated as a dichotomous variable in a cross-tabulation). Strictly speaking, these values are not exactly comparable since the number of cells in each table is not the same, but they still depict the basic trend. "Other" and "Unknown" entries have been excluded from all computations. In statistical terms I am concerned with the strength of the association rather than its significance. On the contingency coefficient, see Sidney Siegel, *Nonparametric Statistics for the Behavioral Sciences* (New York, 1956), pp. 196-202; and Charles M. Dollar and Richard J. Jensen, *Historian's Guide to Statistics* (New York, 1971), pp. 80-81.

13. It is improper to compute the value of the contingency coefficient C for Tables 2-6 through 2-9, however, since the expected cell frequencies are too low.

14. To be precise, Tables 2-6 through 2-9 display data on party affiliation, status, and the total number of terms served during the course of an entire lifetime—not merely during the time period in question. Elections won either before or after relevant time periods are counted in the lifetime total, on the grounds that a person who is just beginning a long career in politics is probably just as professional in outlook as a person who has already had a long tenure in parliament.

Table 2-6. Party, Status, and Professionalism, 1904-15
(% of Legislative Types in Each Party)

Party	No. deputies	Aristocrats[a]			Nonaristocrats[a]		
		% amateurs	%semi-professionals	%hard-core professionals	% amateurs	%semi-professionals	%hard-core professionals
Unión Nacional	11	72.7	9.1	9.1	0.0	0.0	9.1
Unido	26	30.8	11.5	46.2	3.8	0.0	7.7
Autonomista	13	38.5	30.8	15.4	15.4	0.0	0.0
PAN	29	27.6	10.3	31.0	17.2	3.4	10.3
Conservatives[b]	19	21.1	26.3	21.1	21.1	10.5	0.0
UCR	36	27.8	27.8	8.3	30.6	5.6	0.0
Oficial	69	21.7	15.9	11.6	26.1	20.3	4.3
Unión Popular	15	13.3	13.3	20.0	40.0	6.7	6.7
Popular	10	10.0	20.0	0.0	60.0	10.0	0.0
Other[c]	74	37.8	12.2	9.5	23.0	4.1	13.5
Unknown	31	29.0	19.4	9.7	22.6	6.5	12.9
Total	333	29.4	16.8	15.6	23.1	7.8	7.2

Percentage details may not add up to 100 because of rounding.

[a]Aristocrats are defined according to Appendix A. As explained in the text of this chapter, amateur deputies are those who served only one term; semiprofessionals, those who served two terms; hard-core professionals, those who served three or more terms.

[b]National Conservative party (name varies over time).

[c]Parties with less than 10 deputies each.

The data in Table 2-6 provide an empirical and suggestive glimpse into the breakdown of the nineteenth-century oligarchic system. The older, traditional parties—Unido, Autonomista, PAN—contained substantial professional elements, even of the hard-core type. Nearly one-third of the PAN delegations, for instance, consisted of hard-core professional aristocrats, and another 10 percent were hard-core nonaristocrats; this was a highly durable, experienced, professional group. But the successor to the PAN, the so-called Partido Oficial, with the largest single deputation in the Chamber (N=69), presented only a small hard-core professional cadre: 11.6 percent aristocrats, 4.3 percent nonaristocrats, 15.9 percent in total. Nor was there much professionalism within the UCR, whose spokesmen first won election in 1912: over half the Radicals were amateurs, especially amateurs of nonaristocratic background (who accounted for 30.6 percent of the party total). In general, 1904-15 was an era of transition. One system was on the way out, and a new one was not yet in place. As a result, the newer parties showed high turnover and instability of personnel. (The fairly substantial number of hard-core professionals in the Other category is mainly due to the Socialists, most of whom won their second or third terms to office after 1915.)

As parties developed organizational responses to electoral demands after implementation of the Saenz Peña law, the association between party affiliation and parliamentary professionalism became increasingly complex. Table 2-7 presents pertinent data on this matter for the 1916-30 period. Amid the many diverse patterns, it is clear that the Socialist party—a highly disciplined, evidently hierarchical group—had the most professional delegation in the Congress. Nearly two-thirds of all Socialist deputies were in the hard-core category, and 54.2 percent consisted specifically of nonaristocratic three-time winners. Also professional, but in a different way, was the Conservative representation: 14.6 percent were in the aristocratic semiprofessional category, and over twice as many (37.5 percent) in the aristocratic hard-core group.

Differing from both the Socialists and the Conservatives, the UCR was showing its own signs of professionalization. Although the biggest Radical contingent consisted of nonaristocratic amateurs (45.5 percent), the second largest being aristocratic amateurs (17.3 percent), many of these amateurs were doubtless party loyalists and hacks. Positions of leadership within the UCR appear to have resided in the professional ranks, where—in contrast to the Conservatives—nonaristocrats prevailed. One gets the impression that by this time the UCR had become a generally bureaucratic organization which provided upward mobility for many leaders and which, in the era of its triumph, used seats in the Chamber as a kind of payoff for loyalty or campaign contributions.

Table 2-7. Party, Status, and Professionalism, 1916-30
(% of Legislative Types in Each Party)

Party[b]	No. deputies	Aristocrats[a]			Nonaristocrats[a]		
		% amateurs	% semi-professionals	% hard-core professionals	% amateurs	% semi-professionals	% hard-core professionals
UCRAP	4	50.0	25.0	0.0	0.0	0.0	25.0
Conservatives	48	20.8	14.6	37.5	8.3	8.3	10.4
PDP	34	26.5	11.8	14.7	20.6	11.8	14.7
Local Radicals	50	30.0	10.0	8.0	42.0	8.0	2.0
Local Conservatives	50	18.0	10.0	16.0	32.0	10.0	14.0
UCR	266	17.3	9.8	4.1	45.5	13.9	9.4
Independent Socialists	8	0.0	25.0	0.0	62.5	12.5	0.0
Socialists	24	0.0	0.0	8.3	25.0	12.5	54.2
Unknown	4	25.0	0.0	25.0	25.0	0.0	25.0
Total	488	18.9	10.2	10.0	37.1	11.9	11.9

Percentage details may not add up to 100 because of rounding.
[a]Aristocrats are defined according to Appendix A. As explained in the text of this chapter, amateur deputies are those who served only one term; semiprofessionals, those who served two terms; hard-core professionals, those who served three or more terms.
[b]On party groupings see Appendix B, Table B-3.

In 1932-42 the correlation between party, status, and professionalism took a somewhat different turn, as shown in Table 2-8. Now the national Conservatives, bastion of upper-class interests, recruited a substantial number of their spokesmen from the nonaristocratic professional ranks (6.5 percent and 10.1 percent). The UCR, still dominated by the one-term types, also showed an increase in the incidence of nonaristocratic professionalism (now up to 23.2 percent and 12.8 percent). Partly because of internal schisms the Socialists suffered a sharp decline in the degree of professional leadership (from 54.2 percent in 1916-30 down to 22.4 percent in the hard-core nonaristocratic category), but they still fielded one of the most experienced delegations in the Chamber. In contrast to the previous period, when the number of amateurs seems to have corresponded to Radical hegemony, the frequency of one-term deputies now appears to reflect the short-lived success of some parties, rather than deprofessionalization: Local Radicals and Independent Socialists, who collaborated with the early *Concordancia*, at that time the multi-party ruling coalition; and the PDP and the Socialists, both in the opposition, pushed aside when the UCR ended its electoral boycott in 1935. (And since it was impossible for any member of the UCR to win election to more than two full terms during the decade, semiprofessionals might here be counted as equivalent to hard-core types.) Because of all these circumstances, it seems fair to conclude that the degree of nonaristocratic professionalism had increased—and become more evenly distributed among the leading parties.

As already demonstrated in Figure 2-2, the trend towards professionalization came to an abrupt halt under Perón. Table 2-9 clearly reveals the extraordinary unprofessionalization of Peronist deputations in the 1946-55 era. Less than 17 percent of all the Peronists returned to the Chamber for second or third terms, compared to nearly one-third for all the parties of the opposition—which, to say the least, were having trouble at the polls (so many of their one-term representatives were probably professionals too). To a major degree, therefore, parliamentary partisan conflict in 1946-55 corresponded to a struggle between legislative types: amateurs versus professionals, Peronists against the opposition.

SUMMARY

Collective-biographical data and prosopographic techniques have led to several conclusions about changes in the composition of the Argentine Chamber of Deputies between 1904 and 1955. Some of my methods have rested on delicate assumptions, so the findings must be taken as approximate, but they probably yield reliable indications of general trends over time.

Table 2-8. Party, Status, and Professionalism, 1932-42
(% of Legislative Types in Each Party)

Party[b]	No. deputies	Aristocrats[a]			Nonaristocrats[a]		
		% amateurs	% semi-professionals	% hard-core professionals	% amateurs	% semi-professionals	% hard-core professionals
Local Conservatives	14	35.7	14.3	0.0	35.7	14.3	0.0
Conservatives	138	23.2	13.8	17.4	29.0	6.5	10.1
Independent Socialists	10	0.0	20.0	20.0	30.0	10.0	20.0
Local Radicals	28	7.1	10.8	7.1	60.7	14.3	0.0
UCR	125	12.8	8.0	3.2	40.0	23.2	12.8
PDP	22	13.6	4.5	0.0	50.0	22.7	9.1
UCRAP	25	8.0	0.0	4.0	44.0	36.0	8.0
Socialists	58	1.7	0.0	0.0	56.9	19.0	22.4
Unknown	6	16.7	16.7	16.7	33.3	16.7	0.0
Total	426	14.6	8.9	8.0	40.4	16.7	11.5

Percentage details may not add up to 100 because of rounding.

[a] Artistocrats are defined according to Appendix A. As explained in the text of this chapter, amateur deputies are those who served only one term; semiprofessionals, those who served two terms; hard-core professionals, those who served three or more terms.

[b] On party groupings see Appendix B, Table B-3.

Table 2-9. Party, Status, and Professionalism, 1946-55
(% of Legislative Types in Each Party)

Party[b]	No. deputies	Aristocrats[a]			Nonaristocrats[a]		
		% amateurs	% semi-professionals	% hard-core professionals	% amateurs	% semi-professionals	% hard-core professionals
Conservatives	1	0.0	0.0	100.0	0.0	0.0	0.0
UCR	74	10.8	6.8	0.0	60.8	16.2	5.4
Peronists	339	5.3	1.5	0.3	77.9	13.3	1.8
UCRAP	1	0.0	0.0	0.0	0.0	100.0	0.0
PDP	1	0.0	0.0	0.0	0.0	100.0	0.0
Total	416	6.3	2.4	0.5	74.3	14.2	2.4

Percentage details may not add up to 100 because of rounding.

[a]Aristocrats are defined according to Appendix A. As explained in the text of this chapter, amateur deputies are those who served only one term; semiprofessionals, those who served two terms; hard-core professionals, those who served three or more terms.

[b]On party groupings see Appendix B, Table B-3.

1. Given my sixfold typology of deputies, it is evident that aristocrats, professionals as well as amateurs, dominated throughout the 1904-15 period. Nonaristocratic professionals gained ground in 1916-30 and again in 1932-42; nonaristocratic amateurs comprised the largest group in 1946-55.

2. Among deputies, the overall association between social status and political party was never very high, though it intensified as time went on. There may also have been important breaks within the broad time spans employed in this chapter, so I shall return to this question at a later point.

3. Relationships between party, status, and political professionalism were complex and do not lend themselves to facile summary. Data for 1904-15 reveal the displacement of old professionals by new amateurs within the traditional, aristocratic, oligarchic parties. From 1916 onward there was a general tendency for all major parties to find leadership among nonaristocratic professionals, but at differing rates and to differing degrees. In 1916-30 the Socialists were mostly nonaristocratic and professional; the Conservatives were still aristocratic, but professional; and the Radicals contained a cadre of nonaristocratic professionals, plus a large number of amateurs. During the 1932-42 period the number and proportion of nonaristocratic professionals increased, and became more evenly distributed among the major parties. But after 1946 the trend changed direction, as Peronism set about to deprofessionalize (and dearistocratize) the prevailing manner of political recruitment.

4. There are also some negative findings which I have not reported in the body of this chapter. To be precise, neither the age of deputies nor their regional constituencies appear to comprise a clear accompanying characteristic of any of the legislative types.

Aside from specifying the changing character of Argentina's legislative elites, my findings on the legislative typology are important because of the questions they raise: whether, as hypothesized above, there is any connection between the composition and the behavior of parliamentary groups; and whether this connection, if it exists, can stimulate actions or responses by outside groups. Such problems undergo extensive examination in the following pages.

3
Dimensions of Conflict

One of the most fundamental features of any political system concerns the issues which give rise to conflict. What do people—or their leaders—fight about? Exploration of this question, simple as it may seem, offers an important key to comprehending processes of interaction among political elites. With specific reference to the Argentine Chamber of Deputies, this chapter seeks to identify major dimensions of conflict and their change over time.

DATA AND METHODS

In order to deal with this problem I shall examine the varying content and underlying patterns in the roll-call votes (*votaciones nominales*) which occurred in the Chamber between 1904 and 1955. This approach has manifold virtues. A total of 1,712 roll calls took place during this period,[1] and they furnish hard data which are subject to statistical analysis. Such information makes it possible to handle alignments within large groups (such as the 1,571 deputies involved in this study), including anonymous backbenchers as well as men of fame and reputation. And roll-call votes record patterns of explicit action, rather than statements of intent, so the investigation can dispense with rhetoric and focus on modes of actual behavior.

There are disadvantages too. Legislative voting, in and of itself, reveals nothing about the motivation of the deputies. Nor does it yield direct information on the intensity of conflict, obviously an essential aspect of elite interaction.

Roll-call data present empirical as well as conceptual problems, particularly for longitudinal time-series analysis. In the Argentine Chamber of Deputies,

1. Since there is no guide or index for roll calls, I found the votes by culling through nearly 250 volumes of the *Diario de Sesiones*. I may have missed some votes, but my intent was to gather data on every one during the entire period.

for instance, the total number of recorded votes in legislative sessions[2] varied sharply, from a minimum of 19 in 1908-9[3] to a maximum of 324 in 1946-47. This kind of disparity casts doubt upon the comparability of roll-call patterns at different points in time, and presents a serious methodological challenge.

The basic difficulty is that the varying frequency of roll-call voting reveals changes in the meaning of the act itself. The election of officers of the Chamber, for example, called for obligatory roll-call votes; this requirement accounted for approximately two-thirds of all the *votaciones* from 1904 through 1915, although the proportion thereafter declined to 25 percent or less (usually falling in the neighborhood of 10 percent). Attempts to override presidential vetoes also called for compulsory roll-call votes, although such instances were fairly rare. All other recorded votes were optional, and they could be called at any time by one-fifth of those deputies in attendance. As Lee C. Fennell has persuasively argued, the fluctuation in voluntary roll-call voting (especially from 1916 to 1950) depended largely upon the level of political competition, the number of contending groups in parliament, and the deputies' sense of accountability to their constituents.[4] The introduction of an electro-mechanical recording device in 1938 provided further (but temporary) stimulus by cutting down the time required for each division. From 1950 on the Peronist majority, with overwhelming control of the Chamber, seems to have utilized public voting as a means of demonstrating unswerving loyalty to *El Líder* and his movement, and also as a proclamation of popular support. In the early 1950s votes were always one-sided and sometimes unanimous; they amounted to a ritual of affirmation, a continuing sign of solidarity and triumph.

Because of these considerations, and also for some technical reasons, I have restricted my analysis to contested roll calls, identified according to a two-step procedure. First, in dealing with each legislative session, I decided to limit my concern to deputies who voted on at least one-half of the roll calls in that session.[5] Second, I defined a contested or competitive vote as one on which at least 10 percent of the participant deputies took the minority side.

2. Though a new session technically opened every year, I have considered periods during which membership was constant—usually two years long—as single legislative sessions. Annual sessions could run from one calendar year to the next, but for simplicity's sake I shall identify them by the year in which they began.

3. Not counting the one-year sessions of 1930 and 1955, both interrupted by military coups.

4. Lee C. Fennell, "Reasons for Roll Calls: An Exploratory Analysis with Argentine Data," *American Journal of Political Science,* 18, no. 2 (May 1974), 395-403.

5. The relatively low rates of participation prior to the mid-1920s raise some vexing questions about the functional significance of parliamentary absenteeism; at the same time, the secular increase in participation suggests a gradual invigoration of the Chamber of Deputies, in keeping with most of my observations in the final section of Chapter 1. See Appendix B, esp. section 2.

(See Appendix B, especially sections 2 and 3, for a detailed explanation of these rules and their implications.) In keeping with the purpose of this chapter, I shall therefore be working exclusively with demonstrated *instances of conflict*. Uncontested elections of officers, Peronist rituals, and other near-unanimous votes are dismissed from consideration. To illustrate the consequences of this decision, Figure 3-1 traces, over time, the total number of roll calls and the number of contested roll calls in each legislative session.

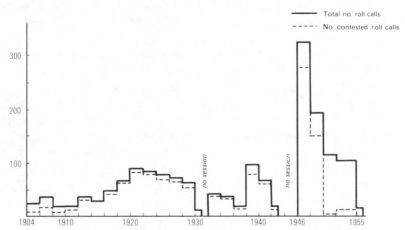

Figure 3-1. Frequency of roll-call voting, 1904-55. In 1914-15 and 1930 the number of contested roll calls was equal to the total number of roll calls; in 1955 there were no contested roll calls.

The trends in frequency bear important substantive implications. Both the absolute and relative numbers of contested roll-call votes reveal an increase in parliamentary competition resulting from the electoral reform of 1912 and continuing, with fluctuations, up to 1930.[6] The comparatively small number of contested votes in the early 1930s testifies to the hegemony of the progovernment *Concordancia;* the return of the Radicals in 1936 led to a brief, competitive resurgence, which then subsided as the Infamous Decade came to an end. Somewhat surprisingly, the first two sessions under Perón reveal marked—and extremely frequent—competition, and this phenomenon will bear close examination throughout the course of this study. Starting in 1950, however, the combined impact of political repression and loyalism led to a drastic decline in the number and proportion of contested votes. In the 1955 session—interrupted by Perón's overthrow—there were no contested divisions at all, so data for this year have been omitted from further analysis.

The substantive content of contested votes provides additional clues about

6. The small number of votes in 1930 was mainly due to the coup of that year, plus delaying tactics which often prevented the formation of quorums.

the Chamber and its occupants. (See Appendix C for a full catalog of contested votes.) Voluntary roll calls in the 1904-15 period, though relatively scarce, deal with such timely issues as electoral reform, resistance to presidential vetoes—a matter rendered sensitive by Josè Figueroa Alcorta's dissolution of Congress in 1908—and the propriety and legality of elections after the reform of 1912.[7] Almost all divisions entailed essentially political matters. While the economy continued to grow at the high rates it maintained during these years, parliamentary leadership gave little thought to social and economic problems.

The Radical triumph of 1916, followed by Hipólito Yrigoyen's accession to the presidency, expanded both the range and frequency of congressional competition. Aside from political questions—which continued to occupy a major share of parliamentary attention—a variety of other issues came up for consideration. In 1916-17 there was a string of votes about the sugar tariff, neutrality in World War I, and agricultural assistance.[8] Similar questions appeared in subsequent years, along with disputes over federal intervention in the provinces, governmental corruption and inefficiency, responses to crises in agriculture and the cattle industry, the nationalization of petroleum, even civil-military relations. It is abundantly clear that, during the 1916-30 period, the Argentine Congress provided quite an open arena for the vigorous articulation and pursuit of contending group interests. (Because of delaying tactics by the opposition, the abortive 1930 session took four months to constitute itself, and then was terminated by the September coup; but even then the exclusively political concern of roll-call voting is revealing, and offers insight into the preoccupations of the moment.)

Despite the installation of the *Concordancia* in 1932, the Chamber continued to fall out over basic current issues. The 1932-33 session gave rise to cleavage over political amnesty, taxes, mortgage regulations, unemployment, and a variety of economic policies.[9] The 1934-35 parliament split over approval for a state of siege and, among other questions, congressional authority for investigating governmental regulation of the meat trade.[10] In 1940-41, with Radicals bolstering the opposition ranks, two major public scandals—one on a War Ministry land purchase deal, another on concessions to a private electric power company—furnished material for roll-call votes.[11] Also during that session, and in 1942 as well, Argentina's stance in World War

7. In Appendix C, see roll call nos. 14-16 in 1910-11; 28-29 in 1912-13; and 2, 10, and 11 in 1914-15.

8. For 1916-17, see roll call nos. 27-31, 36-38, and 44-45.

9. See Table C-15, passim.

10. Roll call nos. 7, 8, and 16 for 1934-35.

11. Roll call nos. 23, 30, and 56 for 1940-41.

II became a matter of congressional dispute.[12] However infamous this decade may have been, deputies argued and struggled over some prominent issues.

After the military interlude of 1943-46, this tradition reappeared in 1946. With a vigorous and outspoken minority, the Chamber cast roll-call votes on an immense variety of issues: Perón's labor policy, intervention in the universities, pensions and patronage, purchase of the British railroads, rent control, commercial functions of the Instituto Argentino de Promoción del Intercambio (IAPI), rights of the political opposition, and many more.[13] It was not until 1950 that an overwhelming preponderance of Peronist deputies brought near-unanimity on most votes, so the number—and substance—of contested issues suddenly became very thin; the same was essentially true of the session from 1952 to 1954.

Aside from its intrinsic significance, the range and diversity in the subject matter of contested divisions cast light in two related areas. First, they provide a kind of substantive inventory to predominant preoccupations of the parliamentary elite: these were issues which (a) at least one-fifth of the Chamber thought worthy of a roll-call vote, and (b) provoked dissent from at least one-tenth of the actively participant deputies. Second, allowing for changes over time, they reveal the Chamber of Deputies to be a remarkably relevant institution for the articulation, if not the resolution, of contemporary national issues. One gets the feeling, from a general acquaintance with twentieth-century Argentine history, that most current public questions of each era found their way into the Chamber—and ultimately became the subject of a roll-call vote. Other than the summary of contested votes in Appendix C, I cannot offer solid proof of this assertion, mainly because it is unprovable. But it is my conviction, as well as my premise, that the overall salience of roll-call voting offers substantial justification for using the Chamber of Deputies to analyze elite interaction in Argentine politics.

At the same time, the roll calls also illustrate a quality of narrowness within the national elite. Particularly during the 1920s and 30s, the Chamber ignored or deemphasized a whole range of social and economic issues: the imbalance of regional development, the need for industrialization, foreign control of resources, the social poverty of displaced migrants and tenant farmers. Urban labor received some consideration, in modest amounts, and some of the other issues came up for discussion without prompting roll-call votes. But the general record is one of neglect. Much of this deemphasis is understandable since, as shown in Chapter 1, members of the Chamber were elected by a limited constituency which did not include foreign-born ele-

12. Roll call nos. 6, 7, 9, 10, 51, and 52 for 1940-41; and nos. 15-17 (possibly also 4 and 5) for 1942.

13. Tables C-21 and C-22, passim.

ments within the middle and lower classes. So if roll calls represent the full breadth of actual preoccupations among political elites, they also demonstrate—by omission—how many issues failed to stimulate intense concern among the country's leadership.

DIFFERENTIATION OF CLEAVAGES

The variety in content of the *votaciones* does not mean, of course, that they each produced unique alignments among deputies. In a highly inflexible atmosphere it would be conceivable for legislators to vote exactly the same way on all issues; the less structured the situation, the more fluid the line-ups. In recognition of this distinction I shall attempt to analyze the level of *differentiation* in congressional alignments. And the question now becomes: What was the level of differentiation in the Argentine Chamber of Deputies, and how did it change over time?

To deal with this problem (and subsequent ones) I have resorted to factor analysis.[14] One task this technique can perform is to specify the number of independent patterns of alignment, or factors (also referred to as dimensions), existing within a given set of roll calls. If there are solid, unwavering blocs in the Chamber, there will be only one dimension in the voting; the greater the variation in alignment, the greater the number of factors. Thus the number of factors corresponds to the degree of differentiation in voting behavior.[15] But since this number is partly a function of the number of roll calls analyzed, and some legislative sessions had more contested roll calls than did others, I have decided to compute the ratio between the number of factors and the number of roll calls, and use this ratio as my index of differentiation. Accordingly, Figure 3-2 traces chronological trends in the factor/roll-call ratio from session to session. The higher the ratio, the higher the level of differentiation.

The results are extremely suggestive. Most notably, there is a clear and steady decline from a high degree of differentiation in the early sessions to a low level by the late 1920s (the relatively high level for 1930 largely resulting

14. See R. J. Rummel, *Applied Factor Analysis* (Evanston, Ill., 1970), esp. Ch. 2 on "Philosophy of Factor Analysis." The specific application.of factor analysis to roll-call data is discussed in Lee F. Anderson et al., *Legislative Roll-Call Analysis* (Evanston, Ill., 1966), Ch. VII; and Duncan MacRae, Jr., *Issues and Parties in Legislative Voting: Methods of Statistical Analysis* (New York, 1970).

15. I am specifically referring to the number of factors with eigenvalues greater than unity. For the measurement of differentiation I have employed this purely statistical criterion for the purpose of achieving comparability over time; but in subsequent portions of the analysis, particularly the search for substantive factors, I have extracted no more than five factors from the roll-call voting pattern in any single legislative session (see Appendix B, esp. section 4).

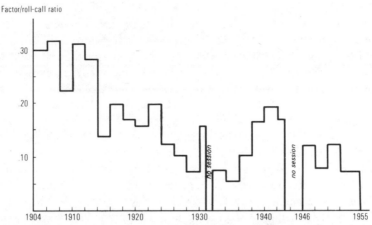

Figure 3-2. Levels of differentiation in roll-call voting, 1904-54. Differentiation in each legislative session is measured by the ratio between the number of factors with eigenvalues greater than unity and the number of roll calls analyzed.

from the small number of roll calls for that year). Prior to the Saenz Peña law, parliamentary behavior seems to have been a bit unstructured; alliances were made, dropped, remade, without any apparent sense of permanence. After 1912, and particularly after 1916, the drop in differentiation suggests that voting took on a more permanent, cumulative quality, as deputies took consistent sides on varying kinds of issues. The intensification of this process during the 1920s offers an important clue to politics under the Radicals, and I shall come back to it again.

The 1932-42 period also shows a marked change, but this time in reverse: a transition from low to moderate differentiation. With the return of the Radicals in 1936 and Roberto Ortiz's inauguration as president in 1938, congressional behavior appears to have acquired flexibility and diversity. Not only were there more roll-call votes, as shown in Figure 3-1; there were also more discernible alignments.

Trends under Perón command a great deal of attention. Despite the widespread tendency to see implacable hostility between Peronists and anti-Peronists in Argentine society since 1946,[16] the moderate levels of differentiation in the legislative sessions of 1946-47 and 1948-49 imply that this picture might well be oversimplified. (Actually, ratios for these sessions may

16. Although this tendency is generalized, it is by no means universal. For analysis of changes during the Peronist years, see Samuel L. Baily, *Labor, Nationalism, and Politics in Argentina* (New Brunswick, N.J., 1967), Chs. IV-VII; Peter Waldmann, "Las cuatro fases del gobierno peronista," and Walter Little, "La tendencia peronista en el sindicalismo argentino: el caso de los obreros de la Carne," both in *Aportes*, 19 (January 1971), 94-106 and 107-24.

be depressed by the very high number of roll calls analyzed.[17] The figures for 1950-51 and 1952-54 are also misleading, since each session had only one factor, but the very small number of contested votes produced an artificial rise in the ratio.) With allowance made for these considerations, the Peronist period comes to reveal a sharp transition from moderate degrees of differentiation in 1946-49 to low degrees of differentiation in 1950-54.

During the first half of this century, the level of differentiation in parliamentary alignment thus underwent important changes over time. On the broadest plane, the general trend shows a two-stage development: first, a gradual decline from high differentiation in the early part of the century to low differentiation in the late 1920s; second, a relatively stable pattern, with fluctuation between low and moderate degrees of differentiation.

Even more generally, such findings clearly demonstrate that there were, in varying measure, manifold alignments in the Argentine Chamber of Deputies. The next problem is to find out whether differing alignments corresponded to specific and identifiable issues.

SUBSTANTIVE CONTENT OF CLEAVAGES

Factor analysis offers an excellent means of approaching this task because it can identify empirical clusters of roll-call votes. Through this procedure, each roll call obtains a statistical score (known as a "loading") demonstrating its relationship to each of the factors: the higher the score, the closer the relationship.[18] In most cases each factor has strong loadings with a variety of roll calls—which can be considered to constitute a cluster, insofar as they produced similar alignments among the deputies.[19] If all the roll calls in the cluster have a common issue orientation, it is furthermore fair to infer that the factor represents, or captures, the common attitudinal dimension which underlies the separate votes. (To take some hypothetical examples: if roll calls involving nationalization of railroads, governance of state-owned petro-

17. On the other hand it has been impossible to analyze all the contested roll calls for 1946-47 and 1948-49 because of limited computer capacity. Consequently, the 90 most contested roll calls in each of these sessions have been selected for analysis, whereas the total number of contested votes was 278 (for 1946-47) and 153 (for 1948-49). This procedure could have produced an upward bias in the factor/roll-call ratio; but other kinds of evidence (such as the total number of factors with eigenvalues greater than unity—respectively 11 and 7) convinces me that this was, indeed, a period of moderate as opposed to low differentiation.

18. Disregarding the sign of the loading, which can be positive or negative, depending upon the particular configuration of the roll-call vote.

19. I speak of clusters in a general sense of the word. Technically there is an important difference between cluster analysis and factor analysis, as outlined in Charles Dollar and Richard J. Jensen, *Historian's Guide to Statistics* (New York, 1971), pp. 215-16.

leum reserves, and restrictions on foreign investment all have strong loadings on a single factor, one might conclude that the factor reflects a pervasive concern with "Economic Nationalism." Similarly, votes on import taxes, anti-trust regulations, and price ceilings might define a "Consumer Protection" dimension.) In practice, the substantive interpretation of factors is difficult and delicate, and it requires a thorough understanding of the latent content of the roll-call votes.

Moreover, factor analysis gives some idea of the relative importance of each factor, in rough correspondence to the proportion of roll calls with high loadings on it.[20] This notion of importance can be deceptive, since it depends upon the particular combination of roll calls subjected to analysis, and changes in these combinations could have considerable impact on the distribution of statistical importance among the factors (the substantive content of the factors could also be affected in this way). The application of uniform criteria for selecting roll calls in each session has somewhat reduced this problem, and the relative prominence of the factors will comprise an integral part of this analysis.[21] The point to remember is that the first factor extracted, referred to as Factor I, is the most important in the statistical sense of the term; Factor II is the next most important, Factor III is the third most important, and so on up through Factor V.

In order to deal with the Argentine data I have constructed several loose categories for identifying the substantive content of factors. One is a so-called "General" type of factor, which has strong loadings with a fairly large number of roll calls representing diverse, apparently unconnected kinds of policy choice or attitudinal dimensions. In most cases the General label applies, if at all, to the most pervasive dimension in the legislative session (that is, Factor I), and it seems to involve support for, or opposition to, the government in power, rather than matters of ideology. (In fact I have been tempted to use a name like "Support for Administration Power and Policies," but this title seems a little too specific; the General label is a bit broader and, I think, more accurate as well.)[22]

Similar to the General factor is a type which I shall call "Unclear," a name

20. More precisely, according to the proportion of variance explained by each factor.

21. Note again that the procedures were not quite uniform, since special procedures had to be adopted for 1946-47 and 1948-49 (see note 17).

22. In many ways these General factors are analogous to the "Presidential Support" factor which Anderson and his colleagues found in the United States Senate, but many of the roll calls associated with the General factors show no clear sign of presidential involvement. Anderson et al., *Legislative Roll-Call Analysis*, pp. 143-64. My General factor also bears a resemblance to the "Partisan Issues" scale which Lee C. Fennell has analyzed in his thesis on "Class and Region in Argentina: A Study of Political Cleavage, 1916-1966" (Ph.D. diss., University of Florida, 1970), but I still prefer the General label; whether or not the factor represented partisan conflict is an empirical question which I shall take up in Chapter 4.

pertaining to factors which have strong loadings with only two or three a priori unrelated roll calls, in contrast to the multitudinous loadings associated with General dimensions. It is possible that the votes relating to Unclear factors share an attitudinal dimension which I have not been able to detect, or that one or more of the high loadings might be spurious and thus exert distorting effect.[23]

Other conventions refer to relatively straightforward situations. (1) If all roll calls with strong loadings on a factor deal with the election of officers for the Chamber, I label this an "Officers" factor. (2) If the election of officers combines with the approval of congressional elections or individual credentials, I conceive of the factor as involving the "Distribution of Parliamentary Power." (3) If the election of officers appears in conjunction with votes on federal intervention in one or more provinces, I see this as affecting, in a somewhat broader sense than the previous type, the "Distribution of Political Power."

These cases aside, all other factors represent reasonably discrete issue areas, some of which may reveal genuine ideological or preferential continua.[24] Even so, the persistence and pervasiveness of ambiguity prompts methodological and conceptual caution. Unless factors appear to be quite pure, I would regard them as reflecting behavioral modes of parliamentary alignment rather than attitudinal scales. This does not, in my view, diminish the usefulness or meaning of factor analysis. And as I shall try to indicate below, lack of clarity can, paradoxically, throw substantial light upon conceptions of congressional behavior.[25]

With all these caveats in mind, I have set out to find and identify prevailing factors. (The raw data for this task, including tables with all factor loadings for each legislative session, are in Appendix C.) Table 3-1 summarizes my

23. Examination of the zero-order correlation coefficients between roll calls with high loadings on Unclear dimensions suggests that a couple of the factors—and some of the loadings on such factors—are statistical artifacts of the factor-analytic method, and in particular they may result from overfactoring. Emphasis upon these intercorrelations might make it possible to label some of the Unclear factors, but with attendant methodological risk.

24. In an effort to gain maximum analytical leverage I have used fairly liberal criteria for identifying substantive factors. For instance, I have not insisted that all votes dealing with a particular issue (such as foreign policy) must have strong loadings on a specific factor in order to label it a "Foreign Policy" factor. For general, but by no means exclusive, guidance I have focused on roll calls having loadings with absolute values equal to or greater than .50.

25. In fact, I think it is wholly unreasonable to expect legislators to cast all votes in accordance with clear and consistent attitudinal preferences. On this point see the fascinating essay by Donald R. Matthews and James A. Stimson, "Cue-Taking by Congressmen: A Model and A Computer Simulation," in William O. Aydelotte, ed., *The Dimensions of Parliamentary History* (Princeton, N.J., forthcoming), as well as other papers in this important volume.

Table 3-1. Substantive Content of Factors, 1904-15

Session	Factor I	Factor II	Factor III	Factor IV	Factor V
1904-05	Alignment for 1905	Officers for 1904	Officers for 1904	–	–
1906-07	Distribution of Political Power for 1907	Distribution of Parliamentary Power for 1906	Vice-Presidents for Late 1907	Comisión de Cuentas, June 1907	Comisión de Cuentas, May 1906
1908-09	Distribution of Political Power	Vice-President for 1909	–	–	–
1910-11	Officers for 1910	Officers for 1911	Distribution of Political Power	Congressional Autonomy	Unclear
1912-13	General	Officers for 1913	Support for President	Unclear	Role and Authority of Congress
1914-15	General	General for 1915	Government Spending on Church	Monetary Policy	–

interpretations for the 1904-15 period, giving summary descriptive labels to each of the factors in each legislative session. The factors are listed in numerical order, I through V, on the basis of their relative statistical importance.

Like the roll calls in these years, most of the factors reflect essentially political concerns. What is interesting—particularly for the first three sessions—is that there are multiple dimensions of any kind. In 1906-7, for instance, the election of parliamentary officers yielded five distinct types of cleavage. For this session, as for some others too, the factors appear to reveal chronologically circumscribed coalitions. Struggles for political preeminence thus seem to have prompted a series of temporary, fluid patterns of alignment.

A separate and recurrent theme concerned "Congressional Autonomy" (see Factor IV for 1910-11 and Factor V for 1912-13). In the face of expanding executive powers, parliamentary prerogative became an issue of its own. The relative clarity of additional factors in 1910-11, 1912-13, and 1914-15 strongly suggests that issue areas were fairly discrete at the time, a finding which complies with data on differentiation in Figure 3-2. But from 1912 onward a new development also begins: the preeminent appearance of across-the-board General alignments.

According to Table 3-2, this trend persisted throughout the Radical period, as General substance characterized at least six out of eight first factors between 1916 and 1930 (the 1920-21 first factor also shared some General characteristics). And there are two additional General dimensions, plus six others which I have had to call Unclear.

This situation strongly implies that, following the establishment of political competition in 1912, deputies began responding to legislative issues in a cumulative fashion. Many votes, regardless of their content, fell along the same behavioral continuum. One might reasonably suspect that this development bore a connection to party strength and coalitions; I shall explore this possibility in Chapter 4.

Paradoxically, though, some issues—usually economic—gave rise to separate alignments. The "Sugar Tariff" factor in 1916-17 is extremely pure and unambiguous. Cleavages over the "Governmental Minimum Wage," "Rent Control," and "Authority for Labor Regulations" are fairly clear, and reveal continuing sources of disagreement over policies toward the working class. By 1930, however, the entire focus was political, both factors dealing with the "Distribution of Parliamentary Power."

What seems to have occurred, between 1916 and 1930, is an expansion and contraction of issue orientations. For several sessions after Yrigoyen's first inauguration, the Chamber demonstrated an inclusive, expansive capacity which allowed specific kinds of cleavage to coexist with predominant General

Table 3-2. Substantive Content of Factors, 1915-30

Session	Factor I	Factor II	Factor III	Factor IV	Factor V
1916-17	General	Sugar Tariff	Well-being of Urban Lower class (?)	Unclear	Legalization of Divorce
1918-19	General	General	Unclear	Rules for Congressional Attendance	Unclear
1920-21	Opposition to Administration	Officers; Congress-ional Autonomy	Government Minimum Wage (?)	Vice-President for January 1922	Rent Control
1922-23	General	Tariffs	Improvements for City of Buenos Aires	Congressional Autonomy	Response to Cattle Crisis
1924-25	General	General	Congressional Procedures and Priorities	Intervention in San Juan	Provisional President
1926-27	General	Congressional Autonomy (?)	Nationalization of Petroleum	Women's Rights	Authority for Labor Regulations
1928-29	General	Unclear	Unclear	Political Tranquillity	—
1930	Distribution of Parliamentary Power	Distribution of Parliamentary Power	—	—	—

factors. After Yrigoyen's second inauguration, the picture quickly changed. Factors emerging in 1928-29 were broad, vague, or political; by 1930 political questions had become completely paramount. As the range of issues lost explicit definition, so the lines of conflict hardened—and Argentina's Congress submerged itself in politics.

In 1932-42, the Infamous Decade, General dimensions returned to the fore, defining all first factors prior to 1942 (the "Foreign Policy" cleavage in that year has broad aspects too). Table 3-3 reveals only a few discernible issue orientations, which are virtually absent from the first three sessions, and some of the definable factors have no genuine policy orientation. The process of contraction thus continued.

Alignments during the Perón era offer much material for speculation. General factors, fraught with partisan overtones, appeared in all the congressional sessions. But in 1946-47 and 1948-49, as shown in Table 3-4, there are also other factors, some fairly discrete, having to do with a variety of governmental policies. Two additional factors (II in 1946-47, III in 1948-49) reflect disagreement over the role and rights of the political opposition. Multiple, reasonably coherent dimensions of cleavage appeared in these sessions, more so than in many previous years. Deputies, at least a large number of them, seem to have been casting ballots independently.

Then this pattern disappeared. In 1950-51 and 1952-54, all roll calls fell along single dimensions. Issue overlap was now complete. Regardless of the question at hand, deputies lined up in a single fashion.

Yet this development came about only after several years, a fact which emphasizes the need to discern and analyze distinct phases within the Peronist regime. Quite clearly, the factor matrices imply a transition from a relatively independent Chamber in the late 1940s to a subservient monolithic organ in the 1950s.

SUMMARY

In this chapter I have attempted to identify the range and character of conflict in the Argentine Chamber of Deputies. Applied to roll-call voting data, factor-analytic techniques have yielded empirical findings on both the *differentiation* and the *substance* of functional cleavages.

1. The differentiation of conflict began at a relatively high level in 1904-5, declined to the end of the 1920s, and wavered from low to moderate thereafter.

2. The substantive content of parliamentary division followed a concomitant pattern. During the early years, voting dimensions reveal the existence of loose and temporary coalitions with little (if any) issue orientation. In 1912 began a pervasive phenomenon: the appearance of across-the-board

Table 3-3. Substantive Content of Factors, 1932-42

Session	Factor I	Factor II	Factor III	Factor IV	Factor V
1932-33	General	General (possible emphasis on economic policies)	Legalization of Divorce	—	—
1934-35	General	General	—	—	—
1936-37	General	Parliamentary Procedures	—	—	—
1938-39	General	Pensions for Police	Unclear	Order of Business	Popular Economic Welfare
1940-41	General	General	Parliamentary Procedures	Confidence in Government Officials	Tax Restitution
1942	Foreign Policy (?)	Unclear	Inheritance Tax	—	—

Table 3-4. Substantive Content of Factors, 1946-54

Session	Factor I	Factor II	Factor III	Factor IV	Factor V
1946-47	General	General (possible emphasis on rights of political opposition)	Economic Policies	Memorial to Hipólito Yrigoyen	Labor Agitation
1948-49	General	Extensions of Government Power	Patronage and Political Opposition	Regulation of Functional Groups	Policies on Real Estate
1950-51	General	—	—	—	—
1952-54	General	—	—	—	—

General cleavages which characterize the first and foremost factor in almost all subsequent legislative sessions. To be sure, there were some clearly defined issue areas too. But for the most part, congressional conflict acquired a cumulative, aggregate, mutually reinforcing quality.

Both of these findings imply a fundamental and far-reaching transformation in elite behavior. Whereas contending groups in the Chamber of Deputies first confronted each other on selective matters, creating *ad hoc* alliances for each kind of question, they eventually came to challenge each other on broad, generalized fronts. This transition began almost immediately after the electoral reform of 1912, accelerated from 1916 to 1930, and continued (albeit with fluctuations and reversals) to 1950—at which time the patterns of cleavage became thoroughly uniform and one-dimensional. Over time, lines of conflict in the Chamber became increasingly fixed. Our next task is to find out what determined those lines.

4
Correlates of Conflict

A central premise of most legislative analyses, including this one, is that the cumulative pattern of individual actions can reveal underlying regularities in collective behavior. Consciously or not, legislators act as members of collective entities; and it is the formation, structure, and duration of these entities which fundamentally define the character and modes of group interaction. The problem, therefore, is to identify the regularities. What gave shape to collective action in the Chamber of Deputies? Did legislators vote in unchanging blocs at all times? Or did alignments vary according to the substance of the issue at hand?

In reference to Argentina, these questions give rise to several possible answers. One plausible proposition might maintain that legislative conflict has taken place along regional lines. Just as federalists from the interior fought against the coastal unitarians throughout the nineteenth century, so their descendants struggled in the twentieth century. After all, as Chapter 1 has shown, the economic modernization of Buenos Aires and the pampas occurred at the expense of the interior, whose inhabitants were bound to feel resentment. Accordingly the regional hypothesis gains credibility from the logic of national development, as well as from its stress upon the continuities of history.[1]

A second general position asserts that elite-level cleavages have responded to the dictates of social class, rather than regional interest. One variation of this argument holds that, from 1890 onward, the country's burgeoning middle sectors challenged the traditional aristocracy in order to reorganize the structure of society; eventually they tried to mobilize support among the

1. See Miron Burgin, *The Economic Aspects of Argentine Federalism, 1820-1852* (Cambridge, Mass., 1946); James R. Scobie, *Argentina: A City and a Nation*, 2nd ed. (New York, 1971); and, for a conceptual discussion of the problem, Joseph L. Love, "An Approach to Regionalism," in Richard Graham and Peter H. Smith, eds., *New Approaches to Latin American History* (Austin, Tex., 1974).

lower classes and lead a broad assault on the historic ruling groups.[2] But the social-class hypothesis can also take another form, maintaining that Argentina's bourgeoisie has consistently cooperated with the aristocracy in an effort to suppress the restless masses. Pursuing a kind of collaborationist policy, the middle class—mobile, prosperous, eager for social recognition— joined the upper class in an alliance against the lower class.[3]

Yet another interpretation might depict political conflict as a struggle between successive generations. I do not know of any systematic application of this theme to Argentine politics, but the prevailing literature customarily makes reference to it. The Generation of 1880 directed the nation on a course of export-import growth; the Generation of 1900 attempted, fitfully, to bring the working class into the mainstream of society;[4] students in the Generation of 1918 led the University Reform which exerted such pervasive influence on higher learning throughout Latin America.[5] Years later, some say, youthful voters cast their ballots overwhelmingly for Juan Perón.[6] Observations of this kind combine to produce the proposition that the nation's politics have witnessed constant, almost Oedipal warfare between fathers and sons, a ceaseless disputation of the young against the old.

Fourth, and finally, there is the commonplace hypothesis that political cleavages in Argentina have followed party lines. Particularly since the electoral reform of 1912, according to this argument, political parties have transcended the specific interests of region, social class, or generations. As heterogeneous organizations they have served to pull various groups together, aggregate their interests, and exert autonomous influence on the definition of conflict. This view has gained widespread adherence in studies of Argentine history; while many writers see parties as representing certain social groups, they nevertheless employ the party as the fundamental unit of analysis.[7]

2. John J. Johnson, *Political Change in Latin America: The Emergence of the Middle Sectors* (Stanford, Cal., 1958), Ch. 6.

3. Jorge Abelardo Ramos, *Revolución y contrarrevolución en la Argentina: las masas en nuestra historia* (Buenos Aires, 1957).

4. Ibid., pp. 296-301.

5. See Richard J. Walter, *Student Politics in Argentina: The University Reform and Its Effects, 1918-1964* (New York and London, 1968); and Alberto Ciria and Horacio Sanguinetti, *Los reformistas* (Buenos Aires, 1968).

6. I have disputed this hypothesis on the basis of aggregate data, and mention it here only to illustrate the emphasis on generational phenomena which pervades the study of Argentine politics. See my article on "The Social Base of Peronism," *Hispanic American Historical Review*, 52, no. 1 (February 1972), 55-73.

7. See, for example, Carlos R. Melo, *Los partidos políticos argentinos*, 3rd ed. (Córdoba, 1964); Alfredo Galletti, *La realidad argentina en el siglo XX: la política y los partidos* (Mexico and Buenos Aires, 1961); Alberto Ciria, *Partidos y poder en la Argentina moderna (1930-46)* (Buenos Aires, 1964); and Darío Cantón, *Elecciones y partidos políticos en la Argentina. Historia, interpretación y balance: 1910-1966* (Buenos Aires, 1973).

Each of these interpretations—that political conflict has responded to dictates of region, class, generation, or party—seems plausible enough. When they are applied to the Chamber of Deputies, the basic question is empirical: Which hypothesis turns out to be correct? It is this problem, beguiling in its simplicity, which I shall now address.

DATA AND METHODS

To test the validity of each hypothesis I shall attempt to correlate the voting records of the deputies with their regional constituency, social background, age, and political party. As a reflection of the voting patterns I shall utilize the numerical scores, known as factor scores, which each deputy receives on each of the roll-call voting factors for each session of the Chamber in which he took part. Every factor provides an independent voting scale, and participant deputies have separate scores on every one. As explained in Chapter 3, the number of extracted factors varies from session to session; some factors can be identified with discrete issue areas, other cannot.[8]

It seems fair to assume that the variation in factor scores corresponds to, and can reveal, fundamental patterns of parliamentary behavior. Deputies with similar scores on a factor comprise a demonstrable voting bloc; those at the other end of the scale comprise another bloc. The immediate task is to find out whether such groupings have common and collective characteristics.

With this in mind, I shall here examine the statistical relationships between factor-scale scores and four sets of attributes:

Region, to see if conflict in the Chamber followed geographical lines. Here I have associated each deputy with the province where he was elected, then put the province into one of five areas: (1) the Federal Capital, being the City of Buenos Aires; (2) the Province of Buenos Aires; (3) the Coast, consisting of Corrientes, Entre Ríos, and Santa Fe; (4) the Northwest, including Catamarca, Jujuy, La Rioja, Salta, and Tucumán; and (5) the Interior, containing all the other provinces. Generally this scheme categorizes regions on the basis of historical and economic development.[9]

Status, with deputies categorized as being either aristocratic or nonaristocratic (according to procedures set forth in Appendix A), to examine the hypothesis that some kinds of cleavage in the Chamber might demonstrate patterns of class conflict. Because of its dichotomous quality this variable

8. On factor scores, see R. J. Rummel, *Applied Factor Analysis* (Evanston, Ill., 1970), Ch. 19; and Lee F. Anderson et al., *Legislative Roll-Call Analysis* (Evanston, Ill., 1966), pp. 165-67. In this study factor scores for individual deputies have been computed by applying a linear transformation to the standardized raw data; as obtained by FACTOR2, the program which I used, scores for every factor have a mean of 0 and a variance of 1.

9. See Scobie, *Argentina*, esp. Ch. 1.

provides a direct test for only one version of the social-class interpretation, the idea that middle- and lower-class leaders joined together in a struggle with the upper class. Yet a near-zero correlation would also be rich with implication: without proving the existence of a middle-upper class alliance, it would at least dispel the notion of a frontal attack upon the aristocracy.

Age at the beginning of each legislative session, to explore the possibility of generational division. I have constructed four categories: up through 35 years old, 36 to 45, 46 to 55, and over 55.

Political Party, to test the general notion that Argentine politics has tended to be highly partisan. For 1904-15, I have retained all the party labels of the period. From 1916 onward I have condensed the many parties into ten groups: Traditional Conservatives (such as the PAN), Conservatives (this being a national party), Local Conservatives, Partido Demócrata Progresista (PDP) and affiliates, the UCR, the UCR Antipersonalista (UCRAP), Local Radicals, Socialists, Independent Socialists, and Peronists. (A complete list of the categories appears in Appendix B, Table B-3.) Naturally, these groups appeared in different combinations at different points in time.

Putting all this information together, the question now becomes: Did Argentine deputies tend to vote according to regional interest, social status, generational solidarity, or party affiliation? If so, to what degree? and on what issues?[10]

AGGREGATE TRENDS

To establish broad chronological trends in parliamentary behavior I have devised indices which purport to measure, in comparable fashion, the degree of association between each of the independent variables and the overall distribution of roll-call votes. Briefly described, my procedure has been to weigh the correlation between each variable and each set of factor scores in each legislative session in accordance with the statistical importance of each factor. (For a detailed explanation, see Appendix B, section 5.) Theoretically the resultant scales range from 0 to 1, but for technical reasons I would consider a score of .50 to be very strong indeed.

Some of the most significant findings are negative. It appears that Status, for instance, never exerted much statistical impact on roll-call voting. For the entire period from 1904 through 1954, the highest aggregate index, in 1934-35, was .12, and for most sessions it was even less than that. (A

10. I must emphasize the fact that this analysis deals with conflict among the deputies themselves, and not among their electoral constituencies. For studies of popular voting behavior, see Cantón, *Elecciones*, and my article on "The Social Base of Peronism."

complete list of all indices appears in Table B-6 of Appendix B.) The conclusion is inescapable: at no time did the Argentine Chamber of Deputies witness protracted conflict between aristocrats and nonaristocrats. If class struggle ever took place within the Chamber, it was not against the aristocracy.

A similar result obtains for Age, which had a maximum index of .19 in 1952-54. As in the case of Status, most of the indices fell substantially below .10. Such figures reveal an almost total absence of generational cleavage among deputies. In short, the young-versus-old hypothesis does not stand up to empirical analysis.

The data on Region begin to show some positive results. The highest index, for 1942, was .24. It was .21 in 1910-11, .20 in 1934-35, and well above .10 in many other sessions. In general, the fluctuations range from low to moderate, and do not reveal any secular trend. Thus regional affiliation never exerted an overwhelming impact on aggregate voting; for whatever reason, the bitter heritage of the nineteenth century did not dominate the halls of Congress.[11] But as I shall demonstrate below, regionalism did bear particular relationships to certain kinds of issues.

By far the highest indices belong to the Party variable. Fourteen of the overall measures for the twenty-four legislative sessions between 1904 and 1954 exceed .50—and, in my view, reveal very strong association between party membership and parliamentary voting. Furthermore, the disparity between the figures for Party and the other variables indicates that *party identification exerted substantial independent effect on legislative alignments*, rather than merely institutionalizing and reinforcing preexisting differences in Region, Status, or Age. To illustrate the chronological dimensions of this situation, Figure 4-1 plots the session-by-session indices for Party over time.

The resulting trends are richly suggestive. First, party affiliation exerted a relatively low influence on roll-call voting from 1904 through 1912. As shown in Chapter 3, shifting, *ad hoc* alliances prevailed at this time; moreover, it is now quite clear that these alliances were not composed primarily of party units. In the absence of further information, I suspect that Argentine deputies joined temporary factions on a highly individual basis. After all, this

11. One possibility is that deputies from the interior fell prey to the manifold attractions of Buenos Aires and, in effect, betrayed their provincial constituencies. As James R. Scobie has written: "Men from the provinces came to the city, drawn by opportunities and offices. Repeatedly these individuals adopted Buenos Aires as their own. After 1880 the congress, largely composed of provincials, lavished funds to transform this large village of low, one-story buildings into Latin America's most elegant metropolis, a Paris of the Southern Hemisphere." Scobie, "Buenos Aires as a Commercial-Bureaucratic City, 1800-1910: Characteristics of a City's Orientation," *American Historical Review*, 77, no. 4 (October 1972), 1038.

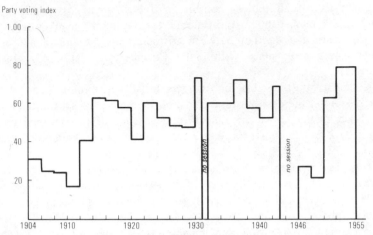

Figure 4-1. Degrees of voting along party lines, 1904-54.

was the era of aristocrats, and as I hypothesized in Chapter 2, aristocrats showed little taste for party politics. Conflict was limited, responsibility to constituents was mitigated by electoral fraud, codes of personal deportment and *dignidad* prevailed. In the clublike atmosphere of the period, ardent loyalty to a political party would have been unseemly and out of place.[12]

In 1912—the year of electoral reform—Party began to assume decisive influence on roll-call voting, and the index climbed rapidly from .18 in 1910-11 to .63 in 1914-15. From 1916 through 1921, the sessions corresponding to Yrigoyen's first presidential term, partisan voting slipped gradually from .61 to .41. The Alvear administration witnessed a similar cycle: the index went back up to .62 in 1922-23, just after the inauguration, tailing off to .49 by 1926-27. Because of the continuing schism within Radical ranks partisanship stayed around .48 in 1928-29, following Yrigoyen's second inauguration, and then shot up to a peak of .76 during the truncated session of 1930.

The overall pattern for 1916-30 shows that party conflict was high, though subject to fluctuation, a finding which lends strength to my impression about the behavior of different types of deputies. If nonaristocratic professionals were coming to the fore, as I have claimed in Chapter 2, the predominance of Party makes a good deal of sense. It seems more than likely that deputies who had climbed up through party ranks would also vote on party lines.

The 1932-42 decade reveals much the same pattern, with a brief increase in partisan voting after the return of the Radicals in 1936 and then a temporary decline. But in general, Party continued to have a strong and stable

12. See also Ramon Columba, *El congreso que yo he visto* (Buenos Aires, 1949), vol. I.

influence on roll-call alignments, as the index ranged from .52 to .74. Despite the relative lack of electoral competition, even during the Radical boycott of the early 1930s, political professionals appear to have retained a sense of party allegiance. To this extent the *Concordancia* was not, as many have thought (and some had hoped), a return to the pre-1912 politics of gentlemanly aristocrats; it was an age of partisan conflict.

Notwithstanding its reputation for blind intransigence, the Perón era shows a startling development: first, a phase of very low degrees of party voting, with indices of .29 and .21 for 1946-47 and 1948-49[13] —a return, in fact, to pre-1912 levels; second, starting in the 1950 session, a phase of extreme, and ultimately unprecedented partisanship. Such erratic behavior conforms precisely to my hypothesis regarding political amateurs, predominant throughout this period (see Chapter 2). For a while they enjoyed some independence, and voted according to personal preferences. Then the leadership exerted more demands, and they submitted willingly to party discipline.

Thus far the analysis has demonstrated that, in the main, roll-call voting in the Chamber of Deputies followed party lines. Moreover, the data reveal that *party conflict became particularly acute just prior to the military coups of 1930, 1943, and 1955.* As reflected in Figure 4-1, the Party indices climbed sharply from the mid-1920s to 1930, when Yrigoyen was thrown out of office; they climbed again from the mid-1930s to the early 1940s, when another coup took place; and the cycle again happened under, and to, Perón. This does not mean that intense partisanship directly caused the coups, which varied in their origin and purpose. But the link is more than mere coincidence: when partisan conflict intensifies, military intervention follows. It would appear that the Argentine army did not step into politics just of its own accord; perhaps, as suggested in the Introduction, it was responding to occurrences in the political system. The character of these occurrences, and the significance of party conflict, will be dealt with later on in Chapter 6.

Despite the manifold importance of partisan allegiance, my techniques for measuring its influence on roll-call voting have been exceedingly robust. It is still conceivable that Status or Age or Region could exert substantial impact on parliamentary voting *within* the party groupings.

COMPLEX RELATIONSHIPS

To explore the possibility that legislative alignments responded to a variety of simultaneous influences, I shall use an open-ended technique which selects, on a purely empirical basis, the optimal combination of independent

13. The voting indices for 1946-47 and 1948-49 may be somewhat depressed by my selection of the 90 most contested roll calls in each session (because of limited computer capacity) rather than dealing with all contested votes, but I suspect that the distortion is not very great.

variables for predicting the values of the roll-call voting scores. Packaged in a computer program called the Automatic Interaction Detector (AID), this routine begins by selecting that dichotomous permutation of the independent variable, such as Party, which has the strongest correlation with the distribution of the factor scores. On this basis it divides the deputies into two groups—for example, the UCR against all other parties. For each of these blocs AID picks the most powerful permutation of another variable (such as Region or Status)—or a different permutation of Party (perhaps separating the Socialists from the Conservatives within the "Other" group)—and breaks down the original partisan groupings into smaller subgroups and splits them up again, according to yet another permutation, and so on in successive iterations until final groupings appear.[14]

These technical matters aside, the point to remember is that this procedure can determine the optimal arrangement of independent variables for explaining roll-call voting scores. AID thus affords several criteria for identifying the existence of discernible groups within broad partisan blocs. First, it tells us which variables come into play after the initial split is made on Party (assuming that this is the case). Second, it indicates how many splits take place according to each variable, that is, how often it comes into play. Third, AID measures the explanatory power of the complex model, according to its degree of accuracy in explaining the distribution of the voting scores (the scale is from 0 to 1). By comparing the coefficient for the complex model with the coefficient for the simple Party model, we can also ascertain the amount of explanatory power gained.

To maximize comparability (and minimize confusion) let us analyze the findings in connection with scores on the first and foremost factor (Factor I) in the successive legislative sessions—usually, but not always, a multipurpose General factor. The results are not strictly comparable regarding issue content, since the substance of votes on the General dimensions varied through the years. They are directly comparable, though insofar as they refer to alignments on the most pervasive dimension in each session.

Table 4-1 sets forth the information from the AID analyses. Reflecting the initial dichotomization of the deputies, entries for the simple models give the name of the variable involved—Party in every case but one—and the coefficient (under the symbol R^2) for its explanatory power. Data on the complex models include the names of pertinent variables; in parentheses, the number of splits made on each variable; and the R^2 coefficient for the entire

14. John A. Sonquist and James N. Morgan, *The Detection of Interaction Effects: A Report on a Computer Program for the Selection of Optimal Combinations of Explanatory Variables* (Ann Arbor, Mich., 1964). See also Appendix B, section 5. Note that AID operates according to the strength of associations between variables, rather than statistical significance.

Table 4-1. Simple and Complex Models for Predicting Dominant Voting Alignments, 1904-54.

Session	Simple model Variable	R^2	Complex model Variables[a]	R^2	Difference in R^2 values[b]
1904-05	Party	.37	no additional splits	.37	.00
1906-07	Party	.25	Party (2), Region (3), Status (1)	.38	.13
1908-09	Party	.26	Party (2), Region (1), Status (1)	.42	.15
1910-11	Region	.26	Region (2), Party (4)	.45	.19
1912-13	Party	.64	Party (3), Region (1)	.81	.17
1914-15	Party	.71	Party (2), Age (1)	.81	.10
1916-17	Party	.87	no additional splits	.87	.00
1918-19	Party	.82	Party (1), Status (1), Region (2)	.89	.07
1920-21	Party	.23	Party (1), Region (1), Status (1)	.41	.18
1922-23	Party	.85	Party (1), Region (1)	.87	.02
1924-25	Party	.81	Party (1), Region (1)	.83	.03
1926-27	Party	.57	Party (3), Region (1), Status (2)	.86	.28
1928-29	Party	.56	Party (2), Region (2)	.68	.12
1930	Party	.81	Party (2), Region (1)	.90	.09
1932-33	Party	.63	Party (4)	.92	.29
1934-35	Party	.53	Party (2), Region (2)	.62	.09
1936-37	Party	.77	Party (2), Region (1)	.81	.04
1938-39	Party	.73	Party (3), Region (2)	.83	.10
1940-41	Party	.75	Party (3), Status (1), Region (2)	.82	.08
1942	Party	.83	Party (1), Region (3)	.90	.07
1946-47	Party	.50	Party (1), Status (1), Region (1), Age (1)	.66	.17
1948-49	Party	.35	Party (2), Region (2)	.42	.07
1950-51	Party	.62	no additional splits	.62	.00
1952-54	Party	.80	no additional splits	.80	.00

[a]Listed in approximate order of appearance in the models.

[b]Figures may vary slightly from the apparent difference in R^2 values because of rounding.

model.[15] The extra explanatory power accruing from the complex analysis is summarized by the difference in R^2 values in the right-hand column.

To an overwhelming degree, the figures demonstrate the pervasive importance of the Party variable. In some instances AID produced no additional breaks beyond the first dichotomization. And where it did, a general rule appears to hold: the greater the incremental gain in R^2, the greater the number of divisions according to Party. For example, the complex models surpass the explanatory power of the simple models by more than .20 in only

15. The optimal multivariate model is considered to be that model with the highest over-all explanatory power (R^2). But because the inclusion of Age greatly reduced the number of observations (deputies) for each legislative session, as shown in Table B-4 of Appendix B, I have included models based upon these populations only if the Age variable appeared in one of the operative splits.

two sessions—1926-27, when three out of six splits were on Party, and 1932-33, when all the splits took place on Party. The basic point is unambiguous: in the Chamber of Deputies, especially from 1912 onward, Party allegiance reigned supreme.[16]

When other variables enter the AID models, the most frequent to appear is Region. Within partisan groupings, regional identification often had a notable impact on voting alignments. And in some cases, Region (or Status or Age) may have been a primary determinant of factor-score configurations. Consideration of this eventuality requires exploration of conflict in discrete issue areas.

SELECTIVE FORMS OF CONFLICT

To permit specific focus on each kind of cleavage, Table 4-2 lists the variables with maximum predictive power—and their respective R^2 coefficients—on all perceptible roll-call alighments in the twenty-four legislative

Table 4-2. Optimal Predictors of Voting Scores on Separate Factors, 1904-54[a]

Session	Factor I	Factor II	Factor III	Factor IV	Factor V
1904-05	Party (.37)	Party (.28)	Region (.18)	—	—
1906-07	Party (.25)	Party (.45)	Age (.07)	Party (.16)	Party (.10)
1908-09	Party (.26)	Party (.18)	—	—	—
1910-11	Region (.26)	Party (.36)	Party (.16)	Party (.08)	Region (.08)
1912-13	Party (.64)	Party (.44)	Party (.29)	Party (.21)	Party (.25)
1914-15	Party (.71)	Party (.59)	Party (.42)	Party (.44)	—
1916-17	Party (.87)	Region (.24)	Party (.41)	Party (.24)	Party (.14)
1918-19	Party (.81)	Party (.41)	Party (.14)	Region (.18)	Region (.30)
1920-21	Party (.23)	Party (.78)	Party (.45)	Party (.16)	Region (.12)
1922-23	Party (.85)	Region (.24)	Age (.13)	Party (.11)	Party (.32)
1924-25	Party (.81)	Party (.41)	Party (.24)	Age (.05)	Party (.30)
1926-27	Party (.57)	Party (.48)	Party (.03)	Party (.05)	Party (.28)
1928-29	Party (.56)	Party (.54)	Party (.20)	Party (.35)	—
1930	Party (.81)	Party (.57)	—	—	—
1932-33	Party (.63)	Party (.70)	Party (.28)	—	—
1934-35	Party (.53)	Party (.67)	—	—	—
1936-37	Party (.77)	Party (.41)	—	—	—
1938-39	Party (.73)	Party (.16)	Party (.22)	Party (.25)	Region (.20)
1940-41	Party (.75)	Party (.39)	Region (.11)	Party (.34)	Region (.10)
1942	Party (.83)	Party (.65)	Age (.06)	—	—
1946-47	Party (.50)	Party (.17)	Party (.13)	Party (.07)	Status (.02)
1948-49	Party (.35)	Party (.22)	Party (.12)	Party (.12)	Party (.10)
1950-51	Party (.62)	—	—	—	—
1952-54	Party (.80)	—	—	—	—

[a]Figures in parentheses represent values of R^2 for the optimal dichotomous permutations of the relevant variables.

16. That is, in comparison to the other variables employed in this study.

sessions between 1904 and 1954. As before, Party emerges with impressive force, explaining the optimal proportion of voting-score variance on 76 out of the grand total of 92 factors. The R^2 values are not always high. Nor do they rule out the possibility that some other variable, not available for this analysis, might show an even greater correlation with parliamentary behavior. Within the limits of this study, however, the over-all supremacy of Party—although in varying degree and permutations—stood unchallenged. (Precisely for this reason, the form and fluctuation of party coalitions will provide the subject of the following chapter.)

The table further demonstrates that Status and Age never had any substantial primary impact on roll-call voting by the deputies. In the rare cases where they came out as optimal predictors, the R^2 values were so low as to be almost meaningless (the maximum for Age, on Factor III of 1922-23, was only .13; the only emergent value for Status, on Factor V of 1946-47, was a paltry .02).[17] *Neither generational differences nor antiaristocratic sentiment appears to have determined any of the voting alignments in the Chamber in any meaningful measure.*[18]

At the same time it is also clear that Region, with optimal predictive power for 13 of the 92 alignments, bore relevant connection to isolated aspects of the roll-call voting. Such frequent exceptions to the predominant rule of partisanship call for explanation.

To this end, Table 4-3 offers summary information on those cases where (a) Region had the maximum explanatory power, (b) the R^2 coefficient for Region exceeded .15, and (c) the factors had an apparent—or approximate—substantive definition. Material in the first three columns identifies the factors by session, number, and content; the right-hand column displays the optimal dichotomous permutation of Region as selected by the AID program. Essentially, the data make it possible to correlate the content and voting alignments on each factor with the operative pattern of regional alignment.

Revealingly enough, three out of the four factors concern economic issues, and two of them refer to tariffs (Factors II of 1916-17 and 1922-23). Both of these latter instances betray clear conflict between producing and consuming areas. The debate of 1916-17 reflected an effort, on behalf of consumers, to lower the protective duty on sugar. Deputies from the urban Capital led the fight in favor of the bill, spokesmen for the Northwest—home of the sugar industry—staunchly resisted it. Apparently regarding sugar as a

17. Throughout this analysis, the R^2 values for Status, Region, and Party have been taken from AID runs excluding data on Age (see note 15).

18. These generalizations refer to conflict *inside* the Chamber of Deputies. It is possible, for instance, that issues may have possessed an antiaristocratic flavor but not produced a clear split between aristocratic and nonaristocratic deputies—especially if, as during the Perón years, there were scarcely any aristocrats left in the parliament.

Table 4-3. Regional Alignment on Selected Factors

Session	Factor no.	Substantive content[a]	Alignment[b]
1916-17	II	Sugar Tariff	Capital, Interior, and Buenos Aires Province vs. Coast and Northwest
1918-19	IV	Congressional Attendance	Interior and Northwest vs. Buenos Aires Province, Coast, and Capital
1922-23	II	Tariffs	Capital vs. Coast, Interior, Buenos Aires Province, and Northwest
1938-39	V	Popular Economic Welfare	Buenos Aires Province, Interior, and Northwest vs. Coast and Capital

[a]For explanatory information see Chapter 3 and Appendix C.
[b]Listed in rank order, according to mean factor scores.

special interest, most delegates from other areas—with the exception of the Coast—took the consumer side.

The tariff question in 1922-23 involved a plan to raise the duties on a variety of goods (including wool, cotton, shoes) as well as on sugar. The results again reveal a split between consumer and producer interests. This time the Capital, consuming center of the nation, stood alone against the rural and producing areas.[19]

Such alignments plainly demonstrate the persistence, and occasional pre-eminence, of regional economic interests, especially regarding tariff schedules. During the nineteenth century, as shown above, this cleavage presented a major obstacle to national unification. No longer quite so critical, it could still shape conflict among political elites.

The other economic dimension—Factor V in 1938-39, which I have

19. For a descriptive analysis of most of the relevant roll calls (specifically nos. 75 and 77-80 as recorded in Appendix C, Table C-10), see Carl Solberg, "The Tariff and Politics in Argentina, 1916-1930," *Hispanic American Historical Review*, 53, no. 2 (May 1973), 276 and 278-79. One interesting consequence of our different methodologies is that Solberg, for no apparent reason, chooses to interpret the votes along party lines (276), whereas I am led to stress the regional factor (see Table 4-2). At the same time his cross-tabulations permit close observation of each roll-call result, while my techniques risk oversimplification in two ways: first by relying on cumulative scales, and secondly by focusing on only the dichotomous split between the regions. As Solberg's data and my scalar scores reveal, delegations from the Coast and Province of Buenos Aires were internally divided on the 1922-23 tariff issue (both having slightly protariff average factor scores of -.16, compared to a positive antitariff mean of +.82 for deputies from the Capital and a protariff score of -.72 for spokesmen from the Northwest), but this fact does not show up in a purely dichotomous scheme.

(hesitantly) labelled "Popular Economic Welfare"—does not yield such unambiguous interpretation. Roll calls with the strongest loadings on this factor concerned provisions for agrarian reform, mainly to stimulate migration to the countryside (or at least to slow down cityward migration), and a wage settlement for railroad workers. Given the configuration of the votes, delegates from rural areas—the Province of Buenos Aires, the Interior, and the Northwest—may have supported the agrarian bill in anticipation of maintaining a substantial population size, and given low priority to the wage agreement since most railroad workers lived in urban communities. Conversely, deputies from the Coast and especially the Capital would be likely to encourage mass migration from the countryside, which would (among other things) augment the power of their political base; and they would also tend to uphold wages for the city-dwelling workers. In a sense, this cleavage represented a regional struggle for the favor—and control—of Argentina's growing working class.

The only noneconomic factor to provoke significant regional dispute, the "Congressional Attendance" dimension of 1918-19, contains a curious twist. The defining votes revolved around the question of whether to make attendance compulsory during extraordinary sessions of the Chamber in January 1919. One possibility is that spokesmen for the Interior and Northwest were seeking prompt consideration of a vital (economic?) bill, though the *Diario de Sesiones* is unclear on this point. It is more likely, I think, that deputies from distant Northwest and Interior provinces simply wanted to bring the extraordinary sessions to a close and go home. Men from the Province of Buenos Aires, Coast, and Capital could afford to engage in delaying tactics because they lived nearby and suffered little personal hardship; those from far-off places did not have this luxury.

All in all, these data indicate that Argentine deputies could sometimes place regional interest above partisan considerations, usually on selected economic matters (but by no means on all economic matters, most of which fell in with General factors). Yet this occurred only between 1916 and 1942, during the era of nonaristocratic professionals—legislators who apparently had some sense of constituent needs. Neither the aristocrats nor the amateurs seem to have acted in this way.

SUMMARY

In this chapter I have tried to find out whether roll-call alignments in the Chamber of Deputies obeyed regularities defined by social origin (Status), generation (Age), geography (Region), or partisan affiliation (Party). Several conclusions have emerged from the analysis.

1. The most prevalent and powerful determinant of roll-call alignments, throughout the entire period from 1904 to 1954, was Party.[20]

2. However the degree of Party influence underwent important changes, from a low-to-moderate level before 1912 to generally high levels from 1916 to 1942 to abruptly changing levels (first low, then high) from 1946 to 1955.

3. Broad trends in Party voting indirectly confirm the idea that different types of legislators would behave in different ways. Aristocrats, it appears, showed disdain for partisan allegiance; professionals, especially nonaristocratic ones, were loyal to their parties; amateurs could be erratic when left alone, but they were highly responsive to strong party leadership.

4. Party conflict became especially severe just prior to the military coups of 1930, 1943, and 1955.

5. The only other variable to have a substantial impact on voting, either alone or in combination with Party, was Region. The importance of regional influence was particularly apparent on economic issues, especially in connection with the age-old question of the tariff.

20. This conclusion sharply modifies one of the generalizations in my *Politics and Beef in Argentina: Patterns of Conflict and Change* (New York and London, 1969), which depicts political struggle as taking place largely between economic interest groups. The most likely explanation for this inconsistency is simply that the beef-industry issue was not fully representative of the political process at large; certain kinds of economic issues may have prompted functional cleavage, at certain times, while other kinds— frequently aired in the Chamber—gave rise to party conflict. It should also be noted that the data in this present study do not lend themselves to an analysis of economic interest (which I would distinguish from occupation), so the relative explanatory power of this variable has not been subjected to a direct test.

5
Patterns of Party Alignment

The discovery that Argentine deputies voted largely along party lines leads directly to another set of questions. How did the parties tend to line up? What kinds of coalitions took shape at what times? Were partisan positions related to specific issues? Was there much variation over time? Skipping over the initial period of generally low party conflict (1904-15), this chapter confronts these problems by exploring patterns of party alignment from 1916 through 1954.[1]

DATA AND METHODS

The basic data for this inquiry come from the factor analysis already used in Chapters 3 and 4. In order to locate a party's scalar position on any dimension of roll-call voting in a given legislative session, as represented by a factor, I shall simply take the mean (or average) of individual scores on the appropriate factor for all deputies belonging to that party. Parties which tend to vote alike on certain factors for whatever reason—tend to have similar mean scores; opposing parties have differing scores. Of course there may be a good deal of fluctuation around the party mean, perhaps reflecting internal disagreement, but (at the risk of some simplification) reliance upon the average score should suit the purpose at hand.[2]

For every congressional session, each party obtains a scale position on each of the factors extracted. This permits us to identify forms of conflict and

1. Though partisan voting was quite strict in 1912-13 and 1914-15, as shown in Figure 4-1, the transitory character of many parties in that period makes analysis extremely difficult.

2. Another problem with reliance on the mean is that averages become very unstable in small groups. Regarding fluctuation around the mean score, it should be possible to use the standard deviation as an indicator of party dispersion, or lack of cohesion, and I shall do so briefly near the end of this chapter.

consensus on various dimensions, and sometimes in relation to specific issue areas, depending upon the content of the factors.

In this context I shall operationally define a party *coalition* as one of the two optimal party groupings formed by Automatic Interaction Detector (AID), the computer program described in the previous chapter (see also Appendix B, section 6); *conflict* will be considered as the fact of location in separate camps. Though mindful of the likelihood of complex cleavages, such as trichotomous groupings, I shall deal only with dichotomous patterns, mainly for the sake of clarity.

1916-30: COALITIONS AND CONFRONTATIONS

To begin the analysis, Table 5-1 summarizes party alignments in the Chamber of Deputies from 1916 to 1930. For each factor in each legislative session, the table presents the following information: (a) the substantive label of the factor, according to my interpretation, (b) the pertinent partisan cleavage, as identified by AID, and (c) in the right-hand column, the coefficient of determination, or R^2, which indicates the extent to which deputies actually voted along the relevant party lines. (As stated in Chapter 4, an R^2 value of .50 shows that the roll-call alignment bore a close relationship to partisan affiliation, in which case the party cleavage merits very strict attention. An index of .20 could be viewed as moderate; anything below .10 basically means that the voting on that factor did not correspond to party allegiance.) A letter *b* after the R^2 figure indicates that some other variable —Age, Status, or Region—had a greater correlation with the scale-score distribution for that factor than did Party.

Perhaps the most obvious finding concerns Factor I, usually General in content and, by statistical definition, always the most pervasive dimension of roll-call voting (see data in Appendix C). Throughout this entire period, the predominant pattern of conflict in the Chamber of Deputies pitted forces of the government against the opposition, the Radicals against a coalition of Conservatives, Socialists, and Progressive Democrats, an alliance opprobrious-

Table 5-1. Variations in Party Cleavage, 1916-30

Factor	Cleavage[a]	Party R^2
	1916-17 Session	
I General	Socialists, all Conservatives, and PDP vs. all Radicals	.87
II Sugar Tariff	Socialists, all Radicals, and Conservatives vs. PDP, Local Conservatives, and Traditional Conservatives	.15[b]
III Well-being of Urban Lower Class	Socialists vs. all Conservatives, all Radicals, and PDP	.41

Table 5-1 *(continued)*

Factor	Cleavage[a]	Party R^2
	1916-17 Session	
IV Unclear	Socialists, Local Conservatives, Traditional Conservative, all Radicals, and PDP vs. Conservatives	.24
V legalization of Divorce	Socialists vs. all Conservatives, all Radicals, and PDP	.14
	1918-19 Session	
I General	All Radicals vs. PDP, all Conservatives, and Socialists	.81
II General	Socialists and all Radicals vs. all Conservatives and PDP	.41
III Unclear	Socialists and Local Radicals vs. UCR, PDP, and all Conservatives	.14
IV Rules for Congressional Attendance	Local Conservatives and all Radicals vs. Conservatives, Socialists, and PDP	.04[b]
V Unclear	All Conservatives and Local Radicals vs. UCR, PDP, and Socialists	.11[b]
	1920-21 Session	
I Opposition to Administration	Socialists, all Conservatives, and PDP vs. all Radicals	.23
II Officers; Congressional Autonomy	Socialists and all Radicals vs. PDP and all Conservatives	.78
III Governmental Minimum Wage	Socialists vs. all Conservatives, PDP, and all Radicals	.45
IV Vice-president for January 1922	All Radicals, all Conservatives, and PDP vs. Socialists	.16
V Rent Control	Socialists and PDP vs. all Radicals and all Conservatives	.06[b]
	1922-23 Session	
I General	All Radicals vs. PDP, Socialists, and all Conservatives	.85
II Tariffs	Socialists, PDP, and all Radicals vs. all Conservatives	.20[b]
III Improvements for City of Buenos Aires	Socialists vs. PDP, all Radicals, and all Conservatives	.12
IV Congressional Autonomy	All Conservatives, all Radicals, and PDP vs. Socialists	.11
V Response to Cattle Crisis	Socialists vs. all Radicals, all Conservatives, and PDP	.32

Table 5-1 *(continued)*

Factor	Cleavage[a]	Party R^2
	1924-25 Session	
I General	All Radicals vs. PDP, all Conservatives, and Socialists	.81
II General	All Conservatives and all Radicals vs. PDP and Socialists	.41
III Congressional Procedures and Priorities	All Conservatives, UCR, and Local Radicals vs. UCRAP, Socialists, and PDP	.24
IV Intervention in San Juan	All Conservatives, Local Radicals, Socialists, UCR, and PDP vs. UCRAP	.04[b]
V Provisional President	All Radicals, all Conservatives, and Socialists vs. PDP	.30
	1926-27 Session	
I General	Socialists, all Conservatives, PDP, UCRAP, and Local Radicals vs. UCR	.57
II Congressional Autonomy	All Conservatives, all Radicals, and PDP vs. Socialists	.48
III Nationalization of Petroleum	Local Radicals, Local Conservatives, and PDP vs. Socialists, Conservatives, UCR, and UCRAP	.03
IV Women's Rights	UCRAP, Socialists, Local Conservatives, and UCR vs. Local Radicals, Conservatives, and PDP	,05
V Authority for Labor Regulations	All Radicals vs. Socialists, PDP, and all Conservatives	.28
	1928-29 Session	
I General	UCR vs. all Conservatives. Local Radicals, Socialists, and Independent Socialists	.56
II Unclear	Socialists, Independent Socialists, and all Radicals vs. all Conservatives	.54
III Unclear	All Conservatives and all Radicals vs. Independent Socialists and Socialists	.20
IV Political Tranquillity	Socialists, All Conservatives, Independent Socialists, and UCR vs. Local Radicals	.35
	1930 Session	
I Distribution of Parliamentary Power	UCR vs. all Conservatives, Local Radicals, Socialists, UCRAP, PDP, and Independent Socialists	.81
II Distribution of Parliamentary Power	All Radicals, Independent Socialists, PDP, and Socialists vs. all Conservatives	.57

[a]Parties and party groupings are listed in approximate order, according to mean factor scores, from positive to negative. (On party groupings see Table B-3 in Appendix B.)

[b]This is a factor-score scale on which Party did not explain maximum amount of variance.

ly nicknamed the *Contubernio*.[3] The struggle cut through many issues and, despite the changing substance of the roll-call votes, it bore a simple stamp: the ins against the outs.

In elaboration of this point, Figure 5-1 plots the relative positions of the parties on the major voting dimensions from 1916 through 1930, as gauged from the differences in average factor scores between the parties and the UCR. Despite impurities in the comparability of such chronological data, the picture yields a number of conclusions. First, the absence of any party position below the UCR axis reveals that the UCR invariably occupied an extreme end of the scale. Second, the Radicals maintained a high degree of cohesion throughout the early years, until the mid-1920s—when a schism occurred between Personalists and Antipersonalists, demonstrated by the defection of Local Radicals in 1926-27.[4] Third, allowing for imprecise measurement, the antigovernment coalition demonstrated a considerable amount of stability. Fourth, on quite a specific level, the Socialist party was not a reluctant partner in the coalition; more often than not, it took a more consistently anti-UCR stance than did Conservatives.[5]

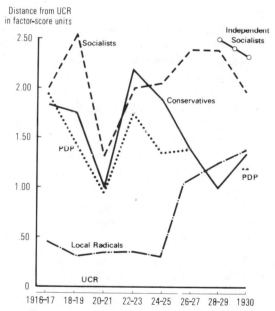

Figure 5-1. Predominant party alignments, 1916-30, in relation to the UCR.

3. In loose translation, *contubernio* means "illegitimate union." For one description by a disillusioned Socialist, see Joaquín Coca, *El Contubernio: memorias de un diputado obrero* (Buenos Aires, 1961).

4. At this time Local Radicals were usually, but not necessarily, Antipersonalists. An extended discussion of the Radical schism appears later in this chapter.

Thus the *Contubernio*, which clearly demonstrates that prevailing party alignments did not fall along a consistent Left-Center-Right continuum at any time throughout this period. Instead, parties of the Left and Right—the Socialists and Conservatives—joined forces against the Radical Center. It therefore appears that ideology did not exercise a determining influence on partisan positioning. Political realities—or, to put it less politely, political opportunism—held the most important key to parliamentary behavior.

In addition to the *Contubernio*, Table 5-1 reveals a secondary kind of coalition which matched Socialists and Radicals against Conservatives. This pattern often appears in General or Unclear dimensions, most notably on Factor II—as in 1918-19, 1920-21, 1922-23 (though this was mainly a regional issue), 1928-29, and 1930.

To this extent, the findings reveal the existence of two basic partisan alignments, the first being a Socialist-Conservative alliance against the UCR and the second being a Socialist-Radical alliance against Conservatives. Neither coalition had clearly defined issue orientations. Instead, they seem to reflect the outcome of parliamentary maneuvering, especially by Socialists. Representing a relatively small party, they chose to maximize their influence through constant dealings and negotiations—at the occasional expense of ideological consistency.

There were times, however, when Socialists found themselves in isolation, especially regarding selected social issues. Factor II in 1916-17 (hesitantly labelled "Well-being of the Urban Lower Class"), Factor III in 1920-21 ("Governmental Minimum Wage"), and Factors III and V in 1922-23 ("Improvements for the City of Buenos Aires," "Response to Cattle Crisis") all demonstrate this tendency. In cases like these, Socialists were seeking legislation in behalf of urban masses—either as wage-earning workers or meat-eating consumers.[6] And for the most part, they were doing it alone.[7]

By implication, of course, this means that Radicals sided with Conservatives on these same issues. As other kinds of evidence have also shown,[8]

5. The extremism of the Socialists could be partly due to their excellent attendance record; Conservatives probably skipped more roll-call votes and, because of my coding conventions (Appendix B, sections 1-2), therefore tended to receive more moderate scores. In Figures 5-1 and 5-3, incidentally, the Conservative bloc includes Local Conservatives as well as national Conservatives (see Table B-3).

6. See my book on *Politics and Beef in Argentina: Patterns of Conflict and Change* (New York and London, 1969), esp. p. 97.

7. Socialists also stood alone on Factor V in 1916-17 and Factor III in 1928-29, which have fairly strong loadings with some roll-call votes on social issues. (See Appendix C.)

8. See, for instance, my book on *Politics and Beef*; Carl Solberg, "Rural Unrest and Agrarian Policy in Argentina, 1912-1930," *Journal of Inter-American Studies and World*

Radicals did not differ sharply with Conservatives on social or economic policy. The two parties stood together on several varying dimensions. To the extent that they disagreed, especially in the early years, it was mainly over political problems.

But Table 5-1 also reveals that, as time went on, the conflict between Conservatives and Radicals intensified. By 1928-29 the parties came to clash on both of the first two dimensions. In 1930, as political questions monopolized parliamentary attention, they opposed each other again. Tacit collaboration, so apparent in the early sessions, seems to have disappeared. A full understanding of political interplay in the 1916-30 period requires close examination of this situation, which implies a change in the Radical party itself.

DIGRESSION: SCHISM AMONG THE RADICALS

As suggested at various points in this analysis, the Radical party began as a thoroughly heterogeneous grouping. Its early leadership consisted of aristocrats (Table 2-2), *nouveaux riches* landowners, and aspiring members of the urban bourgeoisie. Its followers came from a variety of social strata in Argentina's most rapidly developing areas. Its purposes were vague, general, often couched in moralistic language.

This broad-based movement held together throughout Yrigoyen's first presidency, from 1916 to 1922. In the latter year tension began to emerge over the selection of *El Caudillo's* successor, but subsided with the designation—by Yrigoyen himself—of Marcelo T. de Alvear. Strains of discord came back to the surface, however, and in 1924 the party openly divided into two opposing camps: the pro-Yrigoyen Personalists and the pro-Alvear Antipersonalists.[9]

Despite the historical significance of the schism, which wrought great changes in the Radical party, there has been little investigation of its origins. Did Personalists and Antipersonalists disagree over certain issues? Did they come from different areas or social backgrounds? In short, what was the definition of the difference?

At least among the deputies, presumably representative of party leadership in general, legislative roll-call data permit a systematic exploration of these questions. The distribution of factor scores for all Radical legislators (Local

---

Affairs, 13, no. 1 (January 1971), 18-52; and Solberg, "The Tariff and Politics in Argentina, 1916-1930," *Hispanic American Historical Review*, 53, no. 2 (May 1973), 260-84.

9. For a biased but informative description of these events, see Gabriel del Mazo, *El Radicalismo: ensayo sobre su historia y doctrina*, II (Buenos Aires, 1957), pp. 21-82, esp. pp. 21-37.

Radicals as well as members of the UCR) reveals sharp internal division on three major dimensions: Factor II of 1924-25, Factor I of 1926-27, and Factor II of 1926-27.[10] The first two factors were General in content; and the third, Factor II of 1926-27, seems to have involved an essentially political question of "Congressional Autonomy."[11] According to data in Table 5-1, Radicals usually held together on other dimensions of roll-call voting.[12] The implication is unmistakable: by the mid-1920s, at least, *cleavage within the Radical party did not correspond to any particular problem of social policy.* It apparently began as political dispute, then spread across a wide variety of issues.

Who belonged to which side? On this question, Figure 5-2 presents a picture of voting blocs within the Radical party during the 1926-27 legislative session. Specifically, the diagram gives the optimal breakdown of Radical deputies according to the AID criteria, with scores on Factor I (General) as the dependent variable and Region and Status as independent variables (Age never came into play). Given the configuration of the roll-call votes, the more positive the factor score, the more Antipersonalist the stance; the more negative the score, the more Personalist the stance.

Each cell in the figure contains, from top to bottom, (a) the attributes of the group according to the operative independent variable, (b) the average factor score for members of the group, and (c) the number of deputies in the group. As the diagram indicates, AID began with a total sample of 78 Radical legislators having a mean factor score of -.57. The first dichotomous split came on Region, 38 representatives from the Capital and the Province of Buenos Aires having a solid and staunchly Personalist average score of -1.15, 40 men from other areas having a slightly Antipersonalist average of -.03. Within this latter group, a second split took place according to Status, aristocrats tending to be strongly Antipersonalist (+.46) and nonaristocrats holding a fairly central position (-.32, which is quite close to the average for all Radicals of -.57). Simple as it is, this categorization of deputies by Region

10. Histograms reveal clearly bimodal distributions of factor scores for Radical deputies on these factors, in comparison to unimodal (or scattered) distributions on other factor scales. For my purposes the shape of the distribution is much more important than the simple fact of dispersion around the mean, so the standard deviation of within-party factor scores cannot provide a useful guide to the existence of internal conflict. Throughout I have used the factor scores from analyses including all participant deputies; I have not rerun the factor analysis programs on Radicals alone.

11. The Personalist-Antipersonalist schism appears twice in 1926-27 because the two factors essentially correspond to differing alignments among the non-Radical deputies. The distribution of Radical scores on Factors I and II is much the same: a Q-coefficient for a fourfold table, dividing scores on each factor at the zero axis, comes out to .998.

12. By 1928 the Personalists had pretty thoroughly defeated their Antipersonalist rivals, so there is no visible bipolarity among Radical deputies in the legislative sessions for 1928-29 or 1930.

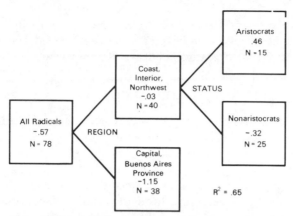

Figure 5-2. Voting blocs within the Radical party, 1926-27.

and Status provides an extraordinarily comprehensive picture of the internal Radical schism, as reflected by the very high R^2 value of .65.

On the basis of these findings, and similar results for the other relevant factors,[13] it seems fair to draw two conclusions about the Radical party split. First, and primarily, it was a regional conflict between Buenos Aires—both city and province, where Yrigoyen had most thoroughly developed his political machine—and the rest of the country.[14] The lines of this division, pitting the coast against the interior, are strongly reminiscent of the nineteenth-century struggle between the unitarians and federalists. The issues appear to have changed, now being more political than economic, but the roots of regional antagonism continued to run deep. In a sense, the Radical movement failed as a party because it failed to overcome this fundamental and historic cleavage in Argentine society.

Second, and secondarily, the Radical rupture was a social conflict: the higher the Status, the more Antipersonalist (or less Personalist) the stance. Among the deputies from the interior, as shown in Figure 5-2, aristocrats firmly favored Alvear, and nonaristocrats occupied an intermediate (slightly Alvearist) position. Within the Buenos Aires delegations, it appears, nonaristocrats were more avidly Yrigoyenist than were the aristocrats.[15] Controlling for the effects of both Party and Region, therefore, Status came to play a

13. AID obtained the same breakdown for Factor II of 1926-27 as for Factor I. The same pattern also appeared on Factor II of 1924-25, the only difference being that Status provided splits within both of the major regional groupings.

14. Using different methods, Lee C. Fennell has obtained a similar finding. "Class and Region in Argentina: A Study of Political Cleavage, 1916-1966" (Ph.D. diss., University of Florida, 1970), p. 138. On the nature of Yrigoyen's political organization see David Rock, "Machine Politics in Buenos Aires and the Argentine Radical Party, 1912-1930," *Journal of Latin American Studies*, 4, no. 2 (November 1972), 233-56.

15. According to the AID breakdown of Radical voting on Factor II of 1924-25.

crucial, if momentary, role in defining the lines of cleavage in Congress.[16] As I shall attempt to indicate in Chapter 6, this development would have serious consequences for the Argentine political system as a whole.

1932-42: DISCORDANT CONCORDANCIA

After the provisional military government which ruled Argentina from 1930 to 1932, power passed to an eclectic regime known as the *Concordancia*—and this transition, it was hoped, would usher in an era of political agreement. The new president was Agustín P. Justo, a military man, well-known Antipersonalist and former minister of war under Alvear. Charged with a delicate balancing act, Justo gave most cabinet appointments to civilians, and aristocrats at that. In the Congress, he leaned upon a progovern-

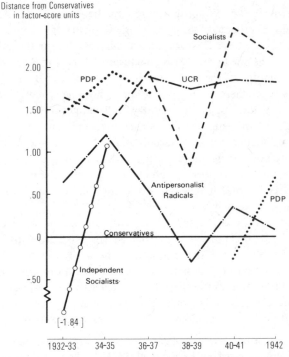

Figure 5-3. Predominant party alignments, 1932-42, in relation to Conservatives. The Antipersonalist category consists of the UCRAP, Local Radicals, and allegedly progovernment members of the UCR who served in the Chamber prior to 1936.

16. The transitory character of this situation is underlined by some of the findings in Chapter 4, which showed Party to be the predominant determinant of parliamentary voting, with relatively little impact coming from Region or Status or Age.

ment coalition between the old-time Conservatives (now known as National Democrats); the Antipersonalist Radicals; and the Independent Socialists. Since Personalist Radicals first chose to boycott elections in protest against pervasive fraud, the early opposition came from only the Socialists, the Progressive Democrats, and the Entre Ríos Radicals.

According to Figure 5-3, which plots party distances on Factor I in relation to Conservatives, bellwether of the *Concordancia*, this pattern was not overwhelmingly stable. The Independent Socialists moved from a thoroughly progovernment position in 1932-33, outflanking even the Conservatives in this respect, over to the opposition ranks in 1934-35—and then they faded from the scene. Antipersonalist Radicals, normally quite loyal, also defected in 1934-35. The PDP and Socialists put up consistent opposition in these early years, but the government's coalition was fast approaching disarray.

The return of the Personalist Radicals, who ended their electoral boycott in 1936, promptly stabilized the situation. The Socialists, UCR, and PDP formed solid—and powerful—ranks, occupying just over half (52 percent) of the seats in the Chamber during the 1936-37 session. Confronted by this challenge, the *Concordancia*— Conservatives and Antipersonalists—began to function as a tightly knit group, and in 1940 even wooed the PDP to its side. Except for this slight shift, however, party alignments maintained a steady course from 1936 through 1942.

Aside from these patterns, other instances of conflict reveal strong continuities with the 1916-30 period. As demonstrated in Table 5-2 (which follows the same format as Table 5-1), the Socialists sometimes found

Table 5-2. Variations in Party Cleavage, 1932-42

Factor	Cleavage[a]	Party R^2
	1932-33 Session[b]	
I General	Independent Socialists, all Conservatives, and Local Radicals vs. UCRAP, PDP, and Socialists	.63
II General (emphasis on economic policies)	Local Radicals, all Conservatives, UCRAP, and PDP vs. Socialists and Independent Socialists	.70
III Legalization of Divorce	Conservatives and Local Radicals vs. Socialists, UCRAP, Independent Socialists, Local Conservatives, and PDP	.28
	1934-35 Session[b]	
I General	All Conservatives and Local Radicals vs. Independent Socialists, UCR, Socialists, PDP, and UCRAP	.53
II General	All Radicals, Independent Socialists, all Conservatives, and PDP vs. Socialists	.68

Table 5-2 *(continued)*

Factor	Cleavage[a]	Party R^2
	1936-37 Session	
I General	Socialists, UCR, and PDP vs. all Conservatives and Local Radicals	.77
II Parliamentary Procedures	UCR, all Conservatives, and PDP vs. Local Radicals and Socialists	.41
	1938-39 Session	
I General	All Conservatives, Local Radicals, and UCRAP vs. Socialists and UCR	.73
II Pensions for Police	Local Radicals, all Conservatives, and UCR vs. UCRAP and Socialists	.16
III Unclear	All Radicals and Conservatives vs. Local Conservatives and Socialists	.22
IV Order of Business	Local Radicals and UCRAP vs. UCR, Socialists, and all Conservatives	.25
V Popular Economic Welfare	All Radicals and all Conservatives vs. Socialists	.10[c]
	1940-41 Session	
I General	Socialists and UCR vs. Local Radicals, UCRAP, all Conservatives, and PDP	.75
II General	PDP, UCR, and all Conservatives vs. UCRAP, Local Radicals, and Socialists	.39
III Parliamentary Procedures	Socialists, Conservatives, Local Radicals, and UCR vs. UCRAP, PDP, and Local Conservatives	.06[c]
IV Confidence in Government Officials	All Radicals and all Conservatives vs. PDP and Socialists	.34
V Tax Restitution	All Conservatives, all Radicals, and PDP vs. Socialists	.06[c]
	1942 Session	
I Foreign Policy	Socialists and UCR vs. PDP, Local Radicals, UCRAP, and Conservatives	.83
II Unclear	All Radicals and Conservatives vs. PDP and Socialists	.65
III Inheritance Tax	Socialists, UCRAP, UCR, and PDP vs. Conservatives and Local Radicals	.05[c]

[a]Parties and party groupings are listed in approximate order, according to mean factor scores, from positive to negative. (On party groupings see Table B-3 in Appendix B.)

[b]In this session, members of the UCR (except the ones from Entre Ríos who won seats in 1934) were actually Antipersonalists. Other factions in the Antipersonalist coalition, as represented in Figure 5-3, were Local Radicals and the UCRAP.

[c]This is a factor-score scale on which Party did not explain maximum amount of variance.

themselves alone on economic questions. Factor II of 1932-33, for example, clearly reflects this situation (and may betray discontent among the Independent Socialists with Justo's economic policies). Factor II in 1934-35, apparently General in content, shows the Socialists in isolation. So do factors on "Popular Economic Welfare" (V, 1938-39) and "Tax Restitution" (V, 1940-41), although the low values for R^2 make these two cases almost meaningless.

What the findings suggest is that, despite their close *political* alliance during this period, Radicals had not come together with the Socialists on *economic* issues. Notwithstanding the results on Factor I, Table 5-2 reveals that the UCR opposed the Socialists on a wide variety of voting dimensions from 1936 through 1942—to be exact, on 8 out of the 11 residual factors. According to data on the party split, displayed above, Personalist Radicals became unaristocratic and possibly antiaristocratic too; but they were not proproletarian.

Despite the absence of class conflict, and the persistence of parliamentary maneuvering, however, party conflict steadily intensified (see Figure 4-1). In 1942 key alignments closely followed party lines, especially regarding sensitive matters of foreign policy in World War II. Concerned about possible abandonment of neutrality, and disdainful of partisan bickering, soldiers overthrew the government in 1943. Three years later Juan Perón became the president.

THE EVOLUTION OF CONFLICT UNDER PERON

The inauguration of Congress in 1946 opened a new era in parliamentary politics. The progovernment Peronists, holding 110 out of 158 available seats, thoroughly dominated the Chamber of Deputies. Other parties, having formed a frontal *Unión Democrática* for the electoral campaign, were firmly united by their opposition to Perón. The lines of struggle appeared to be drawn.

Yet as shown above, especially in Chapter 3, the early legislatures under Perón revealed multiple dimensions of conflict. Table 5-3, summarizing party alignments during the Peronist era, begins to show how this could happen. For most of the factors in 1946-47 and 1948-49 reveal consistent cleavages between Peronists and the opposition; the variation mainly entails shuffling and rearrangement among antigovernment parties. One exception to this rule, Factor IV in 1946-47, concerning a "Memorial to Yrigoyen," rekindled old Personalist-Antipersonalist and Radical-Conservative rivalries. Another exception, and a more important one, Factor II in 1948-49, seems to have dealt with "Extensions of Government Power" (consult Appendix C). Again the UCR was isolated, thus exhibiting internal strain among the opposition forces.

Table 5-3. Variations in Party Cleavage, 1946-54

Factor	Cleavage[a]	Party R²
	1946-47 Session	
I General	UCR, UCRAP, and Conservative vs. Peronists	.50
II General (possible emphasis on rights of political opposition)	Conservative, UCR, and UCRAP vs. Peronists	.17
III Economic Policies	UCRAP, Conservative, and UCR vs. Peronists	.13
IV Memorial to Hipólito Yrigoyen	UCR vs. Peronists, UCRAP, and Conservative	.07
V Labor Agitation	UCR and Conservative vs. Peronists and UCRAP	.02[b]
	1948-49 Session	
I General	Peronists vs. UCR, Conservative, and UCRAP	.35
II Extension of Government Power	UCR vs. Peronists, Conservative, and UCRAP	.22
III Patronage and Political Opposition	UCRAP, Conservative, and UCR vs. Peronists	.12
IV Regulation of Functional Groups	Peronists vs. Conservative, UCR, and UCRAP	.12
V Policies on Real Estate	Conservative and UCR vs. Peronists and UCRAP	.10
	1950-51 Session	
I General	Peronists vs. UCR	.62
	1952-54 Session	
I General	Peronists vs. UCR	.80

[a]Parties and party groupings are listed in approximate order, according to mean factor score, from positive to negative. (On party groupings see Table B-3 in Appendix B.)

[b]This is a factor-score scale on which Party did not explain maximum amount of variance.

Nor were the Peronists free from tension. As a rough measure of internal disagreement, for example, the standard deviation[17] of scores for Peronist deputies on the foremost factor in 1946-47 was .83, compared to only .37 for

17. The standard deviation measures the fluctuation of values around the mean and corresponds, in a sense, to the average distance between individual values and the mean for the group. See, for instance, Charles Dollar and Richard J. Jensen, *Historian's Guide to Statistics* (New York, 1971), pp. 50-54.

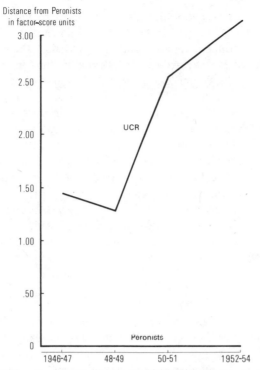

Figure 5-4. Predominant party alignments, 1946-54, in relation to the Peronists.

the (relatively unified) opposition. Similarly, for Factor I of 1948-49 the Peronists had a standard deviation of .82, still higher than the .76 of their opponents.[18]

These data confirm a critical point: the Peronist elite, from 1946 through 1949, represented a fairly loose coalition of diverse political elements.[19] Almost all the deputies (including some aristocrats) were amateurs, as shown in Chapter 2, and they showed a tendency—perhaps out of naiveté—to act with independence. For leaders as well as for the followers, the early Peronist movement was marked by considerable heterogeneity.[20]

18. Fennell has reached the same conclusion for 1946-47; the Peronists show greater cohesion than the opposition on only one out of the eight Guttman scales which he constructed for that session. "Class and Region," Ch. V.

19. AID analyses have defined some blocs within the Peronist ranks according to Region and Status, but such classifications do not explain much of the variance in voting.

20. Peter H. Smith, "The Social Base of Peronism," *Hispanic American Historical Review*, 52, no. 1 (February 1972), 55-73. Gino Germani has disputed my interpretation of Perón's support in the 1946 election, but—for reasons too complex to spell out here—I believe that Germani's own findings actually strengthen my argument instead of

Around 1950, the situation quickly changed. There was only one dimension of conflict in each of the 1950-51 and 1952-54 legislatures. According to Table 5-3, the government forces voted steadily against the opposition, now consisting of the UCR alone. At least as reflected by the Chamber, substantial differences among the Peronists disappeared.[21] And as shown in Figure 5-4, the distance between the UCR and the Peronists sharply and suddenly increased. During the 1950s, polarization became complete.

This finding lends strong support to the idea, recently proposed by other scholars, that the Peronist movement—and conflicts within and around it—underwent significant change over time.[22] Congressional behavior in the 1940s gives signs of parliamentary interplay, multiple alignments, and independence among progovernment deputies. Then this process stopped. From 1950 onward, the Peronist movement seems to have recruited only loyalists. Party discipline grew strict and dissent was suppressed.[23] Beleaguered and weak, the UCR resisted stoutly but ineffectively. It took a military revolt to oust Perón in 1955.

SUMMARY

In this chapter I have examined patterns of party alignment in the Chamber of Deputies from 1916 through 1954. Reliance on AID, which automatically finds the sharpest party cleavage on each dimension of roll-call voting, has produced a number of substantial findings.

1. In 1916-30, the predominant conflict pitted the progovernment Radicals against a coalition of Socialists and Conservatives, known as the *Contubernio*.

2. During this same period, parliamentary jockeying, apparently by the Socialists, sometimes led the Socialists and Radicals to close ranks against Conservatives.

3. On social issues, particularly concerning the urban working class, Radicals and Conservatives lined up against the Socialists.

---

disproving it. Gino Germani, "El surgimiento del peronismo: el rol de los obreros y de los migrantes internos," *Desarrollo Económico*, 13, no. 51 (October-December 1973), 435-88, esp. 437-40.

21. On these factors the standard deviations for Peronist deputies were, respectively, .36 and .34—compared to .83 and .82 for the first factors in 1946-47 and 1948-49.

22. See Samuel L. Baily, *Labor, Nationalism, and Politics in Argentina* (New Brunswick, N.J., 1967); and Peter Waldmann, "Las cuatro fases del gobierno peronista," and Walter Little, "La tendencia peronista en el sindicalismo argentino: el caso de los obreros de la Carne," both in *Aportes*, 19 (January 1971), 94-106 and 107-24.

23. In time, some wayward deputies were excluded or even expelled from the Chamber.

4. The schism which ruptured the Radical party in the mid-1920s was a broad political dispute that cut through many substantive issues. The social character of the struggle bore close relationship to both Region and Status, pitting the interior against the Buenos Aires area and aristocrats against nonaristocrats.

5. The decade from 1932 to 1942 began uncertainly. The Socialist-PDP opposition was firmly united, but the progovernment *Concordancia* showed signs of disarray.

6. The return of the UCR, in 1936, brought stability, if not stalemate: the opposition consistently against the government.

7. As during the previous period, the Socialists usually stood alone on major social issues.

8. The resumption of Congress in 1946 renewed the basic pattern, with very little variation: the opposition against the government, now represented by the Peronists.

9. Between 1946 and 1950 there was substantial flexibility, and even disagreement, among the Peronist deputies. Around 1950—but not before—the movement took on a closed, monolithic character.

One overall impression, related to most of these findings and fore-shadowed in the previous chapter, concerns what I would call the process of rigidification. At the beginning of each period, there was a fair amount of parliamentary give-and-take. Opposition parties usually joined against the government, but this pattern, though important, did not dominate all roll-call voting. But also in each period, this alignment became more and more pervasive. Mounting partisan intransigence, *specifically pitting the government against the opposition*, thus seems to have paved the way for military coups.

A second impression derives from the consistent isolation of the Socialist party on working-class issues from 1916 to 1942. In view of the weakness of the Socialists, based almost entirely in urban Buenos Aires, it is abundantly clear that, during this period, *Argentina's popular masses never found consistent representation in any national party*, not even from the Radicals. One can begin to comprehend the sense of collective deprivation and frustration which would be so well captured, and expressed, by Juan Domingo Perón.[24]

24. For an elaboration of this argument, see my article on "Social Mobilization, Political Participation, and the Rise of Juan Perón," *Political Science Quarterly*, 84, no. 1 (March 1969), 30-49.

6
Elites, Cleavages, and Crises

Now it is time to return to the questions put forth in the Introduction of this book: What happened to politics in Argentina? Given the country's level of socioeconomic development, how could democratic politics give way to an openly authoritarian denouement?[1] As reported in Chapters 2 through 5, my statistical findings on recruitment and conflict in the national Chamber of Deputies have focused only indirectly on this problem. The purpose of this concluding chapter is to reformulate the findings and concentrate directly on the central issue. To do so I shall reach out beyond the empirical bounds of this inquiry, indulge in speculation, and cast broad interpretations.[2]

For an analytical framework I shall employ the concept of "crisis" recently propounded by the Committee on Comparative Politics of the Social Science Research Council. According to this view, political change can be understood as the sequential appearance and resolution (or nonresolution) of political crises in five separate problem areas: identity, legitimacy, participation, penetration, and distribution. A crisis occurs "where a 'problem' arises in one of the problem areas (that is, members of the society are discontented with one of the five aspects of the decisional process), and some new institutionalized means of handling problems of that sort is required to satisfy the discontent."[3]

One virtue of this approach lies in its emphasis upon the importance of historical sequence. The chronological order of crises can vary according to

1. See Introduction, note 1, for a definition of the terms *authoritarianism* and *democracy* as used here.
2. For stylistic convenience I shall refer to empirical findings by merely noting the figure or table in which they are presented; by this I also mean to indicate the accompanying textual discussion.
3. Leonard Binder et al., *Crises and Sequences in Political Development* (Princeton, N.J., 1971); the quote is taken from Sidney Verba's concluding chapter on "Sequences and Development," p. 302.

era and place. They could appear gradually, one at a time, and therefore be presumably susceptible to resolution; or they might appear all at once, challenging political leaders with nearly impossible tasks. Thus the framework is explicitly dynamic and, in principle, suitable for longitudinal time-series analysis.

Another advantage of the scheme, at least for this particular study, stems from the concern with the responsiveness of leadership. As stated in the Introduction, I reject the deterministic notion that political institutions were necessarily overwhelmed in Argentina, either by surging social forces or by a militaristic officer corps. Instead I think that political leaders and institutions met certain crises in certain ways with the ultimate, if indirect, effect of bringing about the demise of the system. Hence my empirical inquiry into the Chamber of Deputies, which provides a documentary record of elite behavior and performance.

Having adopted this framework, I interpret political change in twentieth-century Argentina as involving three basic types of crisis:

1. Crises of *participation*, which occur when sizable segments of the population, heretofore excluded from the system, demand effective participation in the political process.

2. Crises of *legitimacy*, which occur when sizable portions of the politically relevant population challenge or deny the normative validity of claims to authority made by existing leadership.

3. Crises of *distribution*, which occur when sizable portions of the politically relevant population demand a redistribution of societal rewards and benefits, often economic.

I am not claiming that these categories yield a complete understanding of Argentine politics, that their application is unambiguous (how to determine the existence of which crisis?), or that other types of crisis—identity and penetration—bear no relevance at all. I merely maintain that these kinds of crisis, and their conceptual apparatus, provide a useful way of integrating my empirical data into a broad perspective on contemporary politics in Argentina.

My purpose in this chapter is both descriptive and analytical. I am not about to present a theory in any strict sense of that term (nor does the crisis framework constitute a theory in itself). Instead I shall attempt to employ the categories in order to put my data in coherent form.

The key to my analysis consists of three related propositions. One is that political crises can appear as the result of rapid socioeconomic change.[4] As

4. Gilbert W. Merkx has convincingly documented the relationship between short-run economic cycles and political rebellions. "Recessions and Rebellions in Argentina, 1870-1970," *Hispanic American Historical Review*, 53, no. 2 (May 1973), 285-95.

posited above, such crises need not necessarily destroy the system; as argued below, I do not think they did so in the case of Argentina.

My second proposition is that elite reactions to, and even resolutions of, one kind of crisis at one time can give rise to another crisis at another time. Crises do not just appear by themselves; they are structurally, historically, and sequentially interdependent.

That leads to my third proposition, which is that the outcome of a crisis can affect the system's capability for dealing with subsequent crises. Political experience is an integral part of political development. But success does not necessarily beget success, and failure need not always lead to further failure; the successful resolution of one kind of crisis can also reduce the probabilities for successful resolution of another kind of crisis.

For convenience I shall divide Argentine history into three separate phases, the first stretching from 1904 through the electoral reform of 1912 to the military coup of 1930 (thus covering the first two periods dealt with in prior chapters); the second, from 1932 to the coup of 1943, which ultimately brought Juan Perón to power; the third, from 1946 to 1955, the years of Peronist supremacy.

PHASE 1: ELECTORAL REFORM AND DELEGITIMATION

Political processes during the first period, 1904 to 1930, essentially revolve around electoral reform. My proposition here is this: the Saenz Peña law of 1912 constituted an effective short-run response to a crisis of participation; but its unforeseen consequences created a crisis of legitimacy which eventually prompted the 1930 coup.[5] Economic uncertainty contributed to disaffection with the regime, but the Depression did not cause the Yrigoyen government to topple.[6]

Elaboration of this argument begins with an appreciation of the sequential relationship between economic and political development. In Argentina the

5. The argument in this section is more fully documented in my paper on "The Breakdown of Democracy in Argentina, 1916-1930," presented at the Seventh World Congress of Sociology, Varna, Bulgaria (September 1970); a revised version is tentatively scheduled for publication in a volume of essays to be edited by Juan Linz and Alfred Stepan.

6. As stated below, I do not think the Argentine economy was suffering so greatly as of September 1930. But even assuming that it was, as Robert Dahl has pointed out, "other polyarchies were also hit by economic crisis. Some that were also highly dependent on international trade, like Sweden, and even some that were heavy exporters of agricultural products, like Australia and New Zealand, nonetheless met the crisis with actions that retained, restored, perhaps even enhanced, the confidence of their citizens in the effectiveness of their governments. In Argentina, things went differently." Robert Dahl, *Polyarchy: Participation and Opposition* (New Haven and London, 1971), pp. 134-35.

formation of a landowning aristocracy preceded the establishment of constitutional rule in 1853-62. This was the elite which, while in the process of
expansion and consolidation,[7] founded and directed the country's parliamentary system. Throughout the late nineteenth and early twentieth cen-
turies an exclusive circle of aristocrats, epitomized by the Generation of
1880, simultaneously held the keys to economic, social, and political power.
The political system was not meant to provide an independent counterweight
to the distribution of economic power; on the contrary, as implied by the
preponderance of aristocrats in the Chamber of Deputies (Figure 2-1), it was
intended to serve the interests and purposes of exclusive and established
socioeconomic groups.

Expansion of the export-import economy eventually gave birth to middle-
class groups which challenged the political supremacy of the landed elite.
Allying these new social sectors with *nouveaux riches* landowners and some
discontented aristocrats, the Civic Union launched an armed revolt against the
government in 1890. After some supporters came to terms with authorities,
the predominant wing—the Radical Civic Union (UCR)—boycotted elections
in protest against fraud and led open rebellions in 1893 and 1905.

Thus emerged a crisis of participation. No doubt these events also raised
some questions about the legitimacy of the system, but this does not (in my
view) necessarily point to the existence of a legitimacy crisis as such. Most
opponents of the regime, including the Radicals, seem to have believed in the
propriety and desirability of popular elections and constitutional government.
Their complaint concerned the faithless violation of the rules, not the
substance of the rules themselves. Fundamentally, they wanted to take part.

In time, the political leaders of the old elite (whom I shall henceforth call
Conservatives) found a strategy to meet the situation: in 1911-12 they put
through an electoral reform which would give Radicals a share of power,
coopt them into the system, and maintain political stability.

This pattern of challenge and response provides the basis for an interpretive premise: that the electoral reform and consequent redistribution of
political strength were meant—at least by Conservatives—to uphold and com-
ply with longstanding rules of the Argentine political game.[8] Central to this
code was the idea of a balance of power and government by consensus, or
acuerdo. (Most important decisions were reached quietly, behind closed doors
as it were, at the presidential palace or perhaps on someone's elegant *estancia*;

7. See Jacinto Oddone, *La burguesía terrateniente argentina*, 2nd ed. (Buenos Aires, 1936).

8. Documentation for this sort of statement is virtually impossible, since people
rarely announce their adherence to codes which (in many instances) might not have been
consciously perceived. In this case I am imputing attitudes from contemporary behavior
(as in roll-call alignments) and from indirect statements made during and after the fact
(some of which are quoted below).

Figure 3-1 indicates how few roll calls, contested or not, took place prior to 1912.) Whereas power had previously been parcelled out to competing factions within the landed aristocracy, the Saenz Peña law meant that power would now be shared between the aristocracy and rising middle-class groups.

As a result of this understanding, political conflict would retain several traditional features:

1. Fluid patterns of alignment (Figure 3-2), and in particular fluid patterns of party allegiance (demonstrated by the low explanatory power of the Party variable on voting in the Chamber before 1912, illustrated in Figure 4-1).

2. Disregard for class background, shown by the weak predictive power of Status during these same years (Appendix B, Table B-6), and also by the low correlation between Status and party affiliation (Table 2-2).

3. Continued dependence of the distribution of political power upon the distribution of economic power (implied, again, by Figure 2-1).

Though it is doubtful that Radicals struck a conscious bargain of this sort, there is no sign that they were bound and determined to break the code either. Just after 1912 they drew many of their leaders from the same aristocratic ranks as did Conservatives (Table 2-2), and Radical rhetoric constantly emphasized morality in government rather than changes in structure, policy, or procedure. These challengers were seeking power, not the alteration of the social system.

More crucial to my argument is the importance which Conservatives attached to the rules of the game. Congressional debates on the 1912 electoral reform reveal discernible traces of these latent assumptions. Discussion of the provision for guaranteed minority representation in the Chamber of Deputies, for instance, showed the constant conviction that Conservatives would have the majority and direct a kind of coalition government.[9] Thus the reform would guarantee and institutionalize the central tenet of the code: power would be shared among competing factions which would reach decisions by consensus.

Proponents of the reform also appeared to believe that the specific characteristics of traditional conflict would persist. Many looked forward to the reinvigoration of political parties, by this time in disarray, but not to clashes drawn inflexibly on party lines. Legislators should serve the nation, they said more than once, not the interests of party or region. There would be no class warfare: disagreements under the new system ought to be muted, controlled, undemagogic, settled gracefully by gentlemen. By the retention of Conservative majorities, of course, the socioeconomic elite would continue to

9. The congressional debates are conveniently presented in Ministerio del Interior, *Las fuerzas armadas restituyen el imperio de la soberanía popular*, 2 vols. (Buenos Aires, 1946), I, 36-303. See also Darío Cantón, *Elecciones y partidos políticos en la Argentina. Historia, interpretación y balance: 1910-1966* (Buenos Aires, 1973), Ch. 4.

run the political system. As a loyal opposition, furthermore, the Radical party would encourage first- and second-generation immigrants—particularly among the working class—to seek reform by supporting the system, rather than by engaging in anarcho-syndicalist strategies. Revised and strengthened in this fashion, all the basic rules would stay intact.

Thus many aristocratic Conservatives regarded the maintenance of these norms as essential to the legitimacy of the cooptation strategy and open electoral politics in general. To them, democracy would be acceptable only so long as the rules of the game were upheld.[10]

Implementation of the Saenz Peña law brought immediate changes in voting patterns of the electorate,[11] and elites were soon affected too. With increasing frequency political decisions were arrived at openly, even competitively, rather than by the old *acuerdo* system. The number of contested roll calls in the Chamber of Deputies (Figure 3-1) clearly reflected this trend: deputies were becoming accountable, at least to their parties if not to the electorate at large. Government by consensus began to disappear.

Eventually a central tenet of the classic code, the sharing of political power, came to collapse. By the end of the 1920s, the Radicals, whose consecutive victories at the polls stunned complacent Conservatives, were not sharing control of the government with anybody; they held almost all of it themselves. This was partly due to expansion of the electorate, which roughly doubled in size between 1912 and 1930 and gave the Radicals a mass constituency (Figure 1-1). In the Chamber of Deputies they possessed a clear majority by 1920; after the split between the Personalist Yrigoyen wing and the Antipersonalist Alvear faction in 1924, the Yrigoyenist UCR held two-thirds of the seats by 1930. Though the Conservatives managed to prolong their hegemony in the Senate, and thus maintain a power base, time was running out; by 1930 Yrigoyenists had a substantial delegation in the upper chamber and they threatened to gain a full majority in upcoming elections.

Intense partisanship also came to replace the loose party affiliations of the pre-1912 era. Figure 4-1 clearly shows how the association between party identification and roll-call voting in the Chamber of Deputies increased, then reached a peak just prior to the 1930 coup. Recurrent confrontation between progovernment Radicals and the opposition parties along predominantly General factors, cutting across a wide variety of issues (Table 5-1), gave further proof of change. The manners of the gentlemen were gone.

Political conflict moreover acquired subtle social overtones. According to

10. This is a little different from Dahl's version of the credo: "I believe in elections as long as I can be sure that my opponents will not win." Dahl, *Polyarchy*, p. 140. The fact is that Conservatives did accept Radical triumphs in 1916, 1922, and 1928; it was only when these rules were broken that the opposition's victory became intolerable.

11. Darío Cantón, "Universal Suffrage as an Agent of Mobilization," paper presented at the Sixth World Congress of Sociology, Evian, France (September 1966).

Table 2-3, data on deputies for 1916-30 reveal a mild but noticeable association between class status and party affiliation. As shown in Chapter 5 (Figure 5-2), the break between Yrigoyen and Alvear divided Radicals in the mid-1920s along both regional *and social* lines. There is also some evidence that, in 1928 and especially in 1930, the Personalist Radicals tended to gain electoral support from the lower class instead of from the middle class, as the UCR had done before.[12] This does not mean that there was open class conflict on the elite level, since Status (with no control for intervening variables) continued to have weak statistical correlations with roll-call voting alignments in the Chamber of Deputies. But the Radical schism did affect the distribution of effective influence. With the triumph of the unaristocratic Yrigoyenists, and the near-total demise of the Conservative party,[13] the traditional elite lost almost all meaningful access to political power.

Yet the heterogenous quality of the nonaristocracy demands close examination of the specific characteristics of UCR leaders in the late 1920s. They do not seem to have been merchants, farmers, or industrialists who viewed politics as an avocation. As implied in Chapter 2 (Table 2-6), they comprised a special breed: they were political professionals. Biographical data for Yrigoyenist senators and deputies in 1928-30 show that their average age was around forty-five, meaning that this was not the same generation which guided the Radical movement prior to 1916, that they were usually university-trained lawyers, and that they had taken up politics while still in their twenties.[14] There was very little lateral mobility from Argentina's socioeconomic elite into Yrigoyen's political elite during his second administra-

12. Cantón makes this point in his study of *Elecciones*, principally on pp. 149-52. I construe this argument as tentative, however, since Cantón uses rank-order correlation coefficients to measure relationships between conceptually imprecise variables on the provincial level (with 15 observations or less). One of his most intriguing findings is the positive correlation between the Radical vote in 1928 and the Peronist vote in 1946 (+.43, and +.90 when two outlying cases are omitted), but this does not necessarily demonstrate a class basis for the Radical vote. Using different methods, in fact, I have concluded that Perón drew support from heterogeneous sectors of the population in 1946. See Peter H. Smith, "The Social Base of Peronism," *Hispanic American Historical Review*, 52, no. 1 (February 1972), 55-73.

13. One of the great mysteries of Argentine politics is the utter failure of the Conservative party to cope with the realities of electoral competition. This topic is badly in need of research. For a preliminary study of the subject, see Oscar Cornblit, "El fracaso del Conservadorismo en la Argentina," Trabajo Interno no. 14, Centro de Investigaciones Sociales, Instituto Torcuato di Tella, mimeographed (Buenos Aires, 1973).

14. On sources, see the Bibliography and Figure 5-2. I use the term professional in the same sense as in Chapter 2, but with different indicators. Applied to Yrigoyenists of the late 1920s, the number-of-congressional-terms criterion could seriously underestimate professionalism because the coup of 1930 and the UCR's subsequent electoral boycott interrupted, and in some cases truncated, legislative careers.

tion. As one observer recalled with disgust, "The Congress was full of rabble and unspeakable hoodlums. The parliamentary language used up to then had been replaced by the coarse language of the outskirts of the city and the Radicals' committees . . . ."[15] At least regarding leadership, it began to look as though the political system no longer reflected the distribution of power within the economic system.

While political power passed into the hands of new social groups, central government power expanded as well. Threatening to eliminate local pockets of opposition, Radical presidents resorted to federal intervention in the provinces much more than did previous leaders: of 93 such actions from 1862 to 1930, 34 took place during the fourteen-year period of Radical rule.[16] The economic impact of political decision-making also increased. In the decade from 1920 to 1929 federal expenditures climbed from 9 percent of GNP to nearly 19 percent.[17] This fact alone helps explain the intensification of political pressure as the decade wore on. By 1930 there was more at stake than in 1912.

Finally, Yrigoyen and his followers made ambiguous use of their power. On the one hand, Yrigoyen ignored all codes of military discipline by turning the army into a source of patronage, promoting officers because of partisan allegiance rather than because of seniority or merit. Such maneuverings naturally angered many officers who were intensely proud of the army's professional autonomy and honor and who, largely for this reason, supported or abetted the 1930 coup. But most striking is the sequence of events: Yrigoyen intervened in military affairs *before* the army intervened decisively in politics, and the officers responded in *reaction* to his interference.[18]

On the other hand, Yrigoyen's failure to employ power may have been as important as his use (or abuse) of it. There are solid indications that his economic policy would have been acceptable to rural landed interests, as suggested by the affinity between Radical and Conservative deputies on socially definable roll-call voting factors (Table 5-1). This was not the issue; what mattered was the distribution of political power (note the content of relevant factors in Table 3-2). In 1930 the Congress bickered from May until August about the legality of elections in several provinces: the UCR was flaunting its superiority, and the opposition, hopelessly outnumbered, could only boycott sessions in an effort to prevent quorums. As a result, the legislature passed no laws at all in 1930! Though Yrigoyen's physical in-

15. Mariano Bosch, *Historia del Partido Radical: la U.C.R., 1891-1930* (Buenos Aires, 1931), p. 214.

16. Rosendo A. Gómez, "Intervention in Argentina, 1860-1930," *Inter-American Economic Affairs*, 1, no. 3 (December 1947), 55-73.

17. Cámara de Diputados, *Diario de Sesiones*, 1932, 7 (December 1), 142.

18. See the description of events in Marvin Goldwert, "The Rise of Modern Militarism in Argentina," *Hispanic American Historical Review*, 48, no. 2 (May 1968), 189-205.

firmities and the bureaucracy's ineptness undoubtedly slowed down the decision-making process, concern with the allocation of political power brought the parliamentary machine to a total halt. This stalemate and publicity about it no doubt engendered widespread frustration.

In summary, the traditional rules of Argentina's political game had all been seriously violated, particularly after 1928. Despite a setback in the 1930 by-elections, the Radicals' steady accretion of votes destroyed any balance of power in politics. Intense partisan struggles replaced fluid party allegiances. Subtle social alignments, and the displacement of the aristocrats, threatened to end intraclass maneuvering. The political system came to represent an autonomous threat to the socioeconomic system, even in the absence of major disagreements over policy, both through the hegemony of political professionals and through the accumulation of independent political power.

This abandonment of long-standing norms produced an essentially political crisis which, in turn, led to the breakdown of Argentine democracy. There remains the question of why the norms were abandoned. I do not think that Yrigoyen or the Radicals purposely betrayed a conscious agreement or simply changed their minds along the way. In fact, the very *consistency* of the Radicals' behavior did much to weaken the system, since they continued to act like an opposition party once they were in power. The attitudes and tactics which helped them acquire power before 1916 did not help them solidify power after 1916. Catering to military factions served the interests of an opposition, for instance, but undermined the authority of a president; disputes over congressional credentials could dramatize the plight of an opposition but obstruct the administrative need for policy output; intransigence might allow an opposition to bring attention to key issues but, in leading to the defection of the Antipersonalists, weaken a government coalition. It is difficult to say why the UCR maintained this inflexible posture, but I might suggest that (1) for Yrigoyen's own generation, the twenty-six-year experience as an "out" group from 1890 to 1916 had created a firm and antagonistic oppositionist mentality;[19] and (2) for the new generation of Radical party professionals political power represented a channel to upward social mobility, and they were unwilling to share such a precious commodity with other groups.

More important than the Radicals' unchanging stance, however, was the changing structure within which they operated. Almost by definition, democratic politics after 1916 were incompatible with the traditional rules of the game: quite naturally the exercise of universal suffrage gave great power to the mass party, public campaigning and conflict hardened party lines, the

19. As Yrigoyen said near the end of his first presidential term: "I did not expect to end up here. I expected to remain in the agreeable role of an opponent (*el papel simpático de opositor*) . . . ." Félix Luna, *Yrigoyen* (Buenos Aires, 1964), p. 182.

exigencies of electoral politics gave rise to nonaristocratic professional politicians, popular focus on politics produced demands for an autonomous and powerful government. Conservatives wanted democracy to uphold the rules of the game; but the structure was unsuited to this function, and the pursuit of democratic practice led to the violation of those rules. For Conservatives and their allies, in short, democracy became dysfunctional and therefore unacceptable.

So there developed a crisis of legitimacy. The problem was essentially political, and it grew directly out of the methods employed to meet demands for participation in 1912. Thus the resolution of one crisis led to the appearance of another.

Tension in the political sphere was no doubt exacerbated by apprehension over the economic Depression which hit some countries in late 1929. But the deterministic (and retroactive) assumption that declining economic conditions caused the coup does not withstand close scrutiny. By September 1930, Argentina had felt little effects from the Depression—even less so at the time the plotters began conspiring, early in the year. The prices and values of beef exports held firm till 1931. The wheat market was suffering badly, but mainly because of a drought; besides, farmers exerted scant political influence, partly because so many were unnaturalized immigrants (about 70 percent in 1914). In 1930 real wages underwent a brief decline and unemployment was starting to spread, but labor agitation—as reflected by the number of strikes (Figure 1-2)—was still at a moderate level.[20]

Perhaps the most significant piece of evidence is qualitative and negative. While some civilian members of the anti-Yrigoyen conspiracy referred to economic crisis as one reason for their action, most participants failed to mention it or gave it very low priority. In brief, the economic Depression might have emphasized weaknesses within the political system and thus been necessary for the overthrow; but it was not a sufficient cause by itself.

As the crisis over legitimacy deepened, the opposition responded with force. On September 6, a coalition of officers and aristocrats ousted Yrigoyen and set up a provisional government. The new leadership was divided in many ways but all major factions agreed on one point: somehow the traditional rules of the political game should be restored.

One group, led by General Agustín P. Justo—himself an Antipersonalist

20. Data on Argentine exports can be found in Dirección General de Estadística, *Informes*, nos. 11, 24, 33, 34, 40 (Buenos Aires, 1924-33). On the nationality of farmers in the cereal belt, see Carl Solberg, "Rural Unrest and Agrarian Policy in Argentina, 1912-1930," *Journal of Inter-American Studies and World Affairs*, 13, no. 1 (January 1971), 29. On working-class wages and unemployment, see Figure 6-1 below; and the extremely important book by Miguel Murmis and Juan Carlos Portantiero, *Estudios sobre los orígenes del peronismo*, vol. I (Buenos Aires, 1971), p. 85.

Radical—sought a return to pre-1916 (or pre-1912) politics. This faction thought the Yrigoyenists had grossly abused the electoral and parliamentary procedure. With Personalists out of the way, power would revert to the aristocrats, conflict would be restrained, the possibility of class struggle would disappear, the *gente bien* would rule once again. Thus the democratic structure would reassume its normal, proper and legitimate functions.[21]

Another group, led by General José F. Uriburu, had a more drastic solution: the creation of a semifascist corporate state. The problem was not Yrigoyen or his followers, but the system itself. Combining Catholic precepts with admiration of Mussolini's Italy, Uriburu sought to establish a hierarchical order based on social function. He thought the vote should be "qualified" so that the most cultivated members of society would have predominant influence on elections, and he wanted to reorganize Congress in order to take power away from political professionals—"agents of political committees," as he disdainfully called them. In his "functional democracy" legislators would represent not parties but corporate interests—as ranchers, farmers, workers, merchants, industrialists, and so on. A vertical structure of this kind would create a basis for rule by consensus, eliminate class conflict, and perhaps most important—in Argentina—reintegrate the political system with the economic system. Once more, and now by conscious design, the political arena would reflect the distribution of power within the economic arena; the pre-1912 rules of the game would be restated and put into law.[22]

Although Uriburu directed the provisional government, the Justo group eventually won out. Elections took place but, as in the days before Saenz Peña, fraud was undisguised. Deprived of a provincial victory in 1931, Personalist Radicals embarked upon another boycott, and Justo won the presidency over weak opposition. At his inauguration in January 1932, it must have seemed as though the coup had achieved its purpose: politics was as it used to be.

PHASE 2: FRAUDS AND FAILURES

Despite this aura of success, the political manipulations of the 1930s culminated in further historical crises. Justo's pseudodemocratic solution to the pre-1930 legitimacy crisis was as fragile as it was fraudulent; even a

21. Evidence for this interpretation is indirect and circumstantial, since (to the best of my knowledge) Justo and his colleagues issued no clear public statement of political purpose.

22. See José María Sarobe, *Memorias sobre la revolución del 6 de septiembre de 1930* (Buenos Aires, 1957), pp. 19-38, 44-50, 56-78; [José Félix Uriburu], *La palabra del General Uriburu*, 2nd ed. (Buenos Aires, 1933), esp. pp. 22-23, 95-100, 167-68; and the quotation in Peter G. Snow, *Political Forces in Argentina* (Boston, 1971), p. 65.

temporary phase of honest elections could revive the crisis again. Further-more, a system of this sort, conceived in nostalgia, was ill equipped to deal with new demands and challenges. Political practice under Justo may have been logical, according to the momentary context, but it was also unrealistic.

In a parliamentary incarnation of the old *acuerdo* method of decision-making, the Justista coalition dominated Congress through a multiparty *Concordancia*. A fair number of policies came up for public scrutiny, as shown in the frequency of contested roll calls (Figure 3-1), but the prepon-derance of progovernment deputies left little doubt about the ultimate outcome. There were signs of strain within the coalition, particularly regard-ing the Independent Socialists (Figure 5-3, Table 5-2), but for the most part the government groups voted against the opposition.

Yet as shown in Chapter 2, Justo's efforts to remove the military from politics entailed reinstallation of political professionals, even within the ruling coalition (Table 2-5; note also the high percentage of former deputies in the presidential cabinet, shown in Figure 1-5). Especially because of the fraud, deputies in the 1930s gained their seats in the Chamber through loyalty to party machineries, rather than by appealing to public constituencies. One sign of this situation was the generally strong association between party identifica-tion and roll-call voting patterns between 1932 and 1942 (Figure 4-1).

Ultimately, it proved impossible to revive the old rules of the game. One reason for this failure was the expansion of an urban working class which, through strikes and other tactics, made repeated demands upon the govern-ment authorities. And on the elite level, political professionals—committed to partisan interests—simply refused to play by the rules. The return of the Personalist Radicals—professionalism par excellence—laid bare the failure of Justo's attempt. From 1936 onward partisanship mounted sharply in the Congress (Figure 4-1), with Personalists leading a steady attack on the government (Table 5-2). When fraud was brought to a halt by President Roberto Ortiz in 1938, Radicals promptly took over the Chamber of Depu-ties and used it as a forum for constant obstruction, delays, and frustration of presidential policies.

After illness forced Ortiz to leave office in 1940, his successor, Ramón Castillo, archconservative from Catamarca, returned to the use of so-called patriotic fraud. Here was the dilemma: in order to resolve the kind of legitimacy crisis which had appeared by 1930, authorities had to cheat at the polls; but the cheating itself, widely observed and recognized, only served to emphasize the weakness and instability of civilian rule.

The armed forces, by this time more professional than ever, and deeply influenced by the German and Italian examples, watched all these goings-on with a combination of dismay and disdain. As World War II broke out in Europe, military chieftains saw the need for steady, sure, and evenhanded leadership. And there were the politicians, pursuing party interests and committing open falsehood!

What resulted was a new kind of legitimacy crisis, felt most strongly (but not exclusively) within military circles. Several efforts to unseat the Castillo regime took place before the final overthrow in 1943. Despite great differences among the plotting officers, they had one common bond: utter contempt for the civilian government, especially political professionals. On seizing power the triumphant GOU (Grupo de Oficiales Unidos) denounced the Castillo administration for "venality, fraud, peculation, and corruption," and justified its action as a response to popular demand: "We support our institutions and our laws," the officers proclaimed, "persuaded that it is not they but men [i.e., political professionals] who have been delinquent in their application."[23]

Despite this mild gesture of homage to the constitution, it soon became apparent that many officers intended to revamp the entire political structure. After dissolving the Congress, the first provisional president, General Arturo Rawson, proudly announced, "Now there are no political parties, but only Argentines."[24] And in November 1943 the minister of the interior, General Luis Perlinger, spelled out far-reaching aims in a letter of instruction to provincial interventors:

> The meaning of the revolution should reach as soon as possible all social, political, and economic orders . . . . The political aspect should be characterized by an eminently Argentine orientation. *No politician—whatever his affiliation—shall be summoned to collaborate with the government* [my italics]. Through education and energetic action the *régimen* must be broken. The mass of citizens should be disciplined . . . . The political parties are not important now.[25]

The old regime—electoral politics, tainted by fraud—required total transformation and purification. To this end political parties were dissolved by decree the following year, and, except for a couple of "collaborationist" Radicals, political professionals were excluded from the cabinet (Figure 1-5).

In sum, the Justista resolution of the 1930 legitimacy crisis was incomplete. Given the presence of parties and political professionals, as well as the existence of a surging proletariat, it was impossible to return to the pre-1912 politics of gentlemen. The result was a second legitimacy crisis, this time perceived mainly by the military—since it was now the Conservatives, not the Radicals, who were demonstrating the inadequacy and ineffectiveness of electoral institutions.

23. Quoted in Robert A. Potash, *The Army and Politics in Argentina, 1928-1945* (Stanford, Cal., 1969), p. 197.

24. Quoted in K. H. Silvert, "The Costs of Anti-Nationalism: Argentina," in Silvert, ed., *Expectant Peoples: Nationalism and Development* (New York, 1963), p. 356.

25. Quoted in Potash, *Army*, pp. 225-26.

Concurrent with this development was the appearance of a new phenomenon: a distribution crisis. As described in Chapter 1, the 1930s witnessed substantial growth in industry and, equally important, in the urban working class, many of whose members had migrated from the countryside to the city. Literate, mobile, articulate, if not always well organized, the urban proletariat was emerging as a major social force.[26]

It was also a group with grievances. As revealed in Figure 6-1, the upward trend in real wages for workers in the city of Buenos Aires ended abruptly in 1930—and declined slightly in the course of the following decade. Although this reversal was partly due to the Depression, the Argentine economy had pretty much recovered by the mid-1930s—but to encourage investment, *Concordancia* administrations assiduously pursued policies to favor the landed and the moneyed groups.[27] Workers could justifiably complain about relative deprivation. Moreover, they were accustomed to improvements in the

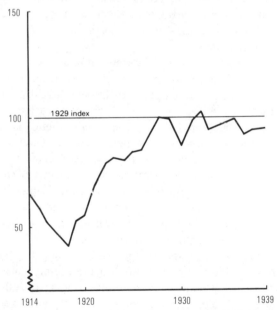

Figure 6-1. Industrial real wages in the city of Buenos Aires, 1914-39. Index: 1929=100. Data from División de Estadística, Departamento Nacional del Trabajo, *Estadística de las huelgas* (Buenos Aires, 1940), p. 21.

26. According to Roberto Cortés Conde, the size of the urban work force actually doubled between 1935 and 1941. See his essay on "Partidos políticos," in Editorial Sur, *Argentina 1930-1960* (Buenos Aires, 1961), p. 138; and Murmis and Portantiero, *Estudios*, esp. Part II.

27. Tulio Halperín Donghi, "Crónica del período," *Argentina 1930-1960*, p. 35, and Murmis and Portantiero, *Estudios*, Part I.

standard of living—and their rising expectations, to use a hackneyed phrase, met with constant frustration during the 1930s.

Not only was it true that workers received no benefits from official government policy.[28] But as shown in Chapter 5, they had no real political representation at all. Social issues came up infrequently in the Chamber of Deputies, as the content of roll-call voting factors implies (Table 3-4); on the few dimensions which reflected labor problems, only the Socialists stood up consistently for the working class (Table 5-2), and they were far too small a group to gain significant support for legislation.[29] (Partly because of this identification with inefficacious parliamentarism, socialism—as party and ideology—lost influence among the laborers, who took another course when it was ultimately offered to them.)

For the working class, the distribution crisis was reinforced and compounded by a problem—if not a crisis—of political participation. The proletariat was rapidly shifting from a predominantly immigrant group to being predominantly native born. Thus workers increasingly possessed the right to vote (Figure 1-1) but, given the operation of the system, they could not find a way to exert effective influence.

One reason for this situation was the fraud. But another reason, even more basic, was the prevailing party structure. All the major parties, even the Radicals and Socialists, had developed their internal organization, operations, and ideology to meet the electoral needs of Argentine society in 1912—when over half the adult male population, and certainly a much larger portion of the lower class, was excluded from the right to vote. Therefore, none of the parties, with the partial exception of the Socialists, came to forge either a clear-cut ideology or a significant working-class base. Established and developed to resolve a distribution crisis in another era, Argentine political parties offered no meaningful outlet for the needs of urban labor. Consequently, the democratic, competitive style of politics, *even without the fraud*, was incapable of meeting or managing the distribution crisis.

Eventually, the lack of a viable political alternative led to the rise of Juan Perón. Using his position as secretary of labor, and later minister of war and also vice-president of the nation, Perón employed a carrot-and-stick method to win the support of industrial workers: old laboring groups as well as new,

28. For a convenient summary of legislative action, see Jerónimo Remorino et al., *Anales de legislación argentina, 1852-1954*, 5 vols. (Buenos Aires, 1953-57). Labor actually made some gains in 1916-30, a fact which probably increased resentment in the 1930s. See Darío Cantón, José L. Moreno, and Alberto Ciria, *Argentina: la democracia constitucional y su crisis* (Buenos Aires, 1972), p. 71.

29. For one case study of this failure, see my article on "Social Mobilization, Political Participation, and the Rise of Juan Perón," *Political Science Quarterly*, 84, no. 1 (March 1969), esp. 36-40, 42-44.

lifelong urban residents as well as recent migrants from the countryside. A hero to the dispossessed, he won the presidential election of 1946 with a solid 54 percent majority—over the indiscreet resistance of the U.S. State Department and, more pertinent to this analysis, the combined opposition of all former national political parties.[30]

PHASE 3: COMPOUNDING CRISES

To meet the distribution crisis, and also integrate workers into the political system, Perón constructed an informal kind of corporate state. Argentine society was thenceforth to be organized according to functional groups: industrialists, farmers, laborers, and so on, with an omnipotent state at the top. Conflicts between the various sectors would be resolved by governmental fiat, presumably to maintain social harmony. As Perón began his term in office, therefore, the state intensified its interventionist role in economic affairs. A host of statutes came forth to regulate the organization of functional groups, institutions sprang up to govern the economy (most notably the Instituto Argentino de Promoción del Intercambio, IAPI, which monopolized the export trade), and the administration even launched a Five-Year Economic Plan.

In general, the overall scheme bears striking resemblance to the corporate utopia envisioned by Uriburu in the early 1930s. This fact alone is not surprising, since both Perón (who took part in the overthrow of Yrigoyen) and Uriburu found ideological inspiration in Mussolini's Italy. Yet the difference was as profound as it was simple: Perón established urban workers as one of the central pillars in his political edifice, along with the armed forces, whereas Uriburu would have relegated labor to a minor place in his scheme.[31]

Clearly, the Peronist plan for a corporate society left little room for political professionals.[32] As shown in Figure 1-5, Perón virtually eliminated former deputies from the presidential cabinet. The Chamber of Deputies

30. On this election, see my article, "The Social Base of Peronism."

31. Until very recently there has been an incredible dearth of scholarly research on the Perón era. In my opinion the best book-length study continues to be George I. Blanksten, *Perón's Argentina* (Chicago, 1953), despite its obvious biases. One good but general discussion of Perón's corporate tendencies appears in Silvert, "Costs," pp. 361-69.

32. Though Perón sought some contact with leaders of the Radical, Communist, and Socialist parties in 1943 and 1944, this seems to have been a passing phenomenon—as suggested by their opposition to his candidacy in 1945 and 1946. See A. Lawrence Stickell, "Peronist Politics in Labor, 1943," in Alberto Ciria et al., *New Perspectives on Modern Argentina* (Bloomington, Ind., 1972), pp. 39-40. Note also Perón's disdainful comments about political parties and their leaders, in *Perón expone su doctrina* (Buenos Aires, 1947), pp. 60, 299, and 301.

filled its halls with nonaristocratic amateurs. A new breed, often reared in labor unions but untrained and inexperienced in politics, thus took over public life.[33]

This change, drastic as it may seem, becomes comprehensible in view of the demonstrated rigidities and obsolescence of the traditional party system. Electoral parliamentarianism, as practiced prior to 1943, had starkly revealed its inability to cope with the mounting distribution crisis. Corporate authoritarianism offered a logical, if possibly pernicious, alternative to worn-out pseudodemocratic politics. And the professionals, men who had made their careers through the traditional parties and the outmoded system, would simply have to step aside.

As a matter of fact, the Perón regime met the distribution crisis decisively and effectively. Using a variety of means, including the encouragement and forced settlement of strikes (note the abrupt rise in strikes and strikers during the mid-1940s in Figure 1-2), Perón brought about a significant reallocation of economic benefits. The wage and salary share of national income, which by one measure fluctuated around 45 percent in the decade prior to 1946, reached an unprecedented height of 60 percent in the years from 1949 through 1954.[34] Rhetorical appeals, exhortations, and lavish attention from the dashing Eva Perón provided psychic benefits as well. The distribution crisis, as it had appeared in the 1930s and early 1940s, came to a resolution.

Though Perón seems to have hoped that his corporate structure would allow him to keep his heterogeneous coalition in a state of permanent equilibrium, his purposes and policies created conflict. From the start, the Chamber of Deputies witnessed a pervasive cleavage between the Peronists and the opposition, a cleavage with multiple dimensions: amateurs versus professionals, ins versus outs, accomplices in corporatism versus practitioners of parliamentarianism. Yet there remained a sense of flexibility. The Peronist group was not overwhelmingly monolithic, and substantial interplay existed among congressional factions (Table 5-3).

Around 1949, however, economic difficulties began to eclipse the visions of lasting social harmony. The exhaustion of foreign reserves, due more to the importing needs of consumer-oriented industry and the costs of welfare programs than to carelessness or corruption (alleged to explain overpayment for British-owned railroads in 1948), started a phase of inflation. Drought curtailed the production of primary goods for export and consumption.

33. Brief portraits of top Peronist leaders appear in Blanksten, *Perón's Argentina*, pp. 343-56.

34. Eldon Kenworthy, "The Function of the Little-Known Case in Theory Formation or What Peronism Wasn't," *Comparative Politics*, 6, no. 1 (October 1973), 40-41; and Clarence Zuvekas, Jr., "Economic Growth and Income Distribution in Postwar Argentina," *Inter-American Economic Affairs*, 20, no. 3 (Winter 1966), 25.

World market prices for key exports fell off, and international demand for Argentina's type of beef began to decline. The rising cost of importables slowed industrial production. As a result, real wages sagged; per capita GNP declined sharply after 1948 and reached a nadir in 1952; by 1955, as Figure 6-2 illustrates, per capita output was still below the levels for 1947-48.

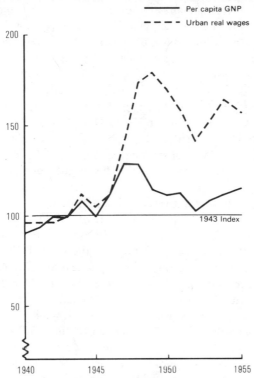

Figure 6-2. Per capita GNP and urban real wages, 1940-55. Indices: 1943=100. Data from Carlos F. Díaz Alejandro, *Essays on the Economic History of the Argentine Republic* (New Haven and London, 1970), p. 538.

The political implications of this situation were extremely grave, since Argentina became involved in a zero-sum game. Increased benefits for labor now came at someone else's explicit expense. An expanding economy made redistributive policies tolerable for relatively less favored groups; a stagnant economy could not. Consequently, there appeared a kind of distributive backlash: under these conditions, resolution of the distribution crisis *for workers* led directly to a distribution crisis *for other sectors of society*, essentially the upper and middle classes.

Perón reacted to this situation in two ways. On the one hand, he loosened state control of the economy. IAPI relaxed its grip on the export sector, the government slowed down its drive to industrialization, and doors were re-opened to foreign investment—as in the celebrated Standard Oil contract of 1954. A series of orthodox measures cut back the rate of inflation.[35] Eventually the government stopped fixing wages and prices and allowed real wages for workers to decline (Figure 6-2).

On the other hand, this liberalization of the economy, as Peter Waldmann has called it,[36] was offset by a tightening of political control. In 1949, the same year that a new constitution was passed and *Justicialista* ideology found explicit formulation,[37] the Peronist party (Partido Peronista) was born. Unlike its predecessors, which exhibited notable internal division, this was a genuine machine: organized, selective, loyal, thoroughly committed to the exaltation of Perón.[38] As though to emphasize the break from the past, one of its central organs was a Tribunal of Party Discipline. In 1951 Perón also established an Escuela Superior Peronista, with two purposes in mind: "The first is the formation of Justicialists," he announced, "and the second the exaltation of Peronist values to serve the Justicialist doctrine in the best way."[39]

After 1949 there followed a series of cathartic actions. Aristocrats disappeared almost entirely from the Peronist elite (Figure 2-1). Unwisely, at least in retrospect, *El Líder* challenged military officers by attempting to indoctrinate cadets with Peronist teachings, upgrade the lower ranks with flashy uniforms, and give preferential promotion to political favorites (such efforts prompted an abortive coup in 1951). After Evita's death in 1952, Perón turned most of his attention from the army to the labor unions, led now by faithful loyalists.[40] Class consciousness mounted and, symbolically enough, a Peronist crowd pillaged the aristocratic Jockey Club in 1953. In its political manifestation, therefore, Peronism transformed itself from a multi-class corporate coalition into a sectarian movement, based upon the working class[41] and headed by the charismatic figure of Perón himself.

35. Thomas E. Skidmore, "The Populist Politician as Inflation-Fighter: The Stabilization Policies of Juan Perón, 1943-1955" (unpublished manuscript).

36. Waldmann, "Las cuatro fases del gobierno peronista," *Aportes*, 19 (January 1971), 101 and passim.

37. A clear exposition of Justicialist doctrine is in Blanksten, *Perón's Argentina*, pp. 276-305.

38. On the tension between organization and charisma, see Alberto Ciria, "Peronism and Political Structures, 1945-1955," in Ciria et al., *New Perspectives*, pp. 1-14; and Walter Little, "Party and State in Peronist Argentina, 1945-1955," *Hispanic American Historical Review*, 53, no. 4 (November 1973), 644-62.

39. Blanksten, *Perón's Argentina*, p. 342.

40. See Walter Little, "La tendencia peronista en el sindicalismo argentino: el caso de los obreros de la Carne," *Aportes*, 19 (January 1971), 107-24.

41. Compare the equations in my article on "The Social Base of Peronism," suggesting that Perón had heterogeneous support in the 1946 election, with correlations

In an ironic way, this development culminated the uneven, decades-long process which had been leading to the separation of political power from socioeconomic power. Essentially, Perón was attempting a balancing act: returning the socioeconomic structures of power to their former leaders, while reserving control of the political system for his movement and its members. In the phrase of one historian, this trade-off led him to abandon the workers' nation in regard to economic policy,[42] at the same time that he elevated union leaders and *descamisados* (shirtless ones) to a singular position of importance and prestige in politics.

The establishment of Peronism as a sectarian movement had clear and far-reaching consequences in the national Chamber of Deputies. From 1950 onward flexibility was most conspicuous by absence. Flaunting their triumph and power, Peronist deputies used roll-call votes to intimidate the opposition and to demonstrate their solidarity. The few contested votes, regardless of issue content, all corresponded to a single partisan alignment. The degree of polarization also increased: as time progressed, Peronists and Radicals moved steadily farther apart (Figure 5-4). As a true sign of the times, progovernment deputies temporarily expelled the opposition in April 1953.

Aside from the backlash-distribution crisis, these developments brought on another legitimacy crisis. Perón's opponents simply refused to recognize the normative basis for his claims to power. Like Yrigoyen, but in a different way, he too had violated all the old rules of the game. Not only was there class conflict in the place of social harmony; political power was now inversely related to economic power, and class struggle was coming to dominate Argentine society.

Tension increased steadily throughout the 1950s.[43] Threatened by a rebellious army in 1955, Perón had only the starkest of alternatives: arming the workers for civil war, or leaving office. Faced by this dilemma, Perón took a boat to Paraguay.

Once in power, the post-Peronist leadership—bolstered mainly by the army, but supported by a wide variety of civilian elements—pursued beguiling logic. Since Peronism had (presumably) caused all the ills in the Argentine body politic, the proper cure would be to extirpate Peronism from the

indicating that he drew votes mainly from the lower class during the early 1950s. See Walter Little, "Electoral Aspects of Peronism, 1946-1954," *Journal of Inter-American Studies and World Affairs*, 15, no. 3 (August 1973), 267-84; Cantón, *Elecciones*, pp. 152-54; and Lars Schoultz, "A Diachronic Analysis of Peronist Electoral Behavior" (Ph.D. diss., University of North Carolina, 1973), esp. Ch. II.

42. Samuel L. Baily, *Labor, Nationalism, and Politics in Argentina* (New Brunswick, N.J., 1967), Ch. VII, entitled "Perón Abandons the Workers' Nation."

43. One could almost argue that there was an identity crisis as well, given the sectarian conflict between people who, seeing themselves primarily as Peronists and anti-Peronists, often ceased to recognize their common identity as Argentines.

national life. Purges took place in the military, the bureaucracy, the universities, and elsewhere. When elections were resumed in 1958, Peronist candidates were not allowed to run. And if they were allowed to run, as in 1962, they were not allowed to win (the military promptly annulled the results). Inevitably enough, the anti-Peronist crusade brought on yet another kind of crisis, this time one of participation. To all intents and purposes the Argentine working class, or at least a major part of it, had been systematically stripped of its political rights.

Since the early 1950s, in short, Argentina has undergone an incremental accumulation of political crises. Resolution of the distribution crisis (for workers) brought on another distribution crisis (for others). Perón's effort to tighten control brought on a legitimacy crisis. And the anti-Peronist campaigns since 1955 created a participation crisis.

Not only have the crises mounted in this fashion, each one adding to the other, but there has also developed a quality of permanence, equilibrium, and interdependence, so that efforts to alleviate one of the crises have actually aggravated one or both of the others. In the eyes of the military, for instance, allowing Peronist candidates to run for office (to meet the participation crisis) has cast doubt upon the legitimacy of the electoral process. Post-Peronist policies to alter income distribution, mainly to the detriment of laborers,[44] has only drawn attention to the denial of working-class participation in politics—and invited challenges to governmental legitimacy. So the form of crisis has changed, but the level of crisis has not. Thus the politics of deadlock: like the economy, the political system has fallen victim to the ruthless mathematics of a zero-sum equation.[45] (It seemed unlikely, at the time of writing, that Juan Perón's remarkable reelection to the presidency in September 1973 represented a departure from this vicious circle.)

SUMMARY AND CONCLUSIONS

In a crude attempt to recapitulate the thrust of this analysis, Figure 6-3 offers a schematic outline of successive trends, events, and crises in twentieth-century Argentine politics. The top row depicts "Socioeconomic Variables," broadly construed, which affected the nature and intensity of demands on the political system. The next row, "Political Variables," presents a catchall category for prevailing practices, policies, and policy outcomes. The

44. Note the data in Leopoldo Portnoy, *La realidad argentina en el siglo XX: análisis crítico de la economía* (Mexico and Buenos Aires, 1961), p. 10.

45. A brilliant analysis of the post-1955 situation—based on a different but complementary conceptual framework—appears in Guillermo A. O'Donnell, *Modernization and Bureaucratic-Authoritarianism: Studies in South American Politics* (Berkeley, Cal., 1973), esp. Chs. III and IV. Also see Tulio Halperín Donghi, *Argentina: la democracia de masas* (Buenos Aires, 1972).

"Type of Crisis" summarizes my attempts to identify the specific character of challenges made upon the system. "Elite Response" describes the reaction of political leaders (civilian or military) to the crises at hand. In order to stress the dynamic processes of interaction, a "Time" continuum appears on the bottom line, although (for reasons of space) it does not constitute a true chronological scale. In an extremely loose sense of the term, arrows represent causality throughout.

Despite the simplifications inherent in any such diagram, Figure 6-3 underscores the enormous complexity of Argentina's recent history. Socioeconomic developments exerted mounting pressures of one sort or another although, as stated before, it was not the pressures per se which led to instability and crisis; it was the manner in which they were filtered through, and processed by, the political system itself. Nor did military coups occur as a logical or necessary consequence of internal professionalization; they came in answer to crisis.

What the diagram does reveal is the importance of elite response as an autonomous independent variable. Throughout this chapter, in fact, there has gradually emerged a fundamental, paradoxical conclusion, as anticipated in one of my propositions at the outset of this chapter: the successful management of a crisis at one time has directly or indirectly brought on the appearance of another kind of crisis at a subsequent time. Resolution of the pre-1912 participation crisis led to a legitimacy crisis; partial resolution of that legitimacy crisis led to another one, now compounded by a distribution crisis; resolution of the distribution crisis, under Perón, led to another distribution crisis and yet another legitimacy crisis. Finally, this process of crisis accumulation—exacerbated by yet another crisis of participation in the post-Peronist era—has given way to a structural deadlock in which crises have not been resolved; they have been merely traded off against each other.

This kind of sequence suggests, in a sense, that the basic question about Argentine politics should not merely be, What went wrong?; the question now becomes, What may have gone right at one point in time, and what problems or crises did it bring about at a subsequent point in time? The Saenz Peña law was a perfectly understandable, and even appropriate, response to the participation crisis of that period; unforeseen, of course, was the legitimacy crisis which grew out of it. Likewise, Perón's economic policies offered quite a reasonable short-run solution to the distribution crisis of the 1930s and 40s; but they helped create the groundswell of resentment that forced him out of office.

In another sense, a sequential perspective on Argentine politics uncovers an evolutionary augmentation and complication in the structure and alignment of contending elites. The electoral reform of 1912 represented an effort by aristocrats to strike a bargain with some sectors of the middle class. What

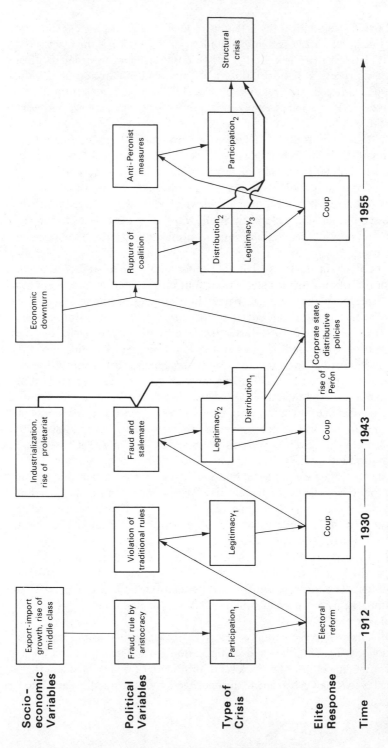

Figure 6-3. Schematic outline of political change in Argentina.

it did, however, was create a cadre of political professionals—against whom both aristocrats and the military formed an alliance in 1930. Contrary to its purposes, political practice during the *Concordancia* reinstalled professionals, even in progovernment ranks, and it was largely against this group that the military (mainly on its own) took action in 1943. But in the 1930s another elite was emerging: leaders of organized labor, novices in politics but demanding just reward. Seizing the opportunity, Perón forged an alliance between labor and the military, with novices and soldiers dominating politics, ultimately subjugating both old-time professionals and aristocrats. By 1955 a new alignment had appeared: almost everyone—aristocrats, professionals, military officers, even industrialists and the church—against the amateur politicians and the labor syndicates.

In a way, these patterns suggest that the pathological approach to Argentine politics, which has dominated so much of the literature on the subject, is misplaced and ill-conceived. If the succession of crises, responses, and policy outcomes offers little to cheer about, it does not invite scorn or pity either. The buildup of crises and the attempts to manage them are, I think, comprehensible phenomena which reflect purposive and rational actions and reactions of elites with understandably conflicting outlooks and interests.[46]

Specifically, the transition from the democracy of 1916-30 to authoritarianism under Perón begins to make sense when it is viewed as a dynamic process. As the roll-call analysis has led me to conclude, Argentina's national parties were quite incapable of dealing with the distribution crisis of the 1930s. Stimulated by the electoral reform of 1912, the parties were staffed and directed by political professionals whose outlooks and constituencies were historically middle-class. Their central concern was political power, as implied by the content of the roll-calls and their underlying factors (Chapter 3); social change occupied a modest place on the agenda in the Chamber of Deputies.

Moreover, the system had already revealed its susceptibility to recurrent crises of legitimacy, which (in my view) sparked the military coups of 1930, 1943, and, less directly, 1955. Democratic institutions, placed in a context never envisioned by the founders, and therefore made fraudulent, could not be responsive to the crises which developed over time. Since 1930, disputes over legitimacy thus seem to have presented a consistent, if not chronic, difficulty for the political system. They have sometimes been reinforced, complemented, or augmented by simultaneous crises over distribution or participation. But a historical constant—presumably a key to Argentine politics—lies in the problem of legitimacy.

Moreover, legitimacy crises have concurred with, and apparently precipitated, interventions by the military. But if such crises have brought on the

46. And see the remarks in O'Donnell, *Modernization*, pp. 193-96.

fact of intervention, the *pattern* of military intervention has been largely determined by the recruitment, structure, and organization of the armed forces. As José Luis de Imaz has argued,[47] the Argentine army has engaged in a form of incomplete intervention—taking over the government temporarily and then stepping out. Such behavior stems, in large part, from the high degree of military professionalization. Largely of middle-class background, army officers have owed their status and careers to the military establishment and have been thoroughly inculcated with its ideals. As soldiers, concerned about the welfare and security of the nation, they developed great disdain for politicians who seemed to place partisan interests above the honor of the nation. (Note, again, the exacerbation of party conflict in the Chamber of Deputies prior to each coup.) At times the military would therefore intervene. But by the same token, their professional values told them not to stay in office very long, because good soldiers should not mix with politics.[48] The difficulties inherent in ruling Argentina have also threatened to make any government look incompetent after a while, and proud officers have wanted to avoid this stigma. So the military has responded to legitimacy crises, but largely because of its manner and degree of professionalization, only with transitory measures up to now.[49]

Given the historic weaknesses of democratic institutions in Argentine society, and the susceptibility to military intervention, the country's authoritarian denouement need not come as a surprise or a betrayal. To recapitulate one of my principle contentions: the constitutional system did not collapse because it was overwhelmed by impossible demands resulting from social or economic trends; the system collapsed because it proved to be incapable of responding to demands which were intrinsically manageable.

But in a sense this merely begs the question. If the system failed because it was weak, what made the system weak? What was the cause of this cause?

As I have persistently maintained, part of the explanation is political. Paradoxically, the resolution of a participation crisis precipitated a series of legitimacy crises with which the system could not cope. Success in 1912 led to failure in and after 1930. From the start of this century, crisis resolution in Argentina has possessed a sort of self-destructing quality.

But there were other causes too, and it is in this context that I focus on the linkages between socioeconomic change and political change. Let me

47. José Luis de Imaz, *Los que mandan* (Buenos Aires, 1964), pp. 45-84.

48. For example, see the quote in Potash, *Army*, p. 243, which helps explain why the military government decided to hold the elections of 1946.

49. Here I have ignored internal splits within the military for the sake of clarity. On this point, see Edwin Lieuwen, *Generals vs. Presidents: Neomilitarism in Latin America* (New York, 1964), pp. 10-25; and O'Donnell, *Modernization*, pp. 154-61. Internal cohesion would be a major influence on the likelihood of a long-run military takeover (as in Brazil) at some point in the future.

stress the notion of *change*. I see no inherent reason why Argentina's *level* of socioeconomic development and its coexistence with political authoritarianism should stamp the country as a theoretically deviant (presumably incomprehensible) case. For the problem is not really one of levels, it is one of interactive processes. More important than literacy, GNP per capita, and other static signs of material well-being is the dialectical relationship between the patterns of socioeconomic development and the patterns of political transition.[50]

Argentine democracy did not break down despite the level of economic development. In a way it broke down—or, more precisely, failed to increase its responsive capability—because of the *kind* of socioeconomic development which took place in Argentina and the *sequence* between socioeconomic and political change, since these factors conditioned both the shape of political crises and the nature of elite response. The growth of a beef-and-wheat export economy concentrated socioeconomic power in the hands of a landed elite which believed that the political order should reflect the socioeconomic order, rather than provide some sort of counterweight to it. By taking place prior to the establishment of democratic institutions, these processes helped lay down the traditional rules of the political game—which democratic structures went on to break in 1916-30, provoking some sectors to seek salvation (and restoration) in a corporate society.

Furthermore, the high proportion of immigrants among the urban laborers made it possible for the country's leadership to meet the pre-1912 participation crisis, and establish competitive politics, without having to effectively enfranchise the working class. These economic and demographic conditions thus gave rise to a limited crisis in 1912; they also permitted a response which would prove to be severely limited in its ultimate flexibility and capability.

Paradoxically, the same conditions which facilitated the 1912 solution also aggravated the post-1930 crises. Suddenly, the sons of immigrants, now native Argentines and members of the working class, swelled the ranks of eligible voters—but the traditional parties, save the Socialists, offered no effective representation of their needs. Frustrated by this situation, workers understandably accepted an authoritarian solution when it came. What had facilitated the rise of Argentine democracy, *de facto* exclusion of the working class, also helped bring about its downfall. In the long run, Argentina's pattern of socioeconomic development may have been more conducive to authoritarian, corporatist politics than to a lasting democracy.

50. See also O'Donnell, *Modernization*, Chs. I-II.

Appendices
Bibliography
Index

Appendix A. Identifying Argentine Aristocrats

Almost every analysis of social structure in Latin America makes some reference to an oligarchy or an aristocracy. But in spite of common usage, or possibly because of it, the concept of aristocracy rarely receives strict definition. Generalized associations with the term abound—an aristocracy is landed, wealthy, powerful, probably selfish and degenerate—but it is often unclear whether such characteristics *define* or merely *accompany* the concept at hand.[1] Since this study purports to trace the role and actions of aristocrats in the Argentine Chamber of Deputies, among other themes, problems of analysis and methodology demand straightforward confrontation.

I consider an aristocracy to be a group of people who hold simultaneously predominant shares of economic and social power, who recognize a common bond with other members of the group, and who regulate admission to the group. Economic power stems from the control of money, goods, services, or labor; social power refers to influence on the criteria and allocation of status or prestige. Aristocrats hold both of these commodities at once (it is the virtual monopoly on status, of course, which separates them from the merely rich). Whether or not to pursue political power is a matter of choice, though aristocrats usually view themselves as the only group fit to rule.[2]

The common consciousness of an aristocracy does not necessarily reflect a common interest. Indeed, the extent of conflict and cohesiveness within Argentina's aristocracy constitutes a major theme of this investigation. I simply mean to say that aristocrats recognize each other as aristocrats. In Argentina, as elsewhere, the regular passport to admission has been birth, but

1. James L. Payne, "The Oligarchy Muddle," *World Politics*, 20, no. 3 (April 1968), 439-53.
2. Though some aristocrats may not possess great personal fortunes, they come from families of real or former wealth. I insist that an aristocracy must retain collective economic power, despite the situation of some individuals, or else it will eventually lose its social prestige—and thereby cease to be an aristocracy. For further reference, see L. T. Hobhouse, "Aristocracy," *Encyclopedia of the Social Sciences* (New York, 1937), I, 183-90.

the form of such requirements is incidental. The important point is that, whatever the credentials, aristocrats have a sense of their social identity.

An abstract definition, such as the one I have offered, brings forth a basic question: how to identify aristocrats. It is one thing to speak of a broad social category; it is quite another to pick out individuals as members of the group or not. Argentina's aristocracy did not bear titles, of course, so there are no rosters of a formal peerage.[3] Thus the problem gains an extra dimension: how to identify untitled aristocrats in such a body as the Argentine Chamber of Deputies.

Other scholars have met this challenge in various ways. For his pathbreaking study of the Argentine parliament, Darío Cantón relied on occupation as his operational criterion; the aristocratic stratum consisted of "men of high finance, large property owners and big industrialists."[4] Ezequiel Gallo and Silvia Sigal employed the same technique, and apparently the same data, in order to explore the composition of the Radical party leadership—although they merged the aristocratic group with the next-highest level (other property owners, businessmen, professionals, important executives and employees) as part of a simple dichotomous scale for "economic position."[5]

Though occupational data bear undoubted relevance to socioeconomic status, they are hazardous as well. Not only are they difficult to find, as "missing data" totals often indicate.[6] In addition, and more importantly, the presumed connection between occupation and aristocratic position may well not exist. At the very least, the connection is bound to vary over time.[7] Argentine society underwent fundamental and far-reaching transition during the first half of this century. The occupational structure changed its shape, investments flowed in new directions, cycles of economic growth and recession altered ownership patterns. Even if occupational data on the deputies had become fully available—as they did not—I would have been reluctant to identify an aristocracy upon this basis.[8]

3. See Lawrence Stone, *The Crisis of the Aristocracy, 1558-1641* (London and New York, 1965) for analysis of England's titular peerage.

4. Darío Cantón, *El parlamento argentino en épocas de cambio: 1889, 1916 y 1946* (Buenos Aires, 1966), pp. 41-42.

5. Ezequiel Gallo and Silvia Sigal, "La formación de los partidos políticos contemporáneos: la U.C.R. (1890-1916)," in Torcuato S. di Tella, et al., *Argentina, sociedad de masas* (Buenos Aires, 1965), pp. 166-69.

6. Cantón, *El parlamento*, p. 41.

7. For thorough discussion of these and other matters, see Otis Dudley Duncan, "Methodological Issues in the Analysis of Social Mobility," in Neil J. Smelser and Seymour Martin Lipset, eds., *Social Structure and Mobility in Economic Development* (Chicago, 1966), pp. 51-97; and Duncan, "Social Stratification and Mobility: Problems in the Measurement of Trend," in Eleanor Bernert Sheldon and Wilbert E. Moore, eds., *Indicators of Social Change: Concepts and Measurements* (New York, 1968), pp. 675-719.

8. Problems of reportage are particularly difficult; though many people held several occupations in the course of a lifetime (i.e., landowner, lawyer, banker), only one might appear in biographical dictionaries.

Nor does knowledge about the highest level of education offer much help. By all accounts Argentine universities have, until recently, been reserved for a tiny fraction of the population,[9] and they have been widely regarded as bastions of tradition. Nevertheless, it would be wholly unreasonable to place all deputies with university degrees in an aristocratic group. Argentina's education system has undergone steady, if limited, alteration.[10] There is much evidence to suggest that, even prior to the University Reform of 1918, all students were not aristocrats.[11] And it is most unlikely that nearly all aristocrats attended university, partly because, being aristocrats, they did not need either the training or the credentials to maintain their way of life. Hidebound as the universitities may have been, they cannot provide a means of picking out aristocrats.

The most relevant precedent for this study has been José Luis de Imaz's investigation of the Buenos Aires upper class. Concentrating on people of "social prestige," Imaz first composed a list of names appearing in social registers and one prominent club membership. He then verified the prestige of these individuals by consulting with publishers of an economic magazine and the staff of a genealogical institute. Thus assured, he took 150 names from the list as the sample to be interviewed.[12]

My own efforts have involved two differing criteria: (a) membership in social clubs, and (b) opinions of qualified judges. By dealing with these data in a systematic way, I have attempted to reach a satisfactory empirical definition of aristocracy in the Argentine context.

Here I would argue that these sources and types of information are aptly suited to the problem. As in Imaz's work, they put primary emphasis on social prestige. At the same time, they capture the quality of mutual recognition. Identification by judges, either members or observers of the aristocracy, implies visibility and consequent status. And by definition, admission to an exclusive club entails admission to a self-aware inner circle.

My central assumption is that socially prominent people tend to be rich and that therefore, as aristocrats, they possess both social *and* economic power. Comments by the judges, membership fees in the clubs, and first-hand observation all support this contention. The premise that prestige reflects

9. Compare the data in Peter G. Snow, *Political Forces in Argentina* (Boston, 1971), p. 110, with the overall population figures in Gino Germani, *Estructura social de la Argentina: análisis estadístico* (Buenos Aires, 1955), p. 22.

10. Hobart A. Spalding, Jr., says that universities maintained their aristocratic nature around the turn of the century despite reform, expansion, and changing patterns in enrollment. "Education in Argentina, 1890-1914: The Limits of Oligarchical Reform," *Journal of Interdisciplinary History*, 3, no. 1 (Summer 1972), 31-61, esp. 55-58.

11. Richard J. Walter, *Student Politics in Argentina: The University Reform and Its Effects, 1918-1964* (New York and London, 1968); for more recent figures, showing an overwhelming predominance of middle-class backgrounds among university students, see Snow, *Political Forces*, p. 113.

12. José Luis de Imaz, *La clase alta de Buenos Aires* (Buenos Aires, 1962), esp. pp. 6-12.

wealth is, at any rate, much more tenable than the view that wealth reflects prestige. For this reason, among others, reputation and acceptance furnish more reliable indications of an aristocracy than does occupation.

The procedure for eliciting opinions from the judges was simple. During a trip to Buenos Aires in 1969 I met three individuals with exceptional qualifications for identifying members of the aristocracy. One was a well-known sociologist who happened to come from an upper-class family. Another was the librarian of an exclusive club, with a great personal interest in genealogy and family heraldry. The third judge, from yet another prominent family, a second son to be exact, made a hobby of genealogy.

In separate interviews, I showed each man an alphabetical list of 1,500-plus deputies who served during the 1904-1955 period and asked for identification of the aristocrats among them. None of the judges hesitated over definition although, during the course of conversation, they sometimes made use of different terms: *las familias tradicionales, la clase alta, miembros de la alta sociedad*, and so on. The results are by no means identical, and one judge found more than twice as many aristocrats as did another. Yet it is still safe to say that all three men were giving emphasis to the social preeminence of Argentina's traditional families.[13]

My other step was to look up the names of deputies in membership lists of social clubs.[14] One was the Sociedad Rural Argentina, founded in 1866 and widely recognized as a bastion of wealthy landowners, particularly cattle barons.[15] The *Nóminas de socios* at various intervals were not entirely consistent—names might show up one year, disappear the next, and reappear on the following list.[16] Nevertheless, I managed to identify 169 individuals who held active memberships in the Sociedad at one time or another, a little more than 10 percent of all the deputies under consideration.[17]

The second organization whose roster I consulted was the Jockey Club, long renowned for its exclusiveness, its wine cellar and, until the building was burned down in 1953, its collection of rare books and art.[18] Though the two clubs were about the same size, the Jockey had a more broadly based

13. On the conception of "traditional families," see Imaz, *La clase alta*, pp. 8-10.

14. Gallo and Sigal also make use of such data, but give no explanation of their procedures. "La formación," pp. 168-69.

15. See Peter H. Smith, *Politics and Beef in Argentina: Patterns of Conflict and Change* (New York and London, 1969), pp. 47-50; and Jorge Newton, *Historia de la Sociedad Rural Argentina* (Buenos Aires, 1966).

16. Membership lists were consulted for 1897, 1918, 1932, 1939, 1943, 1948, and 1954. The lists came out as booklets, under the title *Nómina de socios* for the corresponding year, and sometimes were published in the *Anales de la Sociedad Rural Argentina*.

17. Excluding honorary membership, which was automatically granted to the President and key members of his cabinet.

18. Jorge Newton and Lily de Newton, *Historia del Jockey Club de Buenos Aires* (Buenos Aires, 1966). I would have liked to include data for the Círculo de Armas, allegedly the most exclusive club of all, but was unable to find any membership lists.

membership than the Sociedad Rural, including prominent lawyers—and even industrialists—as well as landowners and cattlemen. A total of 254 members of the Jockey occupied seats in the Chamber of Deputies between 1904 and 1955.[19]

One limitation of these membership lists concerns their possible over-emphasis upon the coastal region of Argentina, especially the city of Buenos Aires, and consequent underrepresentation of aristocrats from the interior. (This bias also pertains, though in a lesser degree, to opinions by the three *porteño* judges.)[20] Rosters for the Jockey Club provide a tentative solution to this problem, however, because the club offered honorary membership to all deputies (and senators) during their term of office. Only 257 deputies accepted the invitation. Since these men presumably thought they would feel comfortable in such an atmosphere, one might suppose they were fully as aristocratic as the regular members.[21] This procedure would raise the proportion of deputies associated with the Jockey Club to nearly one-third of the entire group.

Still another method would be to focus on the surnames in club membership lists rather than just upon the names of individuals. The supposition, in this case, is that deputies might have come from aristocratic families without belonging to a club themselves. In recognition of this possibility, I took note of all deputies whose paternal or maternal surnames appeared on the membership lists.[22] This created two additional classifications of aristocrats and nonaristocrats.

Finally, in order to take maximum advantage of all the data, I constructed two composite categories, one of "definite aristocrats" and another of "possible aristocrats." A deputy qualified as a definite aristocrat if: (a) at least two of the three judges placed him in the aristocracy; (b) he obtained full membership in the Sociedad Rural or the Jockey Club prior to 1946, when both organizations seem to have relaxed admissions standards;[23] or (c) one judge placed him in the aristocracy and he joined either the Rural or the

19. I examined the *Nómina de los socios* of the Jockey Club for 1902, 1913, 1925, 1938, 1950, and 1960. "Regular membership," as I shall use the term, includes both active and life members (*socios activos* and *socios vitalicios*).

20. One of the judges referred to old editions of nationwide social registers, such as the *Guía social Palma* and the *Libro azul*, in the course of reaching his decisions. And throughout the interviews, judges often recognized traditional families of the interior.

21. To identify honorary members I scanned lists for every other year from 1904 through 1953, except for unavoidable gaps in 1940-1942, 1946-1949, and 1954-1955.

22. Not counting the following surnames, which appeared too often to be of much use: Acosta, Alvarez, Castro, Díaz, Domínguez, Fernández, García, Gómez, González, Gutiérrez, Hernández, López, Martínez, Molina, Moreno, Moyano, Núñez, Ortiz, Paz, Pérez, Rodríguez, Ruiz, Sánchez. But even with such common names ruled out, the probability of misidentification is uncomfortably high.

23. Apparently in response to pressure from the Perón regime, the Rural increased its membership from approximately 3,000 in 1946 to 5,000 in 1954; membership in the Jockey grew from 3,300 in 1938 to 5,500 in 1950 (by 1960, five years after Perón's fall

Jockey in or after 1946. A person became a possible aristocrat by getting one vote from the judges or by joining either club in 1946 or afterward. All other deputies were classified as nonaristocrats, including those who accepted honorary membership in the Jockey while in office and those who, through similar surnames, may have had kinship ties with active members in either club.

These procedures yielded twelve different operational definitions of aristocracy (it would have been possible to devise several more). As simplified summary, Table A-1 sets forth the categorizations and the number of deputies included under each.

At this point the problem becomes one of choice: Which categorization is the most appropriate? If the different criteria identify completely different groups of individuals, it would be dangerous (if at all possible) to use *any* of the various definitions. But if the groups overlap, there remains some hope of reaching an acceptable decision.

Table A-2 displays a matrix of correlation coefficients for the dozen definitions. (These are product-moment correlations; each classification has been treated as a dichotomous variable, with individuals coded 1 if they belonged to the category in question and 0 if not.) Encouragingly enough, all the correlations turn out to be positive. Some of the high coefficients result from the fact that categories are additive. But it is also clear that the three judges, entirely independently, tended to identify the same sort of people as aristocrats (note the correlations of .37, .40, and .40). Membership in the Sociedad Rural, furthermore, showed considerable coincidence with membership in the Jockey Club, the coefficient being .42.

Variable 11, the "definite" categorization, merits particular attention. Because of its composite quality, it has high correlations with most basic definitions: .51, .61, and .61 with the three judges; .46 with membership in the Rural and .61 with regular members of the Jockey. On the other hand associations with other variables, which include possible relatives and honorary club members in the aristocracy, are fairly low. The "definite" group shows clear correspondence with the relatively exclusive and strict definitions.

In further exploration of the relationships between these definitions, Table A-3 offers a matrix of time-series correlations for the percentage of aristocrats (by every categorization) among entering deputies for each new legislative session from 1904 through 1955. Despite the small number of observations (N = 24) and some built-in redundancy, the results are astonishing. The lowest correlation is .75, and most are over .90! The data clearly lead to one conclusion. *No matter which definition is used, the secular trend of aristocratic representation in the Chamber of Deputies remains essentially the same.*[24]

from office, membership in the Jockey had declined to 5,000). See Smith, *Politics and Beef*, p. 50; José Luis de Imaz, *Los que mandan* (Buenos Aires, 1964), p. 87; and the *Nómina de los socios* for the Jockey Club in 1938 and 1950.

24. There is also a methodological lesson here: beware of aggregate data!

Table A-1. Operational Definitions of Aristocracy

Definition	Abbreviated identification	No. aristocrats	% of all deputies (N=1,549)[a]
PANEL OF JUDGES			
1. Aristocrats according to Judge #1, sociologist and member of upper-class family	Sociologist	206	13.30
2. Aristocrats according to Judge #2, librarian of an exclusive club	Librarian	581	37.51
3. Aristocrats according to Judge #3, second son in an upper-class family	Scion	504	32.54
CLUB MEMBERSHIPS			
4. Members of the Sociedad Rural Argentina	SRA members	169	10.91
5. Members of the Sociedad Rural Argentina plus their possible relatives	SRA relatives	431	27.83
6. Regular members of the Jockey Club	Jockey regulars	254	16.40
7. Regular plus honorary members of the Jockey Club	Jockey honorary	511	32.99
8. Regular plus honorary members of the Jockey Club plus possible relatives of regulars	Jockey relatives	825	53.26
9. Regular members of the Sociedad Rural Argentina or the Jockey Club	Club members	321	20.72
10. Regular members plus possible relatives of members of the Sociedad Rural Argentina or the Jockey Club	Relatives	902	58.23
COMPOSITE CATEGORIES			
11. Definite aristocrats	Definites	518	33.44
12. Definite plus possible aristocrats	Possibles	838	54.10

[a]This total excludes 22 deputies whose names came to my attention after this part of the research was done.

Table A-2. Correlations between Aristocracy Indices
(Among individual deputies; N=1,549)

		1. Sociologist	2. Librarian	3. Scion	4. SRA members	5. SRA relatives	6. Jockey regulars
1.	Sociologist	1.00					
2.	Librarian	.37	1.00				
3.	Scion	.40	.40	1.00			
4.	SRA members	.22	.22	.22	1.00		
5.	SRA relatives	.19	.29	.20	.56	1.00	
6.	Jockey regulars	.31	.36	.31	.42	.28	1.00
7.	Jockey honorary	.26	.28	.34	.29	.18	.63
8.	Jockey relatives	.26	.43	.38	.22	.36	.42
9.	Club members	.29	.34	.28	.68	.43	.87
10.	Relatives	.24	.40	.35	.30	.53	.38
11.	Definites	.51	.61	.61	.46	.36	.61
12.	Possibles	.36	.70	.64	.32	.31	.49

Table A-3. Time-Series Correlations between Aggregate Aristocracy Indices
(As % of entering deputies in each congressional session; N=24)

		1. Sociologist	2. Librarian	3. Scion	4. SRA members	5. SRA relatives	6. Jockey regulars
1.	Sociologist	1.00					
2.	Librarian	.89	1.00				
3.	Scion	.90	.94	1.00			
4.	SRA members	.75	.76	.80	1.00		
5.	SRA relatives	.80	.92	.87	.78	1.00	
6.	Jockey regulars	.88	.92	.96	.87	.89	1.00
7.	Jockey honorary	.83	.87	.88	.85	.86	.93
8.	Jockey relatives	.85	.90	.92	.87	.88	.96
9.	Club members	.86	.89	.93	.93	.87	.98
10.	Relatives	.84	.92	.90	.84	.92	.93
11.	Definites	.92	.96	.98	.85	.90	.98
12.	Possibles	.94	.95	.97	.86	.88	.96

To illustrate this fact, the following figure plots the percentages of incom-
ing deputies who met the aristocratic criteria of three differing definitions:
the opinion of the sociologist, who picked only 206 legislators as aristocrats;
my composite "definite" category, consisting of 518 deputies; and the
"possible" group, with a population of 838. Though the absolute percentages
differ by quite a great deal, the chronological trends are virtually identical.[25]

The data also show that the "definite" categorization occupies a consistently intermediate position over time, ranging from a high of 69.2 percent to

25. It would be possible to cover up percentage differences by taking any one of the
categorizations, setting the figure for one session (say 1930) equal to 100, and con-
structing a standardized index on that basis.

Table A-2 (*continued*)

7. Jockey honorary	8. Jockey relatives	9. Club members	10. Relatives	11. Definites	12. Possibles
1.00					
.66	1.00				
.57	.40	1.00			
.59	.90	.43	1.00		
.47	.49	.68	.48	1.00	
.40	.49	.47	.50	.65	1.00

Table A-3 (*continued*)

7. Jockey honorary	8. Jockey relatives	9. Club members	10. Relatives	11. Definites	12. Possibles
1.00					
.98	1.00				
.92	.95	1.00			
.97	.98	.92	1.00		
.92	.95	.96	.94	1.00	
.93	.96	.96	.95	.98	1.00

a low of 4.9 percent. And among all deputies, as shown in Table A-1, just about one-third satisfied the "definite" requirements for aristocratic classification. This proportion delineates the aristocracy as a minority group, as common sense demands, but it is also sizable enough to constitute an analytically useful variable.[26]

Because of these percentage figures and the strong correlations in Table A-2, I have selected the "definite" categorization as my operational definition of aristocracy. *Throughout this study, when referring to aristocrats in the Argentine Chamber of Deputies, I am referring to those individuals who*

26. To be useful, of course, a variable must vary. A definition of aristocracy which embraced only 1 percent of all deputies would not meet this requirement.

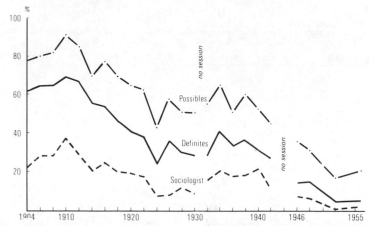

Figure A-1. Aristocrats among entering deputies, 1904-55, by selected definitions. Figures correspondend to the first year in each legislative session, as marked on the horizontal axis (there was no new election for the 1950-51 session, and the 1952-1954 session lasted three years). Breaks in 1930-31 and 1943-46 reflect suspensions of the Congress.

qualified as definite aristocrats according to my composite criteria (in variable 11).

It is by this route, albeit a circuitous one, that I have determined the socioeconomic status of Argentine deputies. The method is hardly ideal. The composite categorization no doubt contains some errors, and the dichotomous classification of legislators as aristocrats and nonaristocrats cannot begin to reflect the varied permutations in the country's social structure. Even so, these techniques have yielded an empirical means of identifying upper-class aristocrats in reasonable accord with an explicit conceptual definition. And the result, as I have tried to show throughout this book, has considerable significance for a comprehension of twentieth-century Argentine politics.

Appendix B.   Procedures for An‡alyzing Roll-Call Data

The manipulation of legislative data has involved complex procedures which have rested upon a series of explicit assumptions and carefully calculated methodological decisions. A full understanding of the significance and limitations of this study, particularly the creation of voting dimensions and scales through factor analysis, must begin with an awareness of the rules and methods employed.

1. CODING ROLL-CALL VOTES

There were two different kinds of roll-call votes in the Argentine Chamber of Deputies: elections for presidents and vice-presidents (and occasional committees) of the assembly, and votes on substantive or procedural issues. Votes for officerships in the Chamber were coded as follows:

1 = a vote in favor of the winner
2 = for the runner-up
3 = for the third-place candidate
4 = for the fourth-place candidate
5 = for the fifth-place candidate
6 = for candidates in sixth or lower place

Votes on other issues received the following code:

6 = yes
8 = no

Deputies who failed to cast ballots, on any kind of vote, were coded accordingly:

0 = ineligible to vote; not yet a member of the Chamber; presiding officer at the time of the vote; known to be dead
7 = abstention; deputy eligible to vote but did not
9 = one of at least five consecutive abstentions; deputy may have been on leave, sick, or even dead

127

In some instances, fortunately few and far between, the *Diario de Sesiones* challenged ingenuity:

7 = deputy reported as having cast two differing ballots (e.g., yes *and* no)
7 = surname belonging to more than one deputy is listed in vote count, but without identifying initials (e.g. Gutiérrez; in such cases all deputies with the surname in question and present at the session would receive 7s)

For the factor analysis, I decided to simplify and standardize the ten-point coding scheme. Yes-no votes were rescored so that

yes = +1
no = -1

In order to include elections of officers, I transformed the codes as follows:[1]

	original code	transformed code
winner	1	+1
loser(s)	2-6	-1

All nonvotes (whether coded as 0, 7, or 9 in the original dataset) were dealt with in the same way and treated as 0.

The advantage of this procedure is that it can include all kinds of votes in a single analysis. For a general study of trends over time, I believe that this device is quite appropriate. And yet collapsing officer elections into "winner" and "loser" categories undoubtedly causes some distortion (though perhaps no more than dichotomous yes-no votes on other issues). Further distortion comes from giving all nonvotes an intermediate position on the revised numerical scale, although it facilitates computation and avoids the problem of missing data.[2]

2. SELECTING DEPUTIES

To create a reliable voting scale, as with factor scores, it is necessary to exclude deputies who cast ballots on a small number of votes. Nonparticipants are really unscalable; they would receive an artifactual central position on the voting scale more as a result of coding conventions (where no vote = 0) than as a reflection of a truly intermediate position.

The problem is empirical: How many votes must a deputy cast in order to obtain a scalar score? My own decision has been to construct scales for only those deputies who voted on *at least 50 percent* of all the roll calls taken

1. Winning candidates customarily voted for someone other than themselves. Since these were almost always courtesy votes, it would be misleading to consider winners as belonging to the opposition—so they were given 7s, which then transformed into 0s for these roll calls.

2. On missing data, see R. J. Rummel, *Applied Factor Analysis* (Evanston, Ill., 1970), pp. 258-65.

Table B-1. Number of Participant Deputies

Session	Total no. deputies[a]	No. participant deputies	% participant deputies
1904-05	124	75	60.5
1906-07	128	82	64.1
1908-09	122	68	55.7
1910-11	122	86	70.5
1912-13	129	73	56.6
1914-15	121	96	79.3
1916-17	125	86	68.8
1918-19	126	80	63.5
1920-21	158	117	74.1
1922-23	160	99	61.9
1924-25	160	118	73.8
1926-27	157	130	82.8
1928-29	156	123	78.9
1930	158	110	69.6
1932-33	160	146	91.3
1934-35	158	126	79.7
1936-37	158	149	94.3
1938-39	159	127	79.9
1940-41	160	128	80.0
1942	157	122	77.7
1946-47	159	129	81.1
1948-49	163	142	87.2
1950-51	154	112	72.7
1952-54	167[b]	148	88.6
1955	167[b]	150	89.8

[a]Refers to the total number of individuals, as distinguished from seats in the Chamber.

[b]Includes about a dozen nonvoting *delegados* from national territories.

during the course of each legislative session. Those casting ballots on less than half the votes were simply dropped from the analysis.

This rule has some important consequences. As shown in Table B-1, it can reduce the number of participant legislators to less than 60 percent of the over-all total (see the figures for 1908-9 and 1912-13). But because the 50 percent criterion is relatively undemanding, it also means that some deputies may obtain scalar scores in relation to the distribution of participation and abstention: a person taking part in 60 percent of all votes could get artificially central scores on some factors, if absent for the roll calls with high loadings on those factors, and similarly extreme scores on other scales.

Perhaps the most fundamental questions concern the relative character of participant and nonparticipant deputies. Do the participants, in their varied forms of behavior, represent the Chamber as a whole? Or do they differ from the nonparticipants? If so, how? If the participants tend to be leaders (which may or may not be true), or at least activists, do they take extreme or moderate positions on substantive issues? Do they influence nonparticipants?

Would committed and well-informed activists vote more independently than passive backbenchers? Or would their roles and obligations lead them to follow group decisions more strictly than nonparticipants? And if participant legislators tend to be professional *políticos*, would career incentives lead them to take more cautious positions than idealistic amateurs? For better or for worse, these issues lie outside the scope of this study. But they raise some critical points and emphasize the limitations of this book.

3. SELECTING ROLL CALLS

In addition to selecting participant deputies, it has also been necessary to devise a rule for including roll-call votes. Unanimous and near-unanimous roll calls reveal little, if anything, about alignment and conflict among deputies. And because of the coding, they produce an artificial kind of differentiation between nonvotes and votes (where the main variation would be between 0 and plus-or-minus 1). For statistical reasons this illusory cleavage would, in turn, lead to the appearance of spurious factors or voting dimensions.

Because of these problems I have decided to include in the factor analysis all roll calls in which *at least 10 percent of the participant deputies, present and voting, lined up on the minority side*. Votes having minorities of less than 10 percent (or majorities greater than 90 percent) were classified as uncontested and removed from further consideration.[3]

The deletion of uncontested roll calls has seriously curtailed the data base for this analysis, reducing the total number of treatable votes from 1,712 to 1,303.[4] And yet as shown in Chapter 3, especially Figure 3-1, the percentage of contested votes (out of all votes) has considerable meaning in itself, and can furnish a useful guide to the intensity of legislative conflict. Similarly, the number of uncontested roll calls can help illustrate the political function and purposes of roll-call voting.

Aside from the exclusion of uncontested votes, I have made no effort to delete or organize roll calls according to substantive content or apparent redundancy. The factor analysis deals with *all* contested votes. This decision (or nondecision) has naturally affected the structure of the factor matrices and, more particularly, the total variances and the relative explanatory power of the factors. Keeping these caveats in mind, however, I have adopted this strategy in an effort to take full advantage of all available data.

3. This rule applied only to participant deputies. It is possible that a roll call which was uncontested among participants could have been contested in the Chamber as a whole (and vice versa).

4. With the FACTOR2 program employed (see below) the computer could handle only 90 roll-call votes at a time; for both 1946-47 and 1948-49 I therefore selected the 90 most contested votes for analysis. This limitation reduced the number of roll calls actually analyzed to 1,052 (61.5 percent of the grand total).

4. CREATING DIMENSIONS AND SCALES

With participant deputies and contested roll calls, I have proceeded (a) to identify underlying dimensions in parliamentary voting, and (b) to use the dimensions as scales for locating the relative positions of individual deputies. Interdependently, these procedures have furnished the basic materials for Chapters 3 through 5.

The very notion of a voting scale demands considerable simplification. Within the chronological span of each analytical unit—in this case, legislative sessions usually stretching over two years[5]—a roll-call scale ignores all change over time. The resulting picture, for each session, is explicitly static. From their voting records (according to the coding scheme employed) deputies obtain scale-score positions; how they got there, possibly by changing views or reference groups, is totally neglected in the process.

It has been customary, in roll-call analysis, to utilize scales as revelations of attitudinal or ideological predilections of the legislators. For this kind of interpretation to be accurate, deputies must be casting ballots in consistent accordance with their attitudes—an assumption which overlooks the possibilities that legislators can (a) be ignorant or ill-informed, (b) change their minds, (c) engage in pork-barrel deals, (d) compromise views for strategic reasons, (e) feel compelled to follow party lines or other collective decisions.

Despite these drawbacks I have constructed voting scales and assigned scale scores for each individual deputy. Since my central concern has been to make longitudinal comparisons between legislative sessions from 1904 through 1955, rather than to explore patterns within any single session, a static picture for each (usually two-year) Congress is quite acceptable. Moreover, I do not conceive of my voting scales as strictly attitudinal. Rather I prefer to interpret them as empirical dimensions of *behavioral* roll-call alignments. This does not mean that they cannot reflect underlying attitudes; I am simply not assuming that they do in every case.

Of the several standard techniques used for making roll-call scales, I have selected factor analysis.[6] Reasons for this choice have been both analytical and practical. Being almost completely open-ended, factor analysis seems ·

5. As explained in Chapter 3, I have used the congressional session as my unit of analysis, instead of the year, in order to maximize potential for interpretation. The one-year sessions of 1930, 1942, and 1955 are due to military coups; three-year sessions were begun in 1952.

6. For discussions of various scaling procedures see Lee F. Anderson et al., *Legislative Roll-Call Analysis* (Evanston, Ill., 1966); Duncan MacRae, Jr., *Issues and Parties in Legislative Voting: Methods of Statistical Analysis* (New York, 1970); and Herbert F. Weisberg, "Scaling Models for Legislative Roll-Call Analysis," *American Political Science Review*, 66, no. 4 (December 1972), 1306-15. Lee Fennell has used Guttman scaling techniques for his analysis of voting patterns in the Argentine Congress, "Class and Region in Argentina: A Study of Political Cleavage, 1916-1966" (Ph.D. diss., University of Florida, 1970).

most appropriate for detecting structure in data which have not been pre-selected according to issue content or some other qualitative criterion. And with the aid of a computer, factor analysis can handle vast amounts of data quickly and efficiently.

To execute the computations I have utilized FACTOR2, a packaged program from the STATJOB series developed at the University of Wisconsin computing center. Obtaining a matrix of product-moment correlations from the roll-call data (with coding as explained above), I employed a principal components procedure in a common factor analysis model.[7] To enhance interpretability and clarity, I have relied on rotated factor matrices resulting from the varimax rotation procedure.

One of my greatest difficulties has been deciding how many factors to rotate.[8] My first idea was to retain those factors which, in a raw (or unrotated) matrix, explained 5 percent or more of the total variance in voting. Examination of the results, however, quickly convinced me that this rule excluded important analytical dimensions for most congressional sessions and would lead to underfactoring. With this in mind I then examined the structure of rotated matrices for all factors having eigenvalues greater than unity. Finally, after considerable reflection, I adopted a uniform criterion for all the legislative sessions: *to rotate factors having eigenvalues greater than unity, up to a maximum of five*. It appears that the eigenvalue-one rule has gained wide recognition as a reasonable solution to the number-of-factors problem. At the possible risk of underfactoring, however, I established the five-factor limit for numerous reasons:

1. For the sake of parsimony, a consideration partly stemming from my intuitive conviction that no Argentine legislature was liable to produce more than five basic voting alignments.

2. Because experimentation showed that extra factors were unstable.

3. Because the percentage of variance explained by additional individual factors made them relatively unimportant (in this context I also used the so-called scree test, which interprets the significance of factors according to their statistical explanatory power).[9]

To illustrate the consequences of this decision, Table B-2 compares the number of factors meeting the eigenvalue-one criterion with the number actually rotated. Figures in the right-hand column indicate the loss in variance

7. Alternatively, one might have used a principal axes procedure, with communality estimates in the diagonals, but the practical difference between the two procedures is usually not very great.

8. See Rummel, *Applied Factor Analysis*, Chs. 15 and 16.

9. In more cases than not, strict application of the scree test would have reduced the number of factors retained for rotation. I therefore believe that, if anything, my operational criterion has led to overfactoring rather than underfactoring. Rummel says that distortions from overfactoring are probably less serious than those from underfactoring, although the evidence is not all in, and that "the researcher should apparently err on the side of too many factors if he errs at all." *Applied Factor Analysis*, p. 365.

Table B-2. Summary of Factor Analysis Procedures

Session	No. roll calls analyzed (A)	Factors with Eigenvalues > 1		Factors rotated		Loss in total variance explained (E-C)
		No. factors (B)	% total variance explained (C)	No. factors (D)	% total variance explained (E)	
1904-05	10	3	63.5	3	63.5	0
1906-07	22	7	75.2	5	65.6	-9.6
1908-09	9	2	60.6	2	60.6	0
1910-11	16	5	68.5	5	68.5	0
1912-13	32	9	75.8	5	60.8	-15.0
1914-15	29	4	72.7	4	72.7	0
1916-17	45	8	78.4	5	70.5	-7.9
1918-19	65	11	78.4	5	65.4	-13.0
1920-21	82	13	78.6	5	61.2	-17.4
1922-23	80	16	77.6	5	58.8	-18.8
1924-25	72	9	77.9	5	71.5	-6.4
1926-27	67	7	79.9	5	76.6	-3.3
1928-29	56	4	82.7	4	82.7	0
1930	13	2	83.0	2	83.0	0
1932-33	41	3	76.3	3	76.3	0
1934-35	37	2	74.8	2	74.8	0
1936-37	19	2	78.7	2	78.7	0
1938-39	79	13	80.5	5	68.0	-12.5
1940-41	58	11	78.1	5	64.9	-13.2
1942	18	3	80.4	3	80.4	0
1946-47	90[a]	11	76.4	5	68.0	-8.4
1948-49	90[a]	7	76.1	5	73.7	-2.4
1950-51	8	1	65.0	1	65.0	0
1952-54	14	1	64.7	1	64.7	0
1955	0	—	—	—	—	—

[a]Maximum capacity of FACTOR 2 computer program (see note 4 to this appendix).

explained because of the five-factor maximum. In no case does the loss exceed 20 percent, and for nearly half the sessions there is no loss at all. With only one exception (1922-23), the total percentage of variance explained by the rotated matrix is never less than 60 percent.

These procedures yielded the factor matrices which allowed me to discern the dimensions of legislative conflict as reported in Chapter 3. In Chapters 4 and 5, the individual factor scores which each partipant deputy receives on each factor furnished the basis for my study of the correlates of conflict and patterns of party alignment. This phase of the analysis raised another series of methodological problems.

5. DETECTING THE CORRELATES OF CONFLICT

As described in Chapter 4, I have employed interval-scale factor scores as the dependent variable in a statistical procedure called Automatic Interaction Detector (AID),[10] with Status, Age, Region, and Party as class-coded independent variables. Here I shall explain the reasons which led me to adopt this technique and some of the difficulties I encountered in its application.

My decision to employ AID rested on various considerations. First, the program relies on analysis of variance, the most powerful and appropriate technique for correlating nominal-scale independent variables with an interval-scale dependent variable (in this case, factor scores). Second, its automatic selection of independent variables according to relative explanatory power is consistent with the open-ended, empirical character of this particular investigation. Third, its reiteration of the analysis-of-variance algorithm can lead to the detection of interactive relationships, controlling for the effect of one or more independent variables.

But perhaps the most attractive feature of AID, for my specific purposes, is its systematic search for the optimal *dichotomous* permutation of each independent variable. The virtue of this procedure is that, in seeking out the variable with the greatest explanatory power, it assures true comparability among all the independent variables. The analysis of variance thus becomes uniform and fair in a way it would not if some independent variables had many more operative categories than others. Of course a drastic imbalance in the number of classes would still present difficulties, even with dichotomous categorizations, because variables with multiple classes would have many more possible permutations than would others. A large number of classes would also raise the possibility of spurious or fortuitous splits.

Nevertheless, AID is aptly suited to an investigation which, like this one, purports to identify the relative explanatory power of independent variables with differing internal categories. As explained in Chapter 4, the Status variable has two classes: aristocrat and nonaristocrat (see also Appendix A).

10. See John A. Sonquist and James N. Morgan, *The Detection of Interaction Effects: A Report on a Computer Program for the Selection of Optimal Combinations of Explanatory Variables* (Ann Arbor, Mich., 1964).

Region has five classes: Federal Capital (City of Buenos Aires), Province of Buenos Aires, Coast, Interior, and Northwest. Age has four classes: up through 35, 36-45, 46-55, and over 55.

The Party variable has presented special problems. For the years from 1904 through 1915 I have simply taken party labels at face value, mainly because I do not know of any historical studies which yield a reasonable a priori categorization. In practice this has meant that Party has had as many as 20 classes—with its concomitant advantage over the other variables, plus the mathematical risk of random dichotomization.[11] (Precisely for these reasons the relatively moderate explanatory power of Party prior to 1912 is particularly striking.)

From 1916 onward I adopted a uniform categorization, drawn from general familiarity with Argentine politics and summarized in Table B-3.

Even with this scheme, the number of classes for Party has varied according to the presence or absence of various partisan groupings. Between 1904 and 1912 the number of classes varied from 7 to 20; from 1916 through 1942 the figure ranged from 6 to 8; there were 4 party groupings in 1946-49, and only 2 in the 1950s. What this means, of course, is that the comparability of the Party variable is somewhat compromised insofar as it concerns (a) comparisons with other variables, and (b) longitudinal comparison of the changing explanatory power of Party over time. Though these drawbacks indicate the need for cautious interpretation, I continue to believe that the overall findings are generally accurate and substantively meaningful.

My application of AID has also been tempered by the relatively small number of observations (deputies) in any single legislative session. This problem is particularly acute for analysis of variance, since the mean scores (or averages) become notoriously unstable as groups become smaller—by common rule of thumb, if the number of individuals in the sample is less than 50. The initial splits in AID resolve part of this problem through the use of dichotomous permutations, which usually keep the number of empirical observations at or near an acceptable level. But as successive iterations take place, the reliability of findings gradually diminishes.[12]

In this particular study the small-N problem has been compounded by missing data, which AID can handle only as a "no data" category for the independent variables involved. To illustrate my practical difficulty, Table B-4 displays the number of observations available for AID runs in each legislative session, and shows the deplorable paucity of data on Age. Eventual-

11. This constitutes willful disregard of Sonquist and Morgan's recommendation that "unordered predictors should not have more than five or six classes." Ibid., p. 79. Unfortunately, the quality of data gave me little choice.

12. I am not referring to statistical significance in the formal sense of the term, since I do not conceive of the deputies as a random or representative sample of some larger population (although I am in some fashion trying to generalize from a restricted sample of "participant" deputies to the entire Chamber). Rather I mean reliability in the sense that factor scores are themselves rather crude, for reasons explained above, and their imprecision is greater in smaller groups.

Table B-3. Party Groupings for 1916-55

Grouping	Parties included[a]
Traditional Conservatives	Partido Autonomista Nacional (PAN), Oficial, Unido, Unión Popular, Unión Nacional, Roquista, Autonomista, Unión Cívica, Constitucionalista, Anticonstitucionalista, Oposición, Junta de N.P.,[b] Situacionista
Conservatives (national organizations)	Conservador, Demócrata Nacional, Oficialista, Concordancia, Concordancia Cívica
Local Conservatives	Autonomista Gubernista, Liberal, Liberal Gubernista, Popular, Demócrata, Provincial, Unión Provincial, Defensa Provincial, Unión Democrática, Coalición, Concentración Conservadora, Concentración Cívica, Concentración Popular, Coalición Liberal Autonomista, Frente Unico, Principista, Autonomista y Liberal Acuerdista; Unión, Comercio y Producción; Popular, Comercio y Producción; popular, Comercio e Industria y Liberal; Independiente
PDP	Liga del Sur, Partido Demócrata Progresista (PDP), Agrario, Alianza Demócrata-Socialista
UCR	Unión Cívica Radical (UCR), UCR Tradicional, Unión Democrática (of the year 1946)
UCRAP	Unión Cívica Radical Antipersonalista
Local Radicals	UCR Concurrencista, Radical Disidente, Radical Azul, Radical Oficialista, Radical Blanco, Radical Situacionista, Radical Negro, Radical Intransigente, UCR Bloquista, UCR Unificada, UCR Federalista, UCR Junta Reorganizadora Nacional, UCR Independiente, UCR Lencinista, UCR de San Juan, UCR de Santa Fe, UCR de Tucumán, UCR Intransigente, UCR del Pueblo, Coalición Radical-Demócrata
Socialists	Partido Socialista
Independent Socialists	Partido Socialista Independiente
Peronists	Laborista, Peronista (name varies)

[a]Listed in approximate order of chronological appearance.

[b]The Junta de N.P. was a small faction, based in the province of Buenos Aires, but I have been unable to ascertain the meaning of the initials.

ly I elected to confront the missing-data dilemma by making every AID run twice: once with all participant deputies having data on Party, Region, and Status; and again with those deputies having data on Party, Region, and Status plus Age, thus eliminating the need for spurious "no data" categories. The disparity in number of observations for the two sets of AID runs further qualifies the comparability of results, both between variables and over time. And yet findings for variables in the two runs do not show any monumental discrepancies, so I suspect that actual distortion is quite minimal.

Table B-4. Observations for AID Runs

Session	No. participant deputies	No. with data on Party, Status, Region	No. with data on all variables, including Age
1904-05	75	45	27
1906-07	82	79	43
1908-09	68	65	32
1910-11	86	81	54
1912-13	73	71	60
1914-15	96	93	71
1916-17	86	86	62
1918-19	80	78	53
1920-21	117	115	71
1922-23	99	99	53
1924-25	118	118	52
1926-27	130	130	57
1928-29	123	122	49
1930	110	109	47
1932-33	146	146	81
1934-35	126	124	77
1936-37	149	148	96
1938-39	127	127	108
1940-41	128	127	101
1942	122	121	88
1946-47	129	129	64
1948-49	142	142	55
1950-51	112	111	33
1952-54	148	148	55
1955	150	————no AID runs made————	

Having met (if not conquered) these various problems, I turned to the analysis. At this stage AID calls for a number of technical decisions, mainly on criteria for truncation of the program, which I made in the following fashion:[13]

Weighting variable (for values of the dependent variable) = none
Split eligibility criterion for candidate groups = .05
Split reducibility criterion for dividing groups = .01
Maximum allowable number of final groups = 11
Minimum number of observations for a group to be considered for splitting = 20

One of the most important results of the AID analysis concerns the relative predictive power of each independent variable on the factor scores. In order to trace changes in predictive power over time, however, I have had to deal with some additional considerations.

In the first place, it is important to understand that genuine comparability

13. Consult Sonquist and Morgan, *Detection*, esp. pp. 114-21.

between results for legislative sessions over time is severely limited by the difference in the composition of the factors. Since roll calls are never quite the same, contents of the cleavages cannot be quite the same (as clearly shown in Chapter 3). To this degree the time-series analysis compares the relationships between fairly stable independent variables and a substantively unstable dependent variable. This predicament forces us to conceptualize the time-series analysis as the tracing of chronological trends in the correlates of observable conflict, *regardless of the substantive content of the issues involved*. A virtue of this approach is that, by being thoroughly empirical and open-ended, it focuses attention on whatever the deputies happened to be fighting about in any given legislative session. In effect, this permits the historical actors to define the scale and scope of inquiry themselves. Nevertheless, the procedure compromises comparability and sharply qualifies the meaning of the findings.

Second, there is the question of selecting the most appropriate measure of over-all predictive value for each independent variable in each legislative session. For this purpose I have worked with two related indices. One is simply the average (mean) value of the R^2 for each independent variable on all the factors for each legislative session. The other is a weighted average, in which the R^2 on each factor is weighted by the statistical importance of the factor itself—as measured by the proportion of factor variance explained by each factor. Table B-5 illustrates the difference between computational procedures for the two indices, both of which vary from 0 to 1.

Table B-5. Sample Computation of Aggregate Indices
for Measuring Explanatory Power of Independent Variables[a]

Factor (A)	Proportion of factor variance explained (B)	R^2 for independent variable (C)	Product[b] of B X C (D)
I	.62	.57	.35
II	.26	.48	.12
III	.05	.03	.00
IV	.04	.05	.00
V	.04	.28	.01

Simple average = average of values in column C = .28.
Weighted average = sum of values in column D = .48.

   [a]This illustration demonstrates actual procedures for computing aggregate indices for the Party variable in the 1926-27 session of the Chamber.
   [b]Minor discrepancies are due to rounding.

Beneath the statistical discrepancies there are, of course, basic conceptual differences. The simple average R^2 treats each voting dimension as a separate, equal entity. The weighted average assigns importance to factors more or less according to the number of roll calls which have strong loadings on it. In some cases this may merely reflect the repetition of roll-call votes on a single issue, rather than uniform alignments on a wide variety of issues. Eventually I opted in favor of the weighted average R^2, however, partly to offset the possible effects of overfactoring. In any case, as shown in Table B-6, the practical disparities are usually quite small.

6. PARTISAN CLEAVAGE AND CONSENSUS

Given the paramount importance of Party as an independent variable—according to both R^2 indices—Chapter 5 proceeds to focus on patterns of partisan alignment. For this sort of enterprise the existence of multiple factors offers a wide variety of analytical strategies. With the average factor score for each party, for instance, it is possible to handle two factors at once. Illustrating this alternative, Figure B-1 represents party positions on both Factor I (General) and Factor II (Tariffs) in the 1922-23 legislative session.

According to this picture, the General factor put the Radicals (both UCR and Local Radicals) against all opposition parties—Conservative, PDP, and Socialist. The Tariffs, however, produced quite a different alignment: the proconsumer Socialists at one extreme, Conservatives at the other, and Radicals and PDP in between. Although the tariff question was more a regional than partisan issue (Table 4-2), Figure B-1 clearly demonstrates the possibilities of multidimensional analysis.

But it also raises a troublesome question: What is conflict? And what is a coalition? Does the distance between the UCR and Local Radicals on Factor I reveal conflict—or a slightly loose alliance? One might be tempted to draw an arbitrary line along the zero axis and declare that parties with positive scores

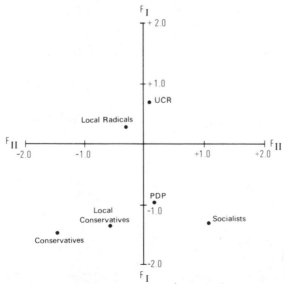

Figure B-1. Party alignments on Factors I and II, 1922-23, according to average factor scores for each party.

Table B-6. Relative Power of Independent Variables for Predicting Voting Scores

Session	No. of factors	Party R² Simple mean	Party R² Weighted mean	Region R² Simple mean	Region R² Weighted mean	Status R² Simple mean	Status R² Weighted mean	Age R²a Simple mean	Age R²a Weighted mean
1904-05	3	.27	.30	.14	.14	.01	.01	.06	.06
1906-07	5	.20	.25	.08	.11	.04	.03	.04	.04
1908-09	2	.22	.24	.05	.04	.04	.05	.02	.01
1910-11	5	.16	.18	.17	.21	.02	.02	.05	.06
1912-13	5	.37	.42	.07	.07	.02	.02	.04	.04
1914-15	4	.54	.63	.13	.13	.07	.04	.04	.03
1916-17	5	.36	.61	.16	.12	.04	.01	.05	.05
1918-19	5	.30	.57	.19	.15	.04	.03	.04	.05
1920-21	5	.34	.42	.10	.12	.03	.04	.05	.05
1922-23	5	.32	.62	.13	.07	.05	.07	.05	.06
1924-25	5	.36	.53	.10	.13	.05	.08	.03	.03
1926-27	5	.28	.49	.12	.19	.05	.07	.03	.02
1928-29	4	.41	.48	.12	.10	.03	.04	.05	.04
1930	2	.69	.76	.12	.13	.03	.02	.05	.05
1932-33	3	.53	.60	.21	.18	.08	.11	.03	.02
1934-35	2	.61	.60	.20	.20	.12	.12	.01	.01
1936-37	2	.59	.74	.08	.12	.08	.10	.01	.01
1938-39	5	.29	.57	.10	.13	.01	.01	.01	.01
1940-41	5	.32	.52	.07	.07	.02	.05	.02	.04
1942	3	.51	.69	.19	.24	.04	.08	.04	.04
1946-47	5	.18	.29	.03	.03	.02	.03	.03	.04
1948-49	5	.18	.21	.02	.03	.01	.01	.06	.06
1950-51	1	.62	.62	.01	.01	.00	.00	.00	.00
1952-54	1	.80	.80	.06	.06	.01	.01	.19	.19

aBased on samples of deputies with data on all variables; all other figures are based on samples with data on Party, Region, and Status (see Table B-4).

constitute one coalition, parties with negative scores another; in two-factor space, as in the figure, one could circumscribe alliances by quadrants. But this strategy can magnify small differences (between -.01 and +.01), minimize large ones (between +.01 and +1.99), and lead to serious distortion. On Factor II, for instance, inspection suggests that the distance between Conservatives and Local Radicals, both with negative scores, is more meaningful than the distance between Local Radicals and the UCR. The zero boundary cannot be sacrosanct.

Fortunately, AID offers partial resolution of the problem. As stated above, AID makes a systematic search for the optimal dichotomous permutation of every independent variable—in this case Party—regardless of the location of the split itself. (On the Tariff factor in 1922-23, AID put Local Radicals together with the UCR, PDP, and Socialists in opposition to the Conservatives.) For this reason, I have operationally defined a *coalition* as *either one of the two party groupings formed by AID*, and *conflict* as the fact of separation. The analysis in Chapter 5 rests upon that foundation.

Notwithstanding the occasionally abstruse and technical character of this appendix, it should be clear that I have had to make a substantial number of critical methodological decisions in the course of this analysis. To one degree or another, they have inevitably led to simplification and distortion. But decisions of this kind comprise an integral part of all historical interpretation, whether or not quantitative methods are employed. In this case the decisions have been consciously made; I would like to think that, because of this fact, gains have been maximized and losses have been minimized.

Appendix C.   Citations, Issue Contents, and Factor Loadings of Contested Roll-Call Votes

This appendix displays the results of factor analysis on contested roll calls in each legislative session from 1904 through 1954 (there being no contested votes in 1955).[1] Twenty-four tables of this sort do not make easy reading, but they are set forth for two basic reasons: first, as supporting documentation for statements in the text, particularly throughout Chapter 3; second, as reference material for students of Argentine politics and history.

All the tables follow a uniform format. In order to identify each roll-call vote, the extreme left column assigns a number according to chronological sequence.[2] The next column gives its location, with abbreviated reference to (a) year of the congressional session, (b) volume number in the annual *Diario de Sesiones*, and (c) page number within the particular volume. The third column gives the day, month, and calendar year of the vote.[3]

The fourth column, labelled "Issue," involves a host of delicate and complex judgments. In many instances—if not most—the issue content of a parliamentary vote is anything but clear. A proposal to move bill C up the agenda ahead of bills A and B, for example, might win approval because: congressmen favored bill C, congressmen opposing bill C wanted to vote it down before it acquired support, congressmen were seeking to postpone consideration of bill A or B. Because of such uncertainties, as explained in Chapter 3, I have usually preferred to think of factors as representing behavioral patterns of cleavage rather than attitudinal dimensions.

As a rule, I have summarized the issue (with only a phrase or two) according to the *general* subject of the relevant debate. This can be mislead-

1. Note, again, that the analysis has been restricted to the 90 most contested votes for the 1946-47 and 1948-49 sessions. A complete catalog of all roll-call votes from 1904 through 1955, uncontested ones as well as contested ones, can be found in the code book on file in the Data and Program Library Service at the University of Wisconsin—Madison.

2. Numbers apply only to contested votes and not to total roll calls in each session.

3. Since pagination sometimes varies from one edition of the *Diario de Sesiones* to another, dates can be helpful for tracing specific roll-call votes.

ing: procedural matters, such as alteration in the agenda, may well have been resolved on procedural rather than substantive grounds. For the most part, however, I suspect that practical preferences affect (if not determine) alignments on procedural questions—at least on contested votes, the only kind considered here. The fact is that roll-call votes take place in some sort of substantive context; and some contexts give rise to more competitive votes (disregarding the particular motion) than do others. And it is the context which usually conditions and determines the response of deputies. In the example above, for instance, I would feel free to consider the roll call as a decision on whether to take up bill C.

Some kinds of votes occur with frequency and have led me to adopt a few conventions:

1. The election of a president and vice-presidents of the Chamber (and, in early years, key committees) involved mandatory roll-calls, and are indicated by the word "Officership," followed by the title of the particular position in question.

2. Under Article 75 of the national constitution the presidential succession went from the president to the vice-president and then to someone chosen by the Congress. At the end of its regular session, the Chamber took a mandatory roll-call vote in order to provide for any such emergency. These votes, if contested, are noted as referring to the "Designate for presidential succession."

3. Many votes concern proposals to bring up matters for immediate debate or to alter the agenda in some other way. Where the proposal refers to a single item (like bill C above), I identify the issue as "Consideration of" item such-and-such. Where it involves a schedule for dealing with more than one item, blatant ambiguities have forced me to see the vote as bearing only a general relationship to the "Order of business."

The right-hand columns, under the title "Factors," present the loadings for each roll call on each rotated factor.[4] For easy reference, loadings of ± .50 or more are enclosed in parentheses. Figures at the bottom of each column indicate the percentage of variance explained by each of the factors.

---

4. As explained in Appendix B, I have (a) rotated factors having eigenvalues greater than unity, up to a maximum of five, and (b) used the varimax rotation procedure in all instances.

Table C-1. Rotated Factor Matrix for Contested Roll Calls in 1904-05

Roll-call no.	Yr./vol./p. in *Diario de Sesiones*	Date of vote	Issue	Factors I	II	III
1	04/I/40	2 May 04	Officership: 2nd vice-president	.24	(.67)	.13
2	04/I/54-55	6 May 04	Officership: Comisión de Cuentas	.07	-.12	(.79)
3	04/I/498	13 July 04	Officership: president	-.01	-.36	(-.68)
4	04/I/499	13 July 04	Officership: 2nd vice-president	.33	(.62)	-.10
5	04/II/5-6	31 Aug 04	Designate for presidential succession	.37	(-.68)	-.12
6	05/I/2	28 Apr 05	Officership: provisional president	(.87)	.17	.22
7	05/I/4	28 Apr 05	Officership: president	(.89)	.14	.22
8	05/I/5	28 Apr 05	Officership: vice-president	(.82)	-.07	-.02
9	05/I/5	28 Apr 05	Officership: 2nd vice-president	(.81)	.12	-.19
10	05/I/1002	15 July 05	Electoral reform	(.51)	.40	.01
			% of total variance explained	34.4	16.5	12.7
			% of factor variance explained	54.1	25.9	20.0

Table C-2. Rotated Factor Matrix for Contested Roll Calls in 1906-07

Roll-call No.	Yr./vol./p. in Diario de Sesiones	Date of vote	Issue	Factors I	II	III	IV	V
1	06/I/53	8 May 06	Officership: president	.03	(.81)	.05	-.05	-.04
2	06/I/53-54	8 May 06	Officership: vice-president	.05	(.85)	-.00	-.00	-.11
3	06/I/54	8 May 06	Officership: 2nd vice-president	.19	(.78)	.16	-.01	-.15
4	06/I/54	16 May 06	Officership: Comisión de Cuentas	.14	(.52)	-.18	-.24	(.54)
5	06/I/78-79	16 May 06	Officership: Comisión de Cuentas	-.21	.36	-.39	-.05	.27
6	06/I/79	16 May 06	Officership: Comisión de Cuentas	-.17	(.64)	.15	.15	.24
7	06/I/79-80	16 May 06	Officership: Comisión de Cuentas	.12	-.17	-.09	-.00	(.65)
8	06/I/469	13 July 06	Officership: 2nd vice-president	-.28	(-.56)	-.11	-.01	.26
9	06/I/860-61	12 Sept 06	Approval of election in Buenos Aires Province	-.03	(-.66)	-.42	.24	-.09
10	07/I/2	29 Apr 07	Officership: provisional president	(.93)	.03	.15	.05	-.10
11	07/I/6-7	29 Apr 07	Officership: president	(.92)	.05	.16	.04	-.08
12	07/I/7	29 Apr 07	Officership: vice-president	(.92)	-.01	-.00	.01	.10
13	07/I/7	29 Apr 07	Officership: vice-president	(.95)	.05	.03	.02	.09
14	07/I/8	29 Apr 07	Officership: 2nd vice-president	(.92)	.06	.19	.04	.09
15	07/I/89	31 May 07	Officership: Comisión de Cuentas	-.25	-.24	.28	.28	.44
16	07/I/90	31 May 07	Officership: Comisión de Cuentas	.12	.02	.46	-.16	-.01
17	07/I/92-93	7 June 07	Officership: Comisión de Cuentas	.14	.07	-.11	(.69)	-.33
18	07/I/93	7 June 07	Officership: Comisión de Cuentas	-.11	-.05	.14	(.80)	.10
19	07/I/93	7 June 07	Officership: Comisión de Cuentas	.17	.08	-.14	(.64)	.09
20	07/I/454	15 July 07	Officership: vice-president	(.58)	.15	(.60)	.08	-.06
21	07/I/454	15 July 07	Officership: 2nd vice-president	.42	.32	(.68)	.18	-.04
22	07/I/1076	16 Sept 07	Intervention in Corrientes	(.70)	.11	.41	.00	-.12
			% of total variance explained	25.7	17.2	8.4	8.2	6.0
			% of factor variance explained	39.2	26.3	12.8	12.6	9.2

Table C-3. Rotated Factor Matrix for Contested Roll Calls in 1908-09

Roll-call no.	Yr./vol./p. in *Diario de Sesiones*	Date of vote	Issue	Factors	
				I	II
1	08/I/2	1 May 08	Officership: provisional president	(.86)	.03
2	08/I/57	7 May 08	Officership: president	(.71)	.16
3	08/I/88	13 May 08	Budget bill	(.81)	.04
4	08/I/632	20 July 08	Officership: vice-president	(.83)	.17
5	08/I/632	20 July 08	Officership: 2nd vice-president	(.79)	.03
6	08/II/998	2 Sept 08	Designate for presidential succession	(.60)	-.19
7	09/I/3	5 May 09	Officership: vice-president	.35	(.69)
8	09/I/308	19 July 09	Officership: vice-president	-.20	(.85)
9	09/I/637	11 Aug 09	Intervention in Córdoba	(.58)	.32
			% of total variance explained	45.1	15.5
			% of factor variance explained	74.4	25.6

Table C-4. Rotated Factor Matrix for Contested Roll Calls in 1910-11

Roll-call no.	Yr./vol./p. in Diario de Sesiones	Date of vote	Issue	Factors				
				I	II	III	IV	V
1	10/I/2	26 Apr 10	Officership: provisional president	(.50)	.11	(.55)	.07	-.03
2	10/I/9-10	2 May 10	Officership: president	(.56)	.15	(.53)	.06	.21
3	10/I/10	2 May 10	Officership: vice-president	.39	-.03	(.60)	.34	.29
4	10/I/10	2 May 10	Officership: 2nd vice-president	.27	-.23	.30	-.00	(.60)
5	10/I/464	15 July 10	Officership: president	(.84)	.03	.16	-.02	-.02
6	10/I/465	15 July 10	Officership: vice-president	(.80)	-.07	-.10	-.05	.03
7	10/I/465	15 July 10	Officership: 2nd vice-president	(.79)	-.12	.08	-.04	.16
8	10/II/309	2 Sept 10	Designate for presidential succession	(.58)	.29	.13	-.01	-.24
9	11/I/573-74	17 July 11	Officership: president	.17	(.90)	-.01	.11	-.09
10	11/I/574-75	17 July 11	Officership: vice-president	.21	(.88)	-.02	.10	-.06
11	11/I/575	17 July 11	Officership: 2nd vice-president	.20	(-.85)	.06	.17	.05
12	11/II/154	21 Aug 11	Investigation of judicial negligence	-.17	-.05	-.22	-.21	(.80)
13	11/II/294-95	1 Sept 11	Designate for presidential succession	(.62)	.33	.13	.06	-.06
14	11/II/872	29 Sept 11	Opposition to presidential objections	-.17	.15	.10	(.82)	.01
15	11/III/338	24 Nov 11	Electoral reform	.15	.19	(-.76)	.24	.20
16	11/IV/994	13 Feb 12	Opposition to presidential objections	.09	-.15	-.18	(.68)	-.33
			% of total variance explained	23.0	16.8	11.2	8.9	8.6
			% of factor variance explained	33.5	24.6	16.3	13.1	12.5

Table C-5. Rotated Factor Matrix for Contested Roll Calls in 1912-13

Roll-call no.	Yr./vol./p. in Diario de Sesiones	Date of vote	Issue	Factors				
				I	II	III	IV	V
1	12/I/2	13 May 12	Officership: provisional president	(.60)	.30	.00	.16	.06
2	12/I/147-48	3 June 12	Officership: president	(.70)	.04	.21	.36	.26
3	12/I/148-49	3 June 12	Officership: vice-president	.21	.39	.38	.21	.29
4	12/I/149	3 June 12	Officership: 2nd vice-president	.35	.31	.37	.21	.45
5	12/I/321	21 June 12	Subsidy for independence celebration	-.04	.22	-.01	(.67)	-.13
6	12/I/527	17 July 12	Officership: president	(.70)	.30	.07	.04	.20
7	12/I/528	17 July 12	Officership: vice-president	.44	.39	.35	.14	.38
8	12/I/528-29	17 July 12	Officership: 2nd vice-president	.47	.38	.41	.07	.35
9	12/III/45-46	5 Aug 12	Taking of national census	.03	.01	.07	.10	(-.69)
10	12/III/175	12 Aug 12	Designation of representative to Spanish celebration	.28	.11	.27	.08	(.50)
11	12/II/477	2 Sept 12	Designate for presidential succession	(.73)	.30	.02	.25	.24
12	12/II/656	10 Sept 12	Presidential decision to live in San Isidro	.03	-.01	(.73)	-.20	.16
13	12/II/932	25 Sept 12	Administrative jobs for deputies	-.21	-.40	-.16	-.20	-.40
14	12/III/5-6	27 Nov 12	Officership: president	(.63)	.09	.13	(.61)	-.06
15	12/III/6	27 Nov 12	Officership: vice-president	.46	.27	.28	(.60)	.11
16	12/III/6	27 Nov 12	Officership: 2nd vice-president	(.54)	.23	.21	(.66)	-.01

17	12/III/646	3 Mar 13	Intervention in Salta	(.58)	.04	.17	.02	.31
18	12/III/902	31 Mar 13	Budget bill	(-.56)	-.06	.27	-.02	.11
19	13/I/2	2 May 13	Officership: vice-president	.10	(.81)	-.03	.25	.13
20	13/I/3	2 May 13	Officership: 2nd vice-president	.16	(.82)	-.03	.12	.11
21	13/I/226	16 May 13	Budget bill	.10	.30	-.15	.23	(.57)
22	13/I/598	29 May 13	Budget bill	(.59)	.29	-.06	.16	-.06
23	13/II/439	16 July 13	Officership: president	(.67)	(.58)	.16	.05	-.01
24	13/II/439	16 July 13	Officership: vice-president	.37	(.74)	.32	.18	.04
25	13/II/440	16 July 13	Officership: 2nd vice-president	.39	(.75)	.35	.08	.09
26	13/II/588-89	23 July 13	Approval of election in Buenos Aires Province	-.32	-.48	(-.51)	-.10	-.19
27	13/III/103	10 Sept 13	Designate for presidential succession	(.77)	.08	.26	.07	.17
28	13/III/722-23, 730	29 Sept 13	Opposition to presidential veto of pensions bill	.06	.11	(.73)	.14	-.00
29	13/III/742	29 Sept 13	Opposition to presidential veto of pensions bill	-.04	.15	(.66)	.15	-.29
30	13/IV/65	5 Nov 13	Interpellation on politics in Buenos Aires Province	-.24	-.49	-.19	-.39	-.12
31	13/IV/153	22 Dec 13	Budget bill	.20	-.01	-.21	(.59)	.26
32	13/IV/369-70	29 Dec 13	Reduction in federal budget	.05	.30	.20	.48	.24
			% of total variance explained	18.9	14.8	10.0	9.5	7.6
			% of factor variance explained	31.1	24.3	16.5	15.6	12.5

Table C-6. Rotated Factor Matrix for Contested Roll Calls in 1914-15

Roll-call no.	Yr./vol./p. in *Diario de Sesiones*	Date of vote	Issue	Factors			
				I	II	III	IV
1	14/I/2	25 Apr 14	Officership: provisional president	(.84)	.18	.11	.17
2	14/I/312	18 May 14	Approval of election in Buenos Aires Province	(.74)	.28	.40	.03
3	14/I/390-91	20-21 May 14	Officership: Ad hoc president	(.65)	.35	-.14	-.31
4	14/I/475-76	22 May 14	Officership: president	(.88)	-.12	.06	-.06
5	14/I/477	22 May 14	Officership: vice-president	(.86)	-.13	.03	-.08
6	14/I/477-78	22 May 14	Officership: 2nd vice-president	(.89)	-.07	.05	-.09
7	14/III/2	15 July 14	Officership: president	(.87)	.15	.20	.16
8	14/III/2-3	15 July 14	Officership: vice-president	(.83)	.10	.16	.18
9	14/III/3	15 July 14	Officership: 2nd vice-president	(.87)	.08	.14	.15
10	14/III/308	24 July 14	Approval of election in Jujuy	(.86)	.16	.19	.05
11	14/III/308	24 July 14	Approval of election in Jujuy	(-.70)	-.42	.20	.19
12	14/III/613-14	7 Aug 14	Monetary policy	.09	-.26	.03	(.80)
13	14/III/997	31 Aug 14	Designate for presidential succession	(.72)	.15	.32	.04
14	14/IV/693-94	23 Sept 14	Appointment of secretary	(.81)	.02	.30	-.15

15	14/V/596	1 Dec 14	Reconsideration of budget	(-.68)	-.05	-.39	.27
16	14/VI/310	16 Dec 14	Government spending on church	.22	-.08	(.77)	-.04
17	14/VI/633	21 Dec 14	Government spending on church	.14	-.13	(.84)	.16
18	15/I/7-8	1 May 15	Officership: president	.21	(.86)	-.02	-.15
19	15/I/8	1 May 15	Officership: vice-president	.42	(.63)	.41	.06
20	15/I/9	1 May 15	Officership: 2nd vice-president	(-.65)	-.30	-.46	.10
21	15/I/591	21 June 15	Antistrike clause in railroad labor law	-.07	(-.52)	.23	.39
22	15/I/685	14 July 15	Officership: president	(.61)	.49	-.03	-.29
23	15/I/686	14 July 15	Officership: vice-president	(.81)	.20	.31	-.02
24	15/I/686	14 July 15	Officership: 2nd vice-president	(.78)	.17	.28	-.05
25	15/III/120	27 Aug 15	Officership: 2nd vice-president	(-.67)	-.11	-.41	.13
26	15/III/124	27 Aug 15	Designate for presidential succession	-.11	(-.88)	-.02	-.07
27	15/IV/734	13 Jan 16	Officership: president	(.59)	-.06	.12	-.40
28	15/IV/735	13 Jan 16	Officership: vice-president	-.08	(.85)	-.01	.01
29	15/IV/880	26 Jan 16	Budget bill	(-.81)	.22	.06	.16
			% of total variance explained	44.3	13.7	9.6	5.2
			% of factor variance explained	60.9	18.8	13.3	7.1

Table C-7. Rotated Factor Matrix for Contested Roll Calls in 1916-17

Roll-call no.	Yr./vol./p. in *Diario de Sesiones*	Date of vote	Issue	Factors				
				I	II	III	IV	V
1	16/I/1-2	26 Apr 16	Officership: provisional president	(.86)	-.06	.01	-.17	.14
2	16/I/62	19 May 16	Approval of election in Buenos Aires Province	(.85)	-.11	.02	.04	.09
3	16/I/87	20 May 16	Approval of election in Jujuy	(.95)	-.07	.01	-.16	.06
4	16/I/308	24 May 16	Officership: president	(.97)	-.09	.03	-.14	.05
5	16/I/310	24 May 16	Officership: vice-president	(-.77)	.32	.29	.29	.15
6	16/I/310	24 May 16	Officership: 2nd vice-president	(.96)	-.08	.06	-.06	.03
7	16/I/607-8	17 July 16	Officership: president	(.89)	-.07	-.11	-.14	.12
8	16/I/608	17 July 16	Officership: vice-president	(-.73)	.27	.36	.29	.03
9	16/I/608-9	17 July 16	Officership: 2nd vice-president	(.85)	-.01	-.05	-.02	.09
10	16/II/1705	1 Sept 16	Designate for presidential succession	(.87)	-.08	.07	-.08	-.01
11	16/III/2408-9	26 Sept 16	Electoral reform in provinces	(-.71)	-.06	-.08	.29	-.09
12	16/III/2572	29 Sept 16	Direct election of intendant (mayor) of Buenos Aires City	-.01	.12	(.77)	-.14	-.18
13	16/IV/3079	26 Dec 16	Support for parochial schools	-.16	-.03	(-.67)	-.11	-.20
14	16/V/4184	15-16 Jan 17	Procedures for debating budget	-.19	-.09	(-.55)	-.17	.08
15	16/V/4339	18 Jan 17	Patent law on alcohol	(.79)	-.17	.13	-.18	.13
16	17/I/1-2	26 Apr 17	Officership: president	(.87)	-.10	.03	-.19	-.08
17	17/I/2	26 Apr 17	Officership: vice-president	(.70)	-.30	-.26	-.33	-.25
18	17/I/3	26 Apr 17	Officership: 2nd vice-president	(.87)	.03	.10	-.11	-.06
19	17/I/766-67	8 June 17	Intervention in Buenos Aires Province	(-.82)	.14	-.21	.22	-.08
20	17/I/774-75	8 June 17	Reading of documents by speakers	(-.77)	.09	-.17	.32	-.02
21	17/I/854	8 June 17	Intervention in Buenos Aires Province	(.90)	-.13	.14	-.22	.07

				F1	F2	F3	F4	F5
22	17/II/194	20 June 17	Legalization of divorce	.24	.27	.11	-.02	(.69)
23	17/II/473	16 July 17	Officership: president	(.91)	-.15	.04	-.08	.03
24	17/II/474	16 July 17	Officership: vice-president	(.70)	-.38	-.29	-.25	-.17
25	17/II/474	16 July 17	Officership: 2nd vice-president	(.82)	-.02	.03	.08	.05
26	17/II/795	27 July 17	Credentials: Enrique Martínez	-.37	.10	.24	(.60)	-.03
27	17/III/127	2 Aug 17	Sugar tariff	-.15	(.81)	.19	.12	-.19
28	17/III/128	2 Aug 17	Sugar tariff	-.14	(.72)	.17	.24	-.30
29	17/III/142	2 Aug 17	Sugar tariff	-.08	(.85)	.20	.03	.17
30	17/III/165	3 Aug 17	Sugar tariff	.00	(-.85)	-.09	.09	-.20
31	17/III/177	3 Aug 17	Sugar tariff	-.15	(.74)	.17	-.12	.42
32	17/III/249	6 Aug 17	Information on banking practices	-.10	.33	(.58)	-.17	-.32
33	17/III/287	8 Aug 17	Intervention in Buenos Aires Province	-.32	.17	.21	(.61)	.08
34	17/IV/285	31 Aug 17	Designate for presidential succession	(.74)	.08	.15	-.28	.07
35	17/IV/519-20	7 Sept 17	Investigation of pension policies	-.03	.16	(.61)	-.04	.17
36	17/VI/27	22 Sept 17	Entrance into World War I	(-.65)	-.14	-.17	.45	.01
37	17/VI/117	24 Sept 17	Diplomatic relations with Germany	(-.54)	.14	.31	.49	.27
38	17/VI/153	24 Sept 17	Diplomatic relations with Germany	(.58)	.16	.09	-.41	-.04
39	17/VII/208	20 Dec 17	Salary of senators	-.15	.35	.33	.13	.17
40	17/VII/746	8 Jan 18	Legal immunity of deputies	(.65)	-.03	.23	-.39	.08
41	17/VII/790	8 Jan 18	Export tax	.19	.19	(.69)	.19	.12
42	17/VIII/526	26 Jan 18	Tariff protection for shoe industry	-.27	-.09	-.38	.34	-.27
43	17/VIII/652	13 Mar 18	Creation of frontier police force	(-.61)	.07	-.25	.49	-.31
44	17/VIII/695	13 Mar 18	Antilocust campaign	(-.63)	.07	.09	.48	-.22
45	17/VIII/697	13 Mar 18	"Agricultural defense" item in budget	(-.60)	-.05	-.28	.41	-.25
			% of total variance explained	41.1	9.5	8.7	7.5	3.8
			% of factor variance explained	58.3	13.4	12.3	10.6	5.3

Table C-8. Rotated Factor Matrix for Contested Roll Calls in 1918-19

Roll-call no.	Yr./vol./p. in *Diario de Sesiones*	Date of vote	Issue	I	II	III	IV	V
						Factors		
1	18/I/2-3	10 Apr 18	Officership: provisional president	(.62)	(.57)	.20	-.02	-.14
2	18/I/98	30 Apr 18	Postponement of judgment on elections in Salta	(.75)	.15	.23	.08	-.12
3	18/I/170	4 May 18	Officership: president	(.59)	(.60)	.05	.05	-.15
4	18/I/170-71	4 May 18	Officership: vice-president	(.82)	.20	-.14	.14	-.10
5	18/I/171	4 May 18	Officership: 2nd vice-president	(.80)	.18	-.10	.11	-.07
6	18/I/570	19 June 18	Information on public debt	(.75)	.10	.16	.19	-.03
7	18/II/122-23	3 July 18	Declaration of national holidays (including 14 July)	-.35	.15	.03	.04	-.16
8	18/II/161-62	15 July 18	Officership: president	(.57)	(.70)	.06	.12	-.15
9	18/II/162	15 July 18	Officership: vice-president	(.83)	.31	-.09	.18	.02
10	18/II/162-63	15 July 18	Officership: 2nd vice-president	(.84)	.34	-.10	.20	.05
11	18/II/445	24 July 18	Officership: 2nd vice-president	(.85)	.28	-.01	.19	.02
12	18/III/252	28 Aug 18	Designate for presidential succession	.48	(.50)	.37	.04	-.23
13	18/IV/510	26 Sept 18	Senate revision of pension bill	.24	(.64)	.18	-.07	.13
14	18/V/4-5	8 Jan 19	Officership: president	(.66)	(.51)	.20	.05	-.28
15	18/V/5	8 Jan 19	Officership: vice-president	(.85)	.26	.07	.08	-.11
16	18/V/6	8 Jan 19	Officership: 2nd vice-president	(.85)	.23	.06	.12	-.13
17	18/V/447-48	30 Jan 19	Designate for presidential succession	(.66)	(.53)	.08	.08	-.21
18	18/VI/261	25 Feb 19	Emission of paper currency	(.51)	-.11	(.54)	.02	.09
19	18/VI/523	20 Mar 19	Strike in port of Buenos Aires	(-.76)	-.16	-.21	.01	-.03
20	18/VI/655-56	9 Apr 19	Extension of 1918 budget	(.75)	.06	.23	.05	.03
21	18/VI/751-52	24 Apr 19	Pensions for railroad workers	.15	-.29	.04	-.10	(.55)
22	18/VI/829	25 Apr 19	Tax exemptions for railroad companies under Mitre Law	-.42	(-.62)	-.10	-.07	-.06
23	19/I/1-2	26 Apr 19	Officership: president	(.57)	(-.58)	.10	.17	.16
24	19/I/2	26 Apr 19	Officership: vice-president	(.71)	.37	.01	.18	.29

#	Reference	Date	Description					
25	19/I/2-3	26 Apr 19	Officership: 2nd vice-president	(.74)	.31	-.03	.21	.28
26	19/I/376-77	4 June 19	Credentials: Federico Pinedo (h.)	.29	.05	.27	.14	(.58)
27	19/II/661-62	3 July 19	Congressional attendance	.27	-.15	.04	(.83)	.02
28	19/II/668	3 July 19	Congressional attendance	.21	-.22	.04	(.84)	.07
29	19/II/678-79	3 July 19	Congressional attendance	-.16	.36	-.07	(-.74)	.02
30	19/II/686-87	4 July 19	Senate revision of 1919 budget bill	.24	.41	.49	.13	.02
31	19/II/712-13	16 July 19	Officership: president	(.59)	(.62)	.14	.07	-.11
32	19/II/713	16 July 19	Officership: vice-president	(.82)	.30	-.03	.11	.04
33	19/II/713-14	16 July 19	Officership: 2nd vice-president	(.83)	.28	-.04	.16	.01
34	19/III/476	7 Aug 19	Military intervention in politics	(-.72)	-.02	-.03	.00	.03
35	19/III/607-8	13 Aug 19	Tax exemptions for railroad companies under Mitre Law	.21	(.82)	-.08	-.14	-.02
36	19/III/613	13 Aug 19	Senate revision in Mitre Law	-.19	(-.77)	.08	.11	.05
37	19/III/743	20 Aug 19	Interpellation on government dealings in gold	(.81)	.21	-.05	.05	.15
38	19/IV/585	12 Sept 19	Grant to Círculo Militar	.14	(-.55)	-.34	-.07	.13
39	19/IV/598	12 Sept 19	Handling of census-related bills	-.10	(-.72)	.07	.34	.00
40	19/IV/746	17 Sept 19	Postal bureaucracy	(-.70)	-.17	-.24	-.06	-.23
41	19/IV/872	18 Sept 19	1914 census and electoral representation	.23	-.34	.05	.05	-.46
42	19/IV/927	19 Sept 19	Postponement of debate on pensions for Desert Campaign	-.03	(.69)	-.19	-.10	.13
43	19/V/738	29 Sept 19	Suspension of debate on budget	(-.51)	-.47	-.08	.02	.23
44	19/V/832-33	30 Sept 19	Abuse in pension payment	.23	(.61)	-.14	-.21	.16
45	19/VI/47	4 Nov 19	Postponement of debate on Catamarca intervention	.44	.17	.36	.22	.16
46	19/VI/526	3 Dec 19	Schedule for taking up political issues	-.24	.03	.29	-.33	-.47
47	19/VI/538-39	3 Dec 19	Political situation in Mendoza	.09	.43	.18	-.12	.12
48	19/VI/700-701	11 Dec 19	Loan to Britain, France, Italy (Germany excluded)	(.76)	.07	.38	.15	.24
49	19/VI/742	17 Dec 19	Postponement of debate on European loan	(-.68)	.19	-.31	.08	-.09
50	19/VI/819	13 Jan 20	Postponement of debate on European loan	(-.85)	-.17	-.20	-.09	-.20

Table C-8. 1918-19 (continued)

Roll-call no.	Yr./vol./p. in Diario de Sesiones	Date of vote	Issue	Factors I	II	III	IV	V
51	19/VI/822	13 Jan 20	Closing of debate on European loan	(.78)	.10	.20	.10	.22
52	19/VI/822	13 Jan 20	Authorization of loan to Germany	(.75)	.16	.32	.13	.40
53	19/VI/824	13 Jan 20	Authorization of loan, but not to Germany	(.75)	.16	.31	.14	.39
54	19/VI/825-26	13 Jan 20	Collective responsibility for repayment of European loan	(-.79)	-.04	-.27	-.04	-.12
55	19/VII/21	14 Jan 20	Withdrawal of funds from Caja de Conversión for European credit	(.73)	.17	.36	.15	.36
56	19/VII/36	14 Jan 20	Tax on agricultural products	.33	.14	.03	.25	.03
57	19/VII/53	14 Jan 20	Reconsideration of decision to exclude Germany from loan	(.82)	.17	.15	.03	.18
58	19/VII/220	21 Jan 20	Homage to José Nestor Lencinas	(.76)	.10	.20	.05	.03
59	19/VII/360-61	26 Jan 20	Compulsory congressional attendance	-.16	-.47	-.24	.02	.07
60	19/VII/591	30 Jan 20	Congressional attendance	.05	(-.57)	-.38	-.19	-.07
61	19/VII/609-10	3 Feb 20	Interpellation on harassment of Socialist party	(-.89)	-.19	.01	.04	-.03
62	19/VII/617	3 Feb 20	Interpellation on harassment of Socialist party	(-.88)	-.14	-.06	.01	-.05
63	19/VII/734	5 Feb 20	Sugar tariff	.08	(.77)	.05	-.01	-.03
64	19/VII/862	6 Apr 20	Resignation by Carlos A. Becú	.29	.44	(.52)	-.06	.04
65	19/VII/886	7 Apr 20	Political situation in Buenos Aires Province	(-.55)	(-.55)	-.26	.08	.18
			% of total variance explained	36.4	15.9	4.6	4.6	3.9
			% of factor variance explained	55.7	24.3	7.0	7.0	6.0

Table C-9. Rotated Factor Matrix for Contested Roll Calls in 1920-21

Roll-call no.	Yr./vol./p. in *Diario de Sesiones*	Date of vote	Issue	Factors				
				I	II	III	IV	V
1	20/I/1-2	6 Apr 20	Officership: provisional president	-.26	(.72)	.06	.02	.02
2	20/I/203	30 Apr 20	Officership: president	-.40	(.70)	-.21	.04	-.15
3	20/I/204	30 Apr 20	Officership: vice-president	-.40	(.70)	-.18	.06	-.15
4	20/I/620-21	8 June 20	Senate revision of wheat export tax	(-.58)	.22	-.14	.13	-.31
5	20/II/872-73	30 June 20	Budget provision for railroad feasibility study	.14	.17	-.19	-.42	.26
6	20/II/889-90	30 June 20	Senate revision of customs tax	.38	.32	.05	-.00	.46
7	20/III/303-4	15 July 20	Officership: president	-.28	(.82)	-.15	-.05	.01
8	20/III/304	15 July 20	Officership: vice-president	-.34	(.79)	-.22	.05	-.07
9	20/III/304-5	15 July 20	Officership: 2nd vice-president	-.38	(.68)	-.40	.15	-.05
10	20/III/627-28	28 July 20	Line of presidential succession	(.75)	-.43	.16	-.10	.12
11	20/III/629	28 July 20	Line of presidential succession	(-.74)	.42	-.17	.09	-.13
12	20/III/665-66	29 July 20	Interpellation of treasury minister	(.64)	-.23	.25	-.06	.27
13	20/III/799	4 Aug 20	Postponement of debate on rent control	-.28	.16	-.11	.22	-.20
14	20/IV/259	17 Aug 20	Investigation of sugar industry and governmental policy	.49	-.48	.48	-.06	.06
15	20/IV/366	19 Aug 20	Duration of rent control (two years)	-.01	.05	.12	-.10	(.85)
16	20/IV/367	19 Aug 20	Applicability of two-year rent control notwithstanding lease provisions	-.09	.09	.14	-.07	(.85)
17	20/IV/621	31 Aug 20	Designate for presidential succession	-.20	(.79)	-.02	-.15	.11
18	20/IV/837	7 Sept 20	Daily congressional sessions	-.41	.45	.36	-.06	.13
19	20/IV/1047-48	9 Sept 20	Investigation of judicial impropriety	.31	(-.71)	.02	.12	-.11
20	20/V/116-17	14 Sept 20	Powers of congressional investigation	(-.50)	.52	-.44	.19	.04
21	20/V/318	21 Sept 20	Debate on agrarian crisis (instead of horse racing)	.02	-.39	-.39	-.05	-.36
22	20/V/455	22 Sept 20	Investigation of financial policies	.43	-.41	.42	-.15	.02
23	20/V/909	30 Sept 20	Senate rejection of public works bill	.44	(-.53)	.42	-.19	.03
24	20/V/921-22	30 Sept 20	Presidential objections to bill for teacher's pension	.29	(-.67)	-.02	.34	-.11
25	20/VI/3	20 Jan 21	Officership: president	-.12	(.81)	.06	.12	.12
26	20/VI/3-4	20 Jan 21	Officership: vice-president	-.30	(.57)	-.41	.35	-.04

Table C-9. 1920-21 (continued)

Roll-call no.	Yr./vol./p. in Diario de Sesiones	Date of vote	Issue	Factors				
				I	II	III	IV	V
27	20/VI/4	20 Jan 21	Officership: 2nd vice-president	-.31	(.56)	-.40	.40	-.06
28	20/VI/88-89	26 Jan 21	Consideration of resolution to censure Yrigoyen	.41	-.43	(.52)	-.20	-.01
29	20/VI/97-98	27 Jan 21	Consideration of resolution to censure Yrigoyen	.41	(-.53)	.49	-.30	-.04
30	20/VI/124	27 Jan 21	Senate revision of wool export tax	-.15	-.03	-.34	.26	-.36
31	20/VI/133-34	28 Jan 21	Investigation of political situation in San Juan	(.59)	-.22	.19	-.35	-.13
32	20/VI/582	25 Feb 21	Intervention in San Juan	(.71)	-.16	.05	-.17	.07
33	20/VI/938	16 Mar 21	Minimum wage for government employees	.31	.03	(.64)	.02	.21
34	20/VII/273	8 Apr 21	Suspension of debate on conduct of treasury minister	(-.66)	.16	-.18	-.08	-.09
35	20/VII/547	20 Apr 21	Debate on conduct of treasury minister	(-.88)	.33	-.15	.01	-.02
36	20/VII/549	20 Apr 21	Debate on conduct of treasury minister	(.87)	-.29	.16	-.04	.02
37	20/VII/802-3	27 Apr 21	Approval for conduct of treasury minister	(-.89)	.34	-.13	.10	-.04
38	20/VII/808-9	27 Apr 21	Approval for conduct of treasury minister	(-.89)	.35	-.14	.08	-.04
39	20/VII/810-11	27 Apr 21	Approval for metal export policies	(-.52)	(.67)	-.40	.22	-.05
40	20/VII/827	29 Apr 21	Temporary budget bill for month of May	(-.52)	(.52)	-.45	.17	-.01
41	21/I/2	26 Apr 21	Officership: president	-.29	(.90)	-.05	-.06	.11
42	21/I/3-4	26 Apr 21	Officership: vice-president	-.46	(.69)	-.44	.19	-.03
43	21/I/4	26 Apr 21	Officership: 2nd vice-president	-.48	(.66)	-.47	.17	-.03
44	21/I/150	1 May 21	Interpellation on police action against workers	(-.77)	.30	-.23	.11	.01
45	21/I/301-2	3 June 21	Consideration of pensions	-.16	-.44	-.05	.14	-.37
46	21/I/434	8 June 21	Interpellation on intervention in San Juan	(-.82)	.26	-.14	.09	-.07
47	21/I/491	9 June 21	Pension for family of deceased deputy	.07	-.01	.11	-.47	.07
48	21/I/600	23 June 21	Intervention in San Juan	(.77)	-.23	.20	-.06	.03
49	21/I/793	6 July 21	Antidumping clause (in antitrust bill)	.20	.28	.46	-.04	.31
50	21/II/10	8 July 21	Intervention in San Juan	(.58)	-.13	.09	-.10	.30
51	21/II/98	15 July 21	Officership: president	-.23	(.81)	-.08	-.11	.20
52	21/II/98-99	15 July 21	Officership: vice-president	-.43	(.58)	(-.50)	.12	.06
53	21/II/99	15 July 21	Officership: 2nd vice-president	-.36	(.51)	(-.57)	.15	.12

No.	Code	Date	Description					
54	21/II/123-24	15 July 21	Interpellation on meat-market policies	.40	-.45	.46	-.19	-.03
55	21/II/132	15 July 21	Interpellation on meat-market policies	.42	-.45	.46	-.20	-.06
56	21/II/238	15 July 21	Interpellation on homestead law	(.70)	-.26	.25	.06	.05
57	21/II/246,256	21 July 21	Information on financial policies	(.52)	-.46	.47	-.06	.01
58	21/II/384	3 Aug 21	Information on national budget accounts	(.81)	-.28	.16	-.05	.03
59	21/II/412-13	3 Aug 21	Reading of message from Yrigoyen	(.52)	-.49	.43	-.14	.04
60	21/II/461-62	4 Aug 21	Closing debate on reading of message from Yrigoyen	(-.84)	.28	-.16	.09	-.03
61	21/II/511-12	11 Aug 21	Investigation of agrarian policies	(.77)	-.27	.15	-.11	-.01
62	21/II/536	11 Aug 21	Investigation of agrarian policies	(.85)	-.26	.17	-.01	.00
63	21/II/699-700	17 Aug 21	Intervention in San Juan	(.74)	-.31	.22	-.16	-.01
64	21/III/96	24 Aug 21	Minimum wage for government employees	.39	-.05	(.56)	-.06	.22
65	21/III/192-98	31 Aug 21	Designate for presidential succession	-.23	(.81)	.04	-.03	.17
66	21/III/323-24	6 Sept 21	Investigation of agrarian policies	(.59)	-.44	.40	-.15	.03
67	21/III/587	14 Sept 21	Budget bill for 1921	-.32	-.01	(-.56)	.24	-.16
68	21/IV/26	20 Sept 21	Order of business	-.36	-.35	-.27	.28	-.25
69	21/IV/78	20 Sept 21	Closing of debate on budget bill	(-.53)	.25	-.42	.15	.07
70	21/IV/161	20 Sept 21	Minimum wage for government employees	.01	.01	(-.50)	-.08	-.07
71	21/IV/193-94	22 Sept 21	Information on government loan from Banco de la Nación	(.73)	-.25	.07	-.04	.03
72	21/IV/195	22 Sept 21	Information on government loan from Banco de la Nación	(.76)	-.35	.16	-.15	.04
73	21/IV/394-95	27 Sept 21	Information on alleged loan from USA	(-.63)	.37	-.25	.23	.04
74	21/IV/447	28 Sept 21	Alleged impropriety by Cabinet members	(-.74)	.37	-.25	.17	.01
75	21/V/5-6	31 Jan 22	Officership: president	-.19	(.76)	.24	.29	-.01
76	21/V/6	31 Jan 22	Officership: vice-president	-.38	(.54)	-.25	(.55)	-.15
77	21/V/6-7	31 Jan 22	Officership: 2nd vice-president	-.36	(.53)	-.25	(.57)	-.16
78	21/V/69	1 Feb 22	Violation of legal immunity for deputies	.47	.10	.08	-.31	-.02
79	21/V/109-10	8 Feb 22	Investigation of disturbances in Santa Cruz	(.56)	.00	.46	-.15	-.01
80	21/V/240	23 Mar 22	Compulsory congressional attendance	.41	.40	.07	-.48	-.00
81	21/V/254	5 Apr 22	Conduct of intervention in San Juan	(.78)	-.08	.10	-.31	-.06
82	21/V/260	5 Apr 22	Removal of tax on agricultural exports	(.70)	-.05	.23	-.18	-.02
			% of total variance explained	27.6	21.2	9.4	4.1	3.7
			% of factor variance explained	41.9	32.1	14.3	6.2	5.6

Table C-10. Rotated Factor Matrix for Contested Roll Calls in 1922-23

Roll-call no.	Yr./vol./p. in *Diario de Sesiones*	Date of vote	Issue	Factors				
				I	II	III	IV	V
1	22/I/1-2	26 Apr 22	Officership: provisional president	(.68)	.29	.08	-.19	.30
2	22/I/223-24	15 May 22	Postponement of debate on elections in Santiago del Estero	(-.81)	.01	.17	.11	.14
3	22/I/229	15 May 22	Officership: president	(.61)	.28	.09	-.33	.33
4	22/I/230-31	15 May 22	Officership: vice-president	(.84)	-.02	-.18	-.03	-.12
5	22/I/231	15 May 22	Officership: 2nd vice-president	(.85)	-.01	-.18	-.06	-.13
6	22/I/764	14 July 22	Officership: president	(.66)	.31	.08	-.17	.37
7	22/I/764-65	14 July 22	Officership: vice-president	(.82)	-.04	-.15	.09	.03
8	22/I/765	14 July 22	Officership: 2nd vice-president	(.83)	-.03	-.15	.08	.03
9	22/II/72	19 July 22	Information on petroleum and government policy	(.81)	-.16	.04	-.03	-.04
10	22/II/231	20 July 22	Information on petroleum and government policy	(-.87)	.06	.00	-.03	.04
11	22/II/319	21 July 22	Investigation of sisal industry	(.73)	-.02	-.04	.31	-.08
12	22/II/451-52	28 July 22	Information on petroleum and government policy	(-.89)	.13	.00	.10	.04
13	22/III/237	17 Aug 22	Construction of drainage system in Buenos Aires City	-.28	.11	.37	-.32	.14
14	22/III/472-73	24 Aug 22	Construction of drainage system in Buenos Aires City	-.11	.14	(.68)	.07	.01
15	22/III/484	24 Aug 22	Construction of drainage system in Buenos Aires City	.31	-.14	(-.66)	-.09	.01
16	22/III/554-55	31 Aug 22	Designate for presidential succession	(.60)	.24	.04	-.19	.40
17	22/III/644-45	1 Sept 22	Order of business; intervention in Córdoba	(-.71)	.15	.22	.01	.09
18	22/III/811-12	13 Sept 22	Information on public debt	(-.74)	-.09	.10	-.01	.14
19	22/IV/23-24	14 Sept 22	Order of business; violation of parliamentary community	(-.78)	.08	.12	.00	.14

No.	Code	Date	Description					
20	22/IV/74-75	15 Sept 22	Order of business; information on public debt	(-.74)	-.12	.06	-.10	.33
21	22/IV/156	20 Sept 22	Order of business	(-.80)	.03	.15	.07	.07
22	22/IV/412	21 Sept 22	Presidential message on divorce	(-.86)	.01	.12	.04	.05
23	22/IV/420	21 Sept 22	Order of business; intervention in Córdoba	(-.73)	.16	.02	.11	-.28
24	22/IV/827-28	27 Sept 22	Budget bill	.23	-.36	.09	.32	.06
25	22/V/2	4 Dec 22	Officership: president	(.64)	.35	.13	-.17	.37
26	22/V/2-3	4 Dec 22	Officership: vice-president	(.83)	-.02	-.17	.08	-.01
27	22/V/3	4 Dec 22	Officership: 2nd vice-president	(.78)	-.04	-.17	.04	.01
28	22/V/283-84	15 Dec 22	Information on government policy concerning gold	(-.83)	-.16	.11	-.21	.10
29	22/V/797	19 Jan 23	Violation of parliamentary immunity	.48	-.02	-.01	(.52)	.01
30	22/V/797-98	19 Jan 23	Violation of parliamentary immunity	(-.85)	.00	.20	-.07	.09
31	22/V/807	19 Jan 23	Violation of parliamentary immunity	(-.51)	.12	.32	.30	.04
32	22/VI/190	1 Feb 23	Budget bill	(.61)	-.24	-.30	.11	-.11
33	22/VI/377-78	8 Mar 23	Violation of parliamentary immunity	(-.56)	.15	.15	.09	.04
34	22/VI/413-14	9 Mar 23	Postponement of debate on intervention in Córdoba	(-.80)	-.06	-.02	-.21	.00
35	22/VI/700	15 Mar 23	Intervention in Córdoba	(.86)	.07	-.06	.17	.02
36	22/VI/879	23 Mar 23	Order of business	-.27	.41	.37	-.17	-.16
37	22/VI/897	23 Mar 23	Rent control	.14	-.10	.47	-.01	.38
38	22/VII/211	12 Apr 23	Congressional attendance	.23	-.17	-.41	(.55)	.23
39	22/VII/397	16 Apr 23	Order of business; cattle crisis vs. budget bill	.20	-.34	-.09	-.17	(-.59)
40	22/VII/504	14 Apr 23	Control of meat trade	.05	-.25	.17	-.02	(-.53)
41	22/VII/576-77	19 Apr 23	Order of business; cattle crisis	.07	-.31	-.27	-.19	-.44
42	22/VII/700-701	23 Apr 23	Press coverage of tax decisions	-.44	-.03	.25	-.24	.29
43	23/I/1-2	26 Apr 23	Officership: president	(.83)	-.00	.04	-.08	.29
44	23/I/2	26 Apr 23	Officership: vice-president	(.81)	-.01	.04	-.06	.31
45	23/I/3	26 Apr 23	Officership: 2nd vice-president	(.83)	-.04	.03	-.07	.30
46	23/II/322-24	16 May 23	Erasure of insult from *Diario de Sesiones*	(-.68)	-.03	-.22	.34	-.08
47	23/II/286	1 June 23	Consideration of budget bill	.26	-.12	-.34	-.28	-.43
48	23/II/302-4	1 June 23	Budget for post office	(.81)	.14	-.14	.20	-.10

Table C-10. 1922-23 *(continued)*

Roll-call no.	Yr./vol./p. in *Diario de Sesiones*	Date of vote	Issue	Factors				
				I	II	III	IV	V
49	23/II/736	6 June 23	Budget increase regarding border with Bolivia	(.72)	-.18	-.26	.06	.00
50	23/III/227	11 June 23	Procedure for dealing with budget	(.78)	-.00	-.11	.10	.03
51	23/III/532	14 June 23	Maintenance of quorum	(-.64)	-.01	.13	-.20	-.05
52	23/IV/78	22 June 23	Violation of parliamentary immunity	-.29	.33	(.50)	-.16	.02
53	23/IV/115	22 June 23	Maintenance of quorum	.07	-.06	.07	-.39	-.10
54	23/IV/559	19 July 23	Officership: president	(.78)	.04	-.27	.07	.03
55	23/IV/560	19 July 23	Officership: vice-president	(.78)	.00	-.29	.08	.03
56	23/IV/560-61	19 July 23	Officership: 2nd vice-president	(.79)	.08	-.27	.05	.00
57	23/V/42	8 Aug 23	Legalization of divorce	-.40	.27	(.54)	-.14	-.14
58	23/V/346-47	23 Aug 23	Allegations of judicial impropriety	.37	-.42	-.23	.12	-.26
59	23/V/431	6 Sept 23	Designate for presidential succession	(.84)	.10	-.13	-.08	.10
60	23/V/654-55	11 Sept 23	Pensions for railroad workers	-.14	.09	(.67)	-.18	.09
61	23/V/775-76	12 Sept 23	Approval of elections in San Juan	(-.57)	.09	.22	.49	.09
62	23/VI/754	27 Sept 23	Investigation of Caja Nacional de Ahorro Postal	(-.50)	-.03	.22	.06	-.05
63	23/VI/815	28 Sept 23	Investigation of Caja Nacional de Ahorro Postal	(-.73)	.05	.25	-.06	-.06
64	23/VII/50	3 Oct 23	Order of business; budget bill	-.10	.16	.02	(-.68)	.08

				F1	F2	F3	F4	F5
65	23/VII/130	4 Oct 23	Order of business	-.17	.35	.39	.03	.25
66	23/VII/195-96	8 Oct 23	Quorum for dealing with budget	(.70)	.09	-.26	.17	-.01
67	23/VII/306	8 Oct 23	Senate revision in 1923 budget bill	(-.53)	-.14	.06	.05	.13
68	23/VII/559	18 Oct 23	Information on commercial tax payments	(-.76)	.16	.23	-.11	-.07
69	23/VII/609-10	19 Oct 23	Consideration of petroleum industry and government policy	(.63)	-.00	-.21	-.07	.02
70	23/VII/643	24 Oct 23	Order of business; pensions	.07	-.37	-.22	.25	-.14
71	23/VII/664	24 Oct 23	Senate revision in 1923 budget bill	(.74)	-.20	.10	.11	.05
72	23/VII/694	24 Oct 23	Minimum wage for workers on state-owned railroads	-.09	.44	.26	-.21	-.03
73	23/VIII/41-42	26 Oct 23	Consideration of federal court system	(.71)	-.19	-.05	.10	.08
74	23/VIII/251-53	7 Nov 23	Order of business; federal courts vs. intervention in Jujuy	(.73)	.01	-.01	-.01	-.01
75	23/VIII/295	8 Nov 23	Senate revision in tariff bill	.12	(.83)	.12	.05	.04
76	23/VIII/296	8 Nov 23	Tariff	.38	(.64)	.13	.00	.27
77	23/VIII/301	8 Nov 23	Tariff	.10	(.81)	-.03	-.10	.04
78	23/VIII/424	15 Nov 23	Sugar tariff	.25	(.78)	.10	.05	.10
79	23/VIII/428	15 Nov 23	Tariff	.24	(.66)	.08	-.01	.38
80	23/VIII/504-7	21 Nov 23	Tariff	-.15	(.58)	.08	.31	.07
			% of total variance explained	38.3	7.0	5.7	3.9	3.9
			% of factor variance explained	65.2	11.9	9.7	6.7	6.5

Table C-11. Rotated Factor Matrix for Contested Roll Calls in 1924-25

Roll-call no.	Yr./vol./p. in *Diario de Sesiones*	Date of vote	Issue	Factors				
				I	II	III	IV	V
1	24/I/4	10 Apr 24	Officership: provisional president	-.33	.07	-.44	-.00	(.54)
2	24/I/240-41	6 June 24	Postponement of debate on elections in Córdoba	(-.92)	.15	-.03	.01	.22
3	24/I/269-70	6 June 24	Postponement of debate on elections in Córdoba	(.92)	-.03	-.02	-.11	-.04
4	24/I/348	10 June 24	Postponement of debate on elections in Mendoza	(.70)	-.43	.42	.12	-.04
5	24/I/369-70	10 June 24	Approval of elections in Mendoza	(-.72)	.42	-.42	-.10	.01
6	24/I/426-27	11 June 24	Motion to adjourn rather than elect officers	(.76)	-.39	.25	.04	-.12
7	24/I/430	12 June 24	Officership: president	(-.72)	.44	-.41	-.04	.18
8	24/I/430-31	12 June 24	Officership: vice-president	-.34	(.87)	-.12	-.03	.09
9	24/I/431	12 June 24	Officership: 2nd vice-president	-.30	(.85)	-.11	.05	.09
10	24/II/438-39	16 July 24	Officership: president	(-.66)	.45	-.43	-.09	.13
11	24/II/439	16 July 24	Officership: vice-president	-.29	(.88)	-.11	-.07	.00
12	24/II/440	16 July 24	Officership: 2nd vice-president	-.29	(.87)	-.10	-.05	-.01
13	24/II/518-19	16 July 24	Publication of congressional committee proceedings	-.10	-.14	(-.56)	.18	.19
14	24/II/798-99	24 July 24	Order of business	(.81)	-.21	.14	.09	-.16
15	24/III/57-58	30 July 24	Approval of elections in Córdoba	(.82)	-.20	.06	.10	-.15
16	24/III/178-79	6 Aug 24	Approval of elections in Córdoba	(.77)	-.21	.13	.09	-.09
17	24/III/229-30	13 Aug 24	Approval of elections in Córdoba	(.77)	-.41	.31	.01	-.14
18	24/III/256-57	14 Aug 24	Approval of elections in Córdoba	(.73)	-.45	.35	.05	-.12
19	24/III/302	14 Aug 24	Approval of elections in Córdoba	(.68)	-.43	.38	.03	-.15
20	24/III/304-5	14 Aug 24	Approval of elections in Córdoba	(-.88)	.26	-.05	-.11	.17
21	24/III/331	14 Aug 24	Approval of elections in Córdoba	(.75)	-.45	.35	.06	-.11
22	24/III/332	14 Aug 24	Approval of elections in Córdoba	(-.92)	.20	-.03	-.12	.13
23	24/III/333-34	14 Aug 24	Approval of elections in Córdoba	(-.92)	.20	-.03	-.12	.13

24	24/III/541-42	22 Aug 24	Order of business; investigation of Banco Hipotecario Nacional	-.47	(.53)	.28	-.03	.08
25	24/V/65	29 Aug 24	Designate for presidential succession	(-.70)	.27	-.34	-.11	.14
26	24/VI/35	16 Sept 24	Allowing deputy to be rector of a university	-.08	(.58)	.40	-.06	-.12
27	24/VI/43-44	16 Sept 24	Approval of leave for Dr. José Arce	-.00	(.61)	.33	.09	-.12
28	24/VI/82	17 Sept 24	Postponement of debate on League of Nations	.31	.01	(.69)	.08	.08
29	24/VI/93-94	17 Sept 24	Membership in League of Nations	-.23	(-.58)	.02	.13	.04
30	24/VI/192-93	19 Sept 24	Order of business	(-.53)	.21	(-.54)	-.05	-.19
31	24/VI/216-17	22 Sept 24	Order of business; rent control	(.60)	-.25	(.55)	-.02	.09
32	24/VI/448	23 Sept 24	Consideration of 1924 budget bill	.27	-.40	(.54)	.21	-.05
33	24/VI/596	24 Sept 24	Intervention in Mendoza	.01	(-.65)	.38	.33	.24
34	24/VI/727-28	26 Sept 24	Presidential objections to salary-payment bill	.12	(.53)	-.30	-.25	-.29
35	24/VI/897-98	29 Sept 24	Social security provisions	(.79)	.09	.09	-.08	.14
36	24/VI/949	30 Sept 24	Order of business	.47	.19	(.53)	.04	.10
37	24/VII/5	21 Nov 24	Officership: president	(-.64)	.32	-.37	.09	.23
38	24/VII/5	21 Nov 24	Officership: vice-president	-.12	(.84)	-.06	.06	.11
39	24/VII/6	21 Nov 24	Officership: 2nd vice-president	-.10	(.81)	-.02	.14	.14
40	24/VII/72	3 Dec 24	Budget	-.04	(-.57)	.07	.45	-.28
41	24/VII/148	10 Dec 24	Speaking time for Romeo David Saccone, for attack on Leopoldo Melo	.41	-.16	(.62)	.06	.09
42	24/VII/295-96	19 Dec 24	Accusation against Leopoldo Melo	(-.65)	.35	(-.53)	-.07	-.01
43	24/VII/300	19 Dec 24	Senate revision of budget bill	.20	(-.81)	.16	.25	-.12
44	25/I/8	7 May 25	Officership: vice-president	.18	(.90)	.08	-.04	.08
45	25/I/8	7 May 25	Officership: 2nd vice-president	.16	(.91)	.12	.02	.09
46	25/I/575-76	3 June 25	Allegations regarding labor law	(-.84)	.04	-.16	.12	-.23
47	25/I/576-77	3 June 25	Allegations regarding labor law	(.80)	-.04	.24	-.10	.21
48	25/I/772	4 June 25	Consideration of elections in Santiago del Estero	-.12	-.10	(-.75)	.02	.14
49	25/II/167-68	18 June 25	Interpellation on application of labor law	(-.53)	-.24	-.19	.25	.08
50	25/II/287	24 June 25	Interpellation on application of labor law	.08	(.58)	.40	.18	-.04

Table C-11. 1924-25 *(continued)*

Roll-call no.	Yr./vol./p. in *Diario de Sesiones*	Date of vote	Issue	Factors I	II	III	IV	V
51	25/II/330	24 June 25	Intervention in San Juan	-.03	-.26	-.05	(.62)	-.06
52	25/II/415	1 July 25	Order of business	-.06	(.68)	.21	-.20	-.01
53	25/II/452-53	3 July 25	Approval of elections in Santiago del Estero	.05	-.29	-.28	-.48	-.14
54	25/II/489	16 July 25	Officership: president	-.17	(.91)	-.08	-.05	.02
55	25/II/490	16 July 25	Officership: vice-president	-.15	(.92)	-.08	-.03	.03
56	25/II/490-91	16 July 25	Officership: 2nd vice-president	-.15	(.90)	-.08	-.01	-.01
57	25/II/682	22 July 25	Consideration of social security law	(.74)	.07	-.00	-.13	.18
58	25/II/565	12 Aug 25	Acceptance of Mario Guido's resignation as Chamber president	.18	(-.87)	.12	.01	.03
59	25/III/585	20 Aug 25	Officership: president	-.27	(.89)	-.01	-.10	-.07
60	25/III/586	20 Aug 25	Officership: vice-president	-.23	(.90)	-.04	-.08	-.09
61	25/III/586-87	20 Aug 25	Officership: 2nd vice-president	-.22	(.90)	-.03	-.06	-.10
62	25/III/832	26 Aug 25	Interpellation on elections in Mendoza	(-.84)	-.05	-.07	.20	-.13
63	25/III/854	26 Aug 25	Postponement of debate on resignation by José A. Núñez	(-.53)	-.19	-.37	.35	.15
64	25/IV/9	27 Aug 25	Consideration of resignation by José A. Núñez	(.56)	.04	.38	-.33	-.07
65	25/IV/163	9 Sept 25	Designate for presidential succession	-.19	(.89)	-.10	-.03	.05
66	25/IV/529-30	17 Sept 25	Expulsion of two Mendoza deputies	-.32	-.35	-.46	-.02	.09
67	25/VI/9	9 Dec 25	Officership: president	(.64)	-.19	.47	.03	.22
68	25/VI/9-10	9 Dec 25	Officership: vice-president	(.66)	-.23	.47	.07	.11
69	25/VI/10	9 Dec 25	Officership: 2nd vice-president	(.67)	-.21	.47	.03	.17
70	25/VI/376	13 Jan 26	Consideration of social security law	(.64)	.23	.16	-.02	.00
71	25/VI/615-16	21 Jan 26	Mismanagement of Caja Nacional de Ahorro Postal	(-.50)	-.41	.08	.15	-.05
72	25/VII/33	27 Jan 26	Order of business; social security vs. budget	(-.69)	-.34	-.17	.24	-.09
			% of total variance explained	29.3	27.3	10.1	2.6	2.1
			% of factor variance explained	41.0	38.2	14.1	3.7	2.9

Table C-12. Rotated Factor Matrix for Contested Roll Calls in 1926-27

Roll-call no.	Yr./vol./p. in *Diario de Sesiones*	Date of vote	Issue	Factors				
				I	II	III	IV	V
1	26/I/10-11	6 Apr 26	Credentials of deputies from Córdoba	(.88)	.26	.18	-.03	-.01
2	26/I/12	6 Apr 26	Officership: provisional president	(.85)	.26	.16	-.09	-.01
3	26/I/294	9 June 26	Postponement of debate on resignation by Romeo David Saccone	(-.80)	-.13	-.06	.04	.27
4	26/I/446	14 June 26	Postponement of debate on election in Buenos Aires Province	.39	(.85)	.13	-.04	.02
5	26/I/447	14 June 26	Approval of election in Buenos Aires Province	-.26	(-.84)	-.12	-.00	-.01
6	26/I/466	16 June 26	Commencement of parliamentary deliberations	(-.85)	-.37	-.21	-.05	.01
7	26/I/596	21 June 26	Approval of elections in Córdoba	(-.87)	-.35	-.14	-.04	.04
8	26/I/617-18	21 June 26	Procedures for considering electoral credentials	(.86)	.36	.08	.06	-.07
9	26/I/664-65	21 June 26	Postponement of vote on credentials: José María Martínez	(-.88)	-.36	-.10	-.06	.09
10	26/I/666	21 June 26	Postponement of debate on credentials: José María Martínez	(.87)	.35	.09	.02	-.11
11	26/I/839	23 June 26	Approval of elections in Jujuy	(.87)	.35	.09	.02	-.11
12	26/II/17	24 June 26	Postponement of debate on elections in Mendoza	(.85)	.34	.12	.05	-.00
13	26/II/28	24 June 26	Approval of elections in San Juan	(-.67)	.42	.04	-.08	.15
14	26/II/28-29	24 June 26	Approval of elections in San Juan	(.87)	.29	.11	.08	.03
15	26/II/140	25 June 26	Officership: president	(.87)	.28	.10	.04	.06
16	26/II/141	25 June 26	Officership: vice-president	(.89)	.34	.12	-.01	-.05
17	26/II/142	25 June 26	Officership: 2nd vice-president	.39	(.88)	.09	-.07	-.01
18	26/II/367	14 July 26	Committee on voter registration	(.87)	.36	.08	.01	-.07
19	26/II/379-80	15 July 26	Officership: president	(-.79)	-.22	-.09	.04	.18
20	26/II/380	15 July 26	Officership: vice-president	(.82)	.42	.05	-.01	-.09
21	26/II/381	15 July 26	Officership: 2nd vice-president	.44	(.80)	.19	-.06	-.07

Table C-12. 1926-27 (continued)

Roll-call no.	Yr./vol./p. in Diario de Sesiones	Date of vote	Issue	Factors				
				I	II	III	IV	V
22	26/III/152-53	29 July 26	Investigation of naval purchases (two battleships)	(.80)	.20	.08	.08	-.10
23	26/III/193-94	30 July 26	Investigation of purchases by state-owned railroads	(.70)	.19	.15	.16	-.09
24	26/III/303-4	3 Aug 26	Congressional responsibility regarding budget	-.33	(-.75)	.05	.12	-.08
25	26/III/313	3 Aug 26	Consideration of budget	-.29	(-.81)	.03	.06	-.06
26	26/III/542	6 Aug 26	Order of business; labor bills	(.57)	-.38	.04	.12	-.39
27	26/III/567	6 Aug 26	Presidential objections to bill to shut businesses by 8 p.m.	.04	-.42	.02	.24	(-.54)
28	26/III/572	6 Aug 26	Senate revision of bill on night-time work in bakeries	-.05	.49	-.05	-.09	(.61)
29	26/III/824	11 Aug 26	Senate revision in 1926 budget bill	.29	(.80)	.13	-.07	.06
30	26/IV/383	24 Aug 26	Women's rights	(-.81)	-.01	-.05	.04	.01
31	26/IV/429	25 Aug 26	Women's rights	.25	-.09	-.00	(.75)	-.21
32	26/IV/429-30	25 Aug 26	Women's rights	.06	-.41	-.09	(.61)	-.04
33	26/IV/718	31 Aug 26	Designate for presidential succession	(.81)	.28	.04	.09	.01
34	26/V/302	9 Sept 26	Consideration of pensions	(-.67)	.39	-.05	-.08	-.12
35	26/VI/242	22 Sept 26	Purchase of armaments	.28	-.48	-.08	.05	.01
36	26/VI/662-63	30 Sept 26	Pension for widow of Leandro N. Alem	(-.70)	.02	.02	.00	(.50)
37	26/VI/692	2 Dec 26	Officership: president	(.84)	.30	.11	.10	-.05
38	26/VI/692-97	2 Dec 26	Officership: vice-president	.40	(.83)	.12	.03	-.03
39	26/VI/696-97	2 Dec 26	Officership: 2nd vice-president	(.85)	.29	.07	.08	-.04
40	26/VI/833-34	9 Dec 26	Interpellation regarding cattle industry	(.73)	.13	.22	.10	.15
41	26/VIII/188	23 Dec 26	Rejection of budget for 1927	.26	(.74)	.12	.04	.15
42	26/VIII/390	18 Jan 27	Consideration of 1927 budget bill	(-.77)	-.09	.02	-.24	.09
43	26/VIII/396	18 Jan 27	Consideration of bill on petroleum	(-.79)	-.18	.01	-.30	.15

No.	Code	Date	Issue	1	2	3	4	5
44	26/VIII/456-57	18 Jan 27	Minimum wage for government employees	(.82)	.28	.15	.28	-.02
45	26/VIII/498-99	18 Jan 27	Consideration of increase in military salaries	(.80)	.22	.18	.34	.05
46	26/VIII/501	18 Jan 27	Increase in military salaries	(-.77)	-.15	-.13	-.36	-.02
47	26/VIII/514-15	18 Jan 27	Increase in governmental salaries	(.82)	.21	.18	.31	.07
48	27/I/11	11 May 27	Officership: vice-president	-.04	(.96)	.08	-.09	.02
49	27/I/234	19 May 27	Investigation of police in Buenos Aires City	(.68)	-.10	.04	.11	-.41
50	27/I/541	8 June 27	Delegation to international labor conference	(-.80)	-.27	-.09	.02	.01
51	27/I/749-50	22 June 27	Interpellation of minister of war (on voter registration)	(-.81)	.32	-.21	-.06	.01
52	27/II/383-84	20 July 27	Officership: president	(.85)	.32	.09	.06	.06
53	27/II/384	20 July 27	Officership: vice-president	.36	(.83)	.11	-.03	.12
54	27/II/385	20 July 27	Officership: 2nd vice-president	(.64)	(.57)	-.22	-.01	.12
55	27/III/20	22 July 27	Presidential designation of national anthem	(-.79)	-.20	-.12	-.08	-.22
56	27/III/207-8	28 July 27	Consideration of petroleum issue	(.84)	.32	.22	.09	.08
57	27/IV/266	1 Sept 27	Designate for presidential succession	(.85)	.21	.16	-.04	.06
58	27/IV/313-14	1 Sept 27	Quorum for debate on petroleum	(-.78)	-.12	-.29	-.03	.01
59	27/IV/359-60	1 Sept 27	Consideration of petroleum issue	(.52)	.37	(-.66)	-.09	.00
60	27/IV/362-63	1 Sept 27	Nationalization of petroleum	-.27	(-.66)	-.16	-.09	-.14
61	27/IV/430-31	7 Sept 27	Nationalization of petroleum	(-.86)	-.25	-.17	-.02	-.04
62	27/IV/457-58	7 Sept 27	Nationalization of petroleum	(-.53)	-.33	(-.69)	.01	.05
63	27/IV/478	7 Sept 27	Nationalization of petroleum	(-.52)	(-.53)	(-.59)	.03	.03
64	27/IV/489	23 Sept 27	Investigation of judiciary in Buenos Aires City	(.66)	-.17	.12	.21	.21
65	27/V/502-3	27 Sept 27	Order of business; petroleum issue	.53	.48	(-.56)	.06	-.05
66	27/V/629	28 Sept 27	Utilization of profits by Yacimientos Petrolíferos de la Nación (YPF)	(.80)	.11	.19	-.05	-.13
67	27/VI/517	29-30 Sept 27	Diplomatic relations with Vatican	(-.52)	.31	-.10	-.39	-.30
			% of total variance explained	47.3	19.7.	3.8	3.0	2.8
			% of factor variance explained	61.7	25.7	5.0	3.9	3.7

Table C-13. Rotated Factor Matrix for Contested Roll Calls in 1928-29

Roll-call no.	Yr./vol./p. in *Diario de Sesiones*	Date of vote	Issue	Factors			
				I	II	III	IV
1	28/I/5, 11	21 May 28	Officership: provisional president	.40	(.71)	.16	.42
2	28/I/246	11 June 28	Officership: president	.28	(.76)	.27	.33
3	28/I/246-47	11 June 28	Officership: vice-president	(.52)	(.53)	.43	.30
4	28/I/247	11 June 28	Officership: 2nd vice-president	(.52)	(.51)	.42	.21
5	28/II/86	6 July 28	Interpellation on meat trade	(-.61)	-.30	-.42	-.17
6	28/II/153	11 July 28	Resignation by Julio A. Roca, deputy from Córdoba	(.62)	(.52)	.24	.36
7	28/II/236	12 July 28	Information on labor dispute	(.62)	.34	.37	.44
8	28/II/239-40	12 July 28	Presidential reaction to political crimes	(.57)	.40	.28	(.53)
9	28/II/285-86	13 July 28	Intervention in San Juan	.27	.08	.13	(.86)
10	28/II/429	18 July 28	Intervention in San Juan	(.69)	.42	.39	.23
11	28/II/745-46	27 July 28	Intervention in Mendoza	(-.60)	-.36	-.45	-.15
12	28/III/117	8 Aug 28	Medals for Olympic fencing team	.42	.16	(.55)	.14
13	28/III/251	10 Aug 28	Relationships with Paraguay	.26	(.79)	.17	.14
14	28/III/446-47	22 Aug 28	Investigation of working conditions in interior	(-.62)	-.35	-.49	-.10
15	28/III/623	29 Aug 28	Investigation of working conditions in interior	(-.60)	-.36	-.46	-.24
16	28/III/677-78	5 Sept 28	Designate for presidential succession	.32	(.86)	.09	-.15
17	28/III/824	5 Sept 28	Nationalization of petroleum	(.72)	.45	.37	.21
18	28/IV/34-35	6 Sept 28	Order of business	(.70)	.46	.37	.16
19	28/IV/159	10 Sept 28	Order of business	(-.63)	-.35	-.43	-.16
20	28/IV/254	13 Sept 28	Order of business	(.73)	.46	.24	.32
21	28/IV/390	17 Sept 28	Nationalization of petroleum	(.76)	.17	(.51)	.10
22	28/V/36	24-25 Sept 28	Senate revision on intervention in San Juan	(-.75)	-.40	-.36	-.23
23	28/V/537	25 Sept 28	Postponement of debate on Código de Comercio	(.73)	.29	.26	.21
24	28/V/574	27 Sept 28	Order of business; interventions	(-.78)	-.41	-.32	-.27
25	28/V/578	27 Sept 28	Sessions over weekend	(.79)	.42	.33	.26

26	28/V/589	27 Sept 28	Order of business; intervention in Santa Fe	(.76)	.44	.27	.28
27	28/V/589-90	27 Sept 28	Order of business; intervention in Entre Ríos	(.77)	.43	.25	.31
28	28/V/590	27 Sept 28	Order of business; intervention in Corrientes	(.78)	.42	.28	.29
29	28/V/591	27 Sept 28	Order of business; intervention in San Luis	(.79)	.39	.30	.26
30	28/V/651	29-30 Sept 28	Closing of debate on resignation by Ernesto Claros	(.80)	.40	.32	.27
31	28/V/656	29-30 Sept 28	Abstention by Alfredo L. Spinetto	(-.75)	-.40	-.31	-.31
32	28/V/657	29-30 Sept 28	Closing of debate on construction of leprosarium	(.76)	.40	.32	.27
33	28/V/690	29-30 Sept 28	Order of business; intervention in Entre Ríos	(-.81)	-.38	-.31	-.27
34	28/V/62-63	29-30 Sept 28	Intervention in Entre Ríos	(.80)	.37	.35	.26
35	28/V/787	29-30 Sept 28	Censure of president of Chamber	(.80)	.37	.32	.28
36	28/V/806-7	30 Sept 28	Intervention in San Juan	(.76)	.33	.36	.31
37	29/I/138	20 May 29	Officership: president	(.76)	.42	.30	.19
38	29/I/138-39	20 May 29	Officership: vice-president	(.78)	.40	.29	.16
39	29/I/139-40	20 May 29	Officership: 2nd vice-president	(.78)	.40	.30	.16
40	29/I/326	12 June 29	Interpellation on agricultural crisis	(-.72)	-.27	-.41	-.21
41	29/I/490	13 June 29	Interpellation on agricultural crisis	(-.74)	-.34	-.34	-.22
42	29/I/589	19 June 29	Interpellation on education policies, mainly regarding private schools	(-.77)	-.34	-.36	-.20
43	29/I/600	19 June 29	Interpellation of treasury minister	(-.75)	-.33	-.37	-.15
44	29/I/604	19 June 29	Reconsideration of proposal to interpellate treasury minister	(-.64)	-.42	-.31	-.06
45	29/II/182	17 July 29	Officership: vice-president	(.54)	.44	.43	.24
46	29/II/183	17 July 29	Officership: 2nd vice-president	(.52)	.44	.42	.28
47	29/II/664-65	16 Aug 29	Reading of agenda	.49	.39	.41	.21
48	29/III/157-58	5 Sept 29	Designate for presidential succession	(.66)	.43	.31	.23
49	29/III/180	5 Sept 29	Interpellation on labor policies	(-.63)	-.35	-.37	-.24
50	29/III/449	13 Sept 29	Interpellation regarding military policies and attitudes	(.73)	.34	.34	.11
51	29/III/533	18 Sept 29	Calling of permanent session	(.56)	.60	.27	.03

171

Table C-13. 1928-29 *(continued)*

Roll-call no.	Yr./vol./p. in *Diario de Sesiones*	Date of vote	Issue	Factors			
				I	II	III	IV
52	29/IV/147	6 Nov 29	Quorum	-.35	-.20	(-.82)	-.11
53	29/IV/147-48	6 Nov 29	Quorum	-.27	-.19	(-.83)	-.10
54	29/IV/154	13 Nov 29	Quorum	(-.57)	-.09	-.48	-.16
55	29/IV/361	12-13 Dec 29	Order of business	(.75)	.33	.40	.27
56	29/IV/504-5	27 Dec 29	Attempt to assassinate Yrigoyen	(.79)	.11	.39	.13
			% of total variance explained	43.6	17.7	14.3	7.1
			% of factor variance explained	52.7	21.3	17.3	8.6

Table C-14. Rotated Factor Matrix for Contested Roll Calls in 1930

Roll-call no.	Yr./vol./p. in *Diario de Sesiones*	Date of vote	Issue	Factors	
				I	II
1	30/I/18	25 Apr 30	Officership: provisional president	(.80)	.29
2	30/I/268	27 June 30	Credentials: Daniel Videla Dorna	(-.89)	-.30
3	30/I/480	16 July 30	Credentials: Daniel Videla Dorna	(-.92)	-.28
4	30/I/500	16 July 30	Credentials: Daniel Videla Dorna	(.96)	.01
5	30/I/666	23 July 30	Approval of elections in Corrientes	.05	(.92)
6	30/II/41	6 Aug 30	Quorum	(-.80)	-.08
7	30/II/50-51	7 Aug 30	Quorum	(-.86)	-.24
8	30/II/77	7 Aug 30	Approval of elections in Mendoza	(.85)	.23
9	30/II/627	29-30 Aug 30	Approval of elections in San Juan	(.89)	.17
10	30/II/660	29-30 Aug 30	Credentials: Carlos R. Porto	(.91)	.25
11	30/II/721	1 Sept 30	Officership: president	(.76)	(.53)
12	30/II/721-22	1 Sept 30	Officership: vice-president	(.75)	(.56)
13	30/II/722	1 Sept 30	Officership: 2nd vice-president	(.76)	(.52)
			% of total variance explained	66.3	16.7
			% of factor variance explained	79.9	20.1

Table C-15. Rotated Factor Matrix for Contested Roll Calls in 1932-33

Roll-call no.	Yr./vol./p. in *Diario de Sesiones*	Date of vote	Issue	Factors I	II	III
1	32/I/4	20 Jan 32	Recess prior to election of provisional president	(.79)	.28	.24
2	32/I/41-42	20 Jan 32	Commencement of session prior to approval of credentials	.49	(.71)	.41
3	32/I/47-48	20 Jan 32	Commencement of session prior to approval of credentials	-.46	(-.69)	-.31
4	32/I/52	20 Jan 32	Officership: president	(.83)	.39	.29
5	32/I/53	20 Jan 32	Officership: vice-president	(.79)	.39	.35
6	32/I/54	20 Jan 32	Officership: 2nd vice-president	(.79)	.41	.31
7	32/II/966-67	8 June 32	Senate revision in commercial tax proposal	.42	(.66)	.34
8	32/IV/299	20-21 July 32	Intervention in Buenos Aires Province	(.78)	.41	.25
9	32/IV/481-82	27 July 32	6% ceiling on agricultural loans by Banco de la Nación	(-.72)	-.21	-.01
10	32/IV/558	29 July 32	Senate revision in municipal bond issue	-.37	(-.70)	-.28
11	32/V/307	19 Aug 32	Political amnesty	(.77)	.33	.22
12	32/V/446	5 Sept 32	Presidential decrees on government of Buenos Aires City	(.83)	.29	.19
13	32/V/862-63	14 Sept 32	Legal rights of employees	(-.70)	-.38	-.11
14	32/VI/207	20 Sept 32	Order of business; debate on sugar industry	(-.76)	-.43	-.19
15	32/VI/283	21 Sept 32	Postponement of debate on legalized divorce	.20	.25	(.76)
16	32/VI/537-38	23-24 Sept 32	Legalization of divorce	-.27	-.26	(-.69)
17	32/VI/743-44	29 Sept 32	Tariff exemptions for Dirección Nacional de Vialidad	-.35	(-.66)	-.37
18	32/VI/1062-63	29 Sept 32	Labor representation on directorate of YPF	-.49	-.46	-.43
19	32/VI/1230-31	30 Sept 32	Consideration of indemnity for job-related injuries	-.40	(-.75)	-.17
20	32/VI/1307-8	30 Sept 32	Senate revision of tariff exemptions for Dirección Nacional de Vialidad	-.26	(-.77)	-.24

21	32/VI/1308-9	30 Sept 32	Postponement of debate on YPF	(-.75)	-.34	-.24
22	32/VII/332	17 Dec 32	Authorization for state of seige	(.76)	.40	.23
23	32/VII/532	22-23 Dec 32	Closing of debate on 1933 budget bill	(.77)	.42	.24
24	32/VII/532-33	22-23 Dec 32	Recess during debate on budget bill	(-.72)	-.47	-.04
25	32/VII/606	23-24 Dec 32	Limitation of debate on military budget	(.74)	.44	.19
26	33/I/1-2	26 Apr 33	Officership: president	(.82)	.40	.22
27	33/I/2-3	26 Apr 33	Officership: vice-president	(.76)	.32	.29
28	33/I/3	26 Apr 33	Officership: 2nd vice-president	(.79)	.35	.24
29	33/I/801	22 June 33	Moratorium on mortgages	(.72)	.44	.17
30	33/II/479	21 July 33	Taxing authority for Dirección General de Obras Sanitarias	.41	(.67)	.19
31	33/II/584	26 July 33	Taxing authority for Dirección General de Obras Sanitarias	(.66)	.15	.32
32	33/II/956	9 Aug 33	Means of combatting unemployment	(-.75)	-.36	-.23
33	33/III/340-41	18 Aug 33	Nationalization of municipal packinghouse	(.77)	.40	.23
34	33/IV/148-49	12 Sept 33	Interpellation on existence of paramilitary groups	-.37	(-.69)	-.44
35	33/IV/446-47	15 Sept 33	Order of business	.44	(.63)	.49
36	33/IV/682	20-21 Sept 33	Creation of new dioceses	.46	(.68)	.47
37	33/IV/684	20-21 Sept 33	Recess in debate on new dioceses	(-.73)	-.38	-.43
38	33/IV/686-87	20-21 Sept 33	Order of business; creation of new dioceses	(.75)	.41	.36
39	33/IV/789-90	21-22 Sept 33	Changes in electoral laws	(.76)	.33	.36
40	33/V/407	25 Sept 33	Senate revision in moratorium on mortgages	.25	(.76)	-.09
41	33/V/798-99	28-29 Sept 33	Minimum wages for government employees	(.76)	.25	.23
			% of total variance explained	42.1	23.6	10.5
			% of factor variance explained	55.2	31.0	13.8

Table C-16. Rotated Factor Matrix for Contested Roll Calls in 1934-35

Roll-call no.	Yr./vol./p. in *Diario de Sesiones*	Date of vote	Issue	Factors	
				I	II
1	34/I/3	10 Apr 34	Officership: provisional president	(.77)	(.57)
2	34/I/135	26 Apr 34	Credentials: Rafael N. Lencinas	(-.61)	-.49
3	34/I/170-71	27 Apr 34	Officership: president	(.78)	(.57)
4	34/I/172	27 Apr 34	Officership: vice-president	(.52)	(.69)
5	34/I/172-73	27 Apr 34	Officership: 2nd vice-president	(.70)	(.53)
6	34/I/245-46	9 May 34	Officership: secretary	.03	(.70)
7	34/I/287-88	9 May 34	Information on state of seige	(.69)	(.56)
8	34/II/461	14-15 July 34	Approval of state of seige	(.70)	(.55)
9	34/III/410	18 July 34	Justice of the peace	(.67)	(.58)
10	34/III/524	19 July 34	Duty-free passage for vessels on religious pilgrimages	(.66)	(.59)
11	34/III/802	1 Aug 34	Interpellation on existence of paramilitary groups	(-.66)	(-.58)
12	34/IV/673	24 Aug 34	Control of commerce in grain	(-.71)	(-.50)
13	34/V/498-99	13 Sept 34	Provincial retention of rights to petroleum	(.57)	(.72)
14	34/V/622-23	18 Sept 34	Order of business; interrogation about YPF	(.51)	(.68)
15	34/VI/354	26-27 Sept 34	Loan to local packinghouse	.49	(.72)
16	34/VI/578	28 Sept 34	Power of congressional investigating committees, especially regarding meat trade	(-.76)	(-.54)
17	34/VI/635	29-30 Sept 34	Order of business	(.56)	(.74)

18	34/VI/638	29-30 Sept 34	Loan to local packinghouse	(.58)	(.70)
19	34/VI/715	29-30 Sept 34	Adjournment	-.44	(-.77)
20	34/VI/826-27	29-30 Sept 34	Consideration of pension bill	-.48	(-.74)
21	34/VII/441	30 Nov 34	Tax-sharing for Buenos Aires City	-.49	(-.59)
22	34/VII/523	3 Dec 34	Provincial taxes and autonomy	-.42	(-.67)
23	34/VII/587	5 Dec 34	10-year duration of tax law	(.55)	(.67)
24	34/VII/703	6 Dec 34	Tax on new grape orchards for producing wine	(.50)	(.61)
25	34/VIII/43-44	20 Dec 34	Sales tax	(.70)	(.54)
26	34/VIII/726	26 Feb 35	Senate revision in bill on pensions	-.38	-.45
27	35/I/2	26 Apr 35	Officership: president	(.62)	(.67)
28	35/I/2	26 Apr 35	Officership: vice-president	(.62)	(.64)
29	35/I/3	26 Apr 35	Officership: 2nd vice-president	(.62)	(.66)
30	35/II/509	9 Aug 35	Consideration of municipal transport bill	(.54)	(.68)
31	35/II/859	22 Aug 35	Tax on new plantings of yerba maté	(.56)	.33
32	35/IV/173-74	24-25 Sept 35	Information on construction of canals	(-.71)	-.44
33	35/IV/209	24-25 Sept 35	Closing debate on national transport bill	(.75)	(.55)
34	35/IV/210-11	24-25 Sept 35	Creation of Comisión Nacional de Coordinación de Transportes	(.64)	(.62)
35	35/IV/348	25-26 Sept 35	Consideration of urban transport bill	(.74)	.45
36	35/IV/640-41	27 Sept 35	Designate for presidential succession	(.86)	.18
37	35/IV/641-42	27 Sept 35	Designate for presidential succession	(.88)	.23
			% of total variance explained	39.2	35.6
			% of factor variance explained	52.4	47.6

Table C-17. Rotated Factor Matrix for Contested Roll Calls in 1936-37

Roll-call no.	Yr./vol./p. in *Diario de Sesiones*	Date of vote	Issue	Factors I	Factors II
1	36/I/7	25 Apr 36	Postponement of debate on credentials: Emilio J. Hardoy	(.97)	-.06
2	36/I/8	25 Apr 36	Officership: president	(.96)	-.06
3	36/I/9	25 Apr 36	Officership: vice-president	(.97)	-.06
4	36/I/9-10	25 Apr 36	Officership: 2nd vice-president	(.96)	-.07
5	36/I/840	17 June 36	Approval of elections in Buenos Aires Province	(-.95)	.10
6	36/IV/410	30 Oct 36	Intervention and elections in Santa Fe	(.88)	-.00
7	36/IV/488	4 Nov 36	Application of Ley de Residencia	(.87)	-.19
8	36/IV/922	9 Dec 36	Intensification of anticommunist campaign	(-.87)	.08
9	35/V/168-69	15 Dec 36	Presidential objections to bill on private chauffeurs	.33	-.23
10	36/V/442	18-19 Dec 36	Increase in size of federal court at La Plata; budget	(-.96)	.02
11	36/VI/106	29-30 Dec 36	Automobile tax; budget	(.73)	-.16
12	36/VI/474	20 Jan 37	Postponement of debate on financial supervision of autonomous institutions	-.43	(.62)
13	37/I/7	5 May 37	Officership: provisional president	(.97)	-.04
14	37/I/8-9	5 May 37	Officership: president	(.97)	-.04
15	37/I/9-10	5 May 37	Officership: vice-president	(.97)	-.03
16	37/I/10	5 May 37	Officership: 2nd vice-president	(.96)	-.03
17	37/I/623	11 June 37	Wages for government workers	(.74)	-.22
18	37/I/1113	4 Aug 37	Quorum	.31	(.83)
19	37/II/686	21-22 Jan 38	Minimum wage for government workers	(.76)	-.24
			% of total variance explained	71.7	7.0
			% of factor variance explained	91.1	8.9

Table C-18. Rotated Factor Matrix for Contested Roll Calls in 1938-39

Roll-call no.	Yr./vol./p. in Diario de Sesiones	Date of vote	Issue	Factors				
				I	II	III	IV	V
1	38/I/8-9	26 Apr 38	Officership: provisional president	(.90)	.26	.24	-.14	.02
2	38/I/16	26 Apr 38	Procedure for incorporation of new deputies	(.90)	.26	.24	-.13	.00
3	38/I/21-22	26 Apr 38	Officership: president	(.90)	.26	.24	-.14	.02
4	38/I/22-23	26 Apr 38	Officership: vice-president	(.90)	.25	.21	-.12	.01
5	38/I/23	26 Apr 38	Officership: 2nd vice-president	(.87)	.25	.18	-.17	.09
6	38/I/147-48	13 May 38	Approval of elections in Entre Ríos	(-.86)	-.25	-.23	.11	-.02
7	38/I/151	13 May 38	Consideration of elections in Entre Ríos	(.57)	.07	.19	-.61	.10
8	38/II/11	14 June 38	Publication of letters on miscarriage of justice	(-.63)	-.09	-.05	.40	.07
9	38/II/483-84	30 June-1 July 38	Approval of elections in San Juan	(.88)	.24	.29	-.08	.02
10	38/III/70	20 July 38	Creation of federal police force	.36	.39	(.53)	-.07	.06
11	38/III/447	3 Aug 38	Subsidy for Círculo Militar	.31	.39	.47	-.04	.19
12	38/III/795	11 Aug 38	Bond issue for municipality of Buenos Aires City	(.80)	.28	.23	-.09	.09
13	38/IV/114	23 Aug 38	Reconstruction of Ferrocarril Trasandino Argentino	(-.81)	-.10	.03	.19	.15
14	38/IV/188	24 Aug 38	Acquisition of Ferrocarril Trasandino	(.90)	.10	.02	-.16	-.13
15	38/IV/454-55	1-2 Sept 38	Acquisition of Ferrocarril Central Córdoba	(.81)	.27	.16	-.05	.01
16	38/IV/460-61	1-2 Sept 38	Financing purchase of Ferrocarril Central Córdoba	(.82)	.30	.12	-.07	-.00
17	38/IV/898	14 Sept 38	Regulations and financing for middle-level schools	(-.64)	-.11	-.27	.35	.23
18	38/IV/902-3	14 Sept 38	Regulations and financing for middle-level schools	(-.59)	-.18	-.27	.44	.16

Table C-18. 1938-39 (continued)

Roll-call no.	Yr./vol./p. in Diario de Sesiones	Date of vote	Issue	Factors				
				I	II	III	IV	V
19	38/V/49-50	15 Sept 38	Senate revision in bill for water exploration in Catamarca	(-.58)	-.27	-.11	-.06	.07
20	38/V/285-86	20-21 Sept 38	7% ceiling on mortgage rates	(-.71)	-.34	-.31	.20	.14
21	38/V/294	20-21 Sept 38	3-year limit on mortgage liability	(-.67)	-.28	-.28	.17	.24
22	38/V/295	20-21 Sept 38	Procedures for default on mortgage payments	(-.73)	-.32	-.27	.13	.16
23	38/V/723	22 Sept 38	Consideration of tax on wine production	(-.63)	-.12	-.24	.46	-.01
24	38/V/754	22 Sept 38	Extension of discussion on antilocust bill	-.09	-.03	.45	-.09	.04
25	38/V/909	26 Sept 38	Consideration of political amnesty	(-.80)	-.19	-.23	.13	-.04
26	38/V/971-72	27-28 Sept 38	Order of business; pensions for police	(.74)	.18	.11	-.03	-.08
27	38/VI/96	28-29 Sept 38	Investigation of Instituto Movilizador de Inversiones Bancarias	(-.73)	-.35	-.19	.16	.04
28	38/VI/144-45	29 Sept 38	Tax on radio advertisements for care of school-age children	-.15	.03	(-.57)	.09	.07
29	38/VI/446-47	15 Dec 38	International postal rates	(-.68)	-.12	-.38	.01	-.03
30	38/VI/452	15 Dec 38	Official welcome for immigrants, especially German Jews	(-.71)	-.08	-.41	.00	-.03
31	38/VI/456	15 Dec 38	Consideration of political amnesty	(-.66)	-.13	-.46	.05	.04
32	38/VI/659	19 Dec 38	Budget bill for 1939	(.81)	.28	.24	-.13	.04
33	38/VI/883	21 Dec 38	Creation of new federal courts	(.67)	.34	.23	-.18	-.08
34	38/VII/488-89	23-24 Dec 38	Salaries for federal judges	.12	-.06	.30	.27	-.24
35	38/VII/492	23-24 Dec 38	Increase in salary for military doctors	(-.64)	-.05	.14	.04	.08
36	38/VII/495	23-24 Dec 38	Order of business; budget	.38	.18	.27	.31	-.30
37	38/VII/540-41	16 Jan 39	Pensions for police in Buenos Aires City	.29	(.89)	-.01	-.06	.03

No.	Reference	Date	Description					
38	38/VII/544	16 Jan 39	Adjournment; pensions for police	.28	(.89)	-.05	-.09	.03
39	38/VII/560	17 Jan 39	Pensions for police in Buenos Aires City	.40	(.76)	.16	-.10	-.10
40	38/VII/599	18 Jan 39	Order of business; pensions for magistrates	(.67)	.41	.18	-.18	-.10
41	38/VII/601	18 Jan 39	Order of business; pensions for sailors and journalists	-.34	-.28	-.20	(.66)	-.03
42	38/VII/625	18 Jan 39	Pensions for magistrates and diplomats	(.63)	.49	.13	-.13	-.09
43	39/I/4	3 May 39	Officership: president	(.87)	.28	.21	-.10	.01
44	39/I/5	3 May 39	Officership: vice-president	(.87)	.26	.21	-.10	.02
45	39/I/5	3 May 39	Officership: 2nd vice-president	(.87)	.26	.20	-.09	.02
46	39/II/116	6 July 39	Order of business; political amnesty	(-.72)	-.20	-.23	.25	-.01
47	39/II/126	6 July 39	Examination of national accounts	(.54)	.04	.28	-.29	.06
48	39/II/266	12 July 39	Spending on official residences and offices	(-.68)	-.30	-.33	.15	-.10
49	39/II/375	14 July 39	Archivist for Chamber of Deputies	.12	.29	.36	-.11	-.10
50	39/II/650	2 Aug 39	Investigation of political repression in Buenos Aires Province	(-.81)	-.21	-.21	.21	-.13
51	39/II/655	2 Aug 39	Investigation of political repression in Buenos Aires Province	(-.82)	-.23	-.23	.16	-.11
52	39/II/714	3 Aug 39	Eviction of colonists from state-owned land	(-.69)	-.24	-.21	.18	-.05
53	39/II/767	4 Aug 39	Consideration of rural colonization bill	.02	.01	.09	-.06	(.73)
54	39/III/143	18 Aug 39	Wage settlements for railroad workers	-.08	.05	.09	-.01	(-.52)
55	39/III/246	23 Aug 39	Order of business	(.85)	.25	.20	-.12	.04
56	39/III/281	23 Aug 39	Wage settlements for railroad workers	(-.72)	-.16	-.03	.05	-.07
57	39/III/284	23 Aug 39	Wage settlements for railroad workers	(.71)	.16	.05	.07	-.00
58	39/III/885	5 Sept 39	Consideration of violation of parliamentary privilege	(.85)	.11	-.02	-.09	.00
59	39/III/897	5 Sept 39	Consideration of violation of parliamentary privilege	(-.80)	-.30	-.18	.09	-.21
60	39/III/903	5 Sept 39	Investigation of violation of parliamentary privilege	(-.59)	-.29	-.27	.03	-.30

Table C-18. 1938-39 *(continued)*

Roll-call no.	Yr./vol./p. in *Diario de Sesiones*	Date of vote	Issue	Factor				
				I	II	III	IV	V
61	39/III/910-11	5 Sept 39	Order of business; to avoid expression of anti-Nazi sympathy	(.72)	.20	.26	-.18	.09
62	39/IV/56	8 Sept 39	Information on intervention in San Juan	(-.76)	-.33	-.18	.11	-.09
63	39/IV/182	13 Sept 39	Order of business	(-.69)	-.24	-.26	.29	-.17
64	39/IV/195	13 Sept 39	Order of business	(.71)	.31	.29	-.06	.17
65	39/IV/196	13 Sept 39	Order of business	(.70)	.30	.29	-.05	.16
66	39/IV/249	14 Sept 39	Order of business	(-.71)	-.20	.22	.01	.08
67	39/IV/254	14 Sept 39	Order of business	(-.66)	-.31	-.19	.12	-.09
68	39/IV/391-92	19 Sept 39	Declaration of political amnesty	(-.90)	-.28	-.25	.13	-.04
69	39/IV/541	21 Sept 39	Order of business	(-.76)	-.29	-.13	.16	-.12
70	39/IV/657	22-23 Sept 39	Revenue-sharing procedures	(.63)	-.01	-.16	-.24	-.12
71	39/V/34	28 Sept 39	Order of business	-.48	-.11	-.15	(.50)	-.12
72	39/V/38	28 Sept 39	Order of business	(-.81)	-.16	-.17	.26	-.05
73	39/V/39	28 Sept 39	Order of business	(.65)	.17	.08	-.12	.31
74	39/V/39-40	28 Sept 39	Order of business	(.82)	.17	.21	-.18	.08
75	39/V/42-43	28 Sept 39	Order of business	(-.84)	-.17	-.22	.20	-.05
76	39/V/65	28 Sept 39	Order of business	.44	.12	.32	.33	.01
77	39/V/191	29-30 Sept 39	National highway system	(.69)	.20	.12	-.08	.38
78	39/V/194	29-30 Sept 39	Tax on petroleum	(-.83)	-.04	-.05	.25	-.03
79	39/V/247	29-30 Sept 39	Granting of pension, despite dubious documentation	(.59)	.06	.22	-.26	.11
			% of total variance explained	47.3	8.0	5.9	4.3	2.4
			% of factor variance explained	69.7	11.8	8.7	6.3	3.6

Table C-19. Rotated Factor Matrix for Contested Roll Calls in 1940-41

Roll call no.	Yr./vol./p. in Diario de Sesiones	Date of vote	Issue	Factor				
				I	II	III	IV	V
1	40/I/2	26 Apr 40	Officership: provisional president	(.88)	.36	.11	-.04	-.09
2	40/I/3-4	26 Apr 40	Officership: president	(.89)	.35	.11	-.02	-.08
3	40/I/4-5	26 Apr 40	Officership: vice-president	(-.79)	(-.54)	-.02	-.20	-.03
4	40/I/5-6	26 Apr 40	Officership: vice-president	(.56)	(.64)	-.02	.34	.04
5	40/I/6	26 Apr 40	Officership: 2nd vice-president	(.55)	(.63)	-.05	.27	.07
6	40/I/198	29 May 40	Consideration of declaring solidarity with Netherlands	(.80)	.29	.12	-.12	-.13
7	40/I/400	7-8 June 40	Prohibition of war propaganda in Argentina	(-.80)	-.37	-.16	.12	.08
8	40/I/400-401	7-8 June 40	Declaring internal disturbances illegal	(-.52)	(-.50)	-.15	.34	.14
9	40/I/402	7-8 June 40	Protection of Argentine neutrality	(.73)	(.57)	.02	.18	.03
10	40/I/403	7-8 June 40	Authorization of measures against war propaganda	(-.81)	-.35	-.09	.12	.04
11	40/II/123	4 July 40	Information on policy for middle-level schools	(-.61)	(-.50)	-.02	-.13	-.11
12	40/II/271	11 July 40	Consideration of survey of Argentine economy	-.13	-.14	-.01	-.30	.13
13	40/II/317-18	12 July 40	Regulations for diphtheria vaccinations	-.27	-.48	.04	-.09	.37
14	40/II/481	19 July 40	Loans to corn producers	.17	.32	-.11	-.22	.06
15	40/II/749	1 Aug 40	Changes in parliamentary procedure	.20	.22	.02	.04	-.20
16	40/II/776	1 Aug 40	Changes in parliamentary procedure	.03	.07	(.94)	-.04	.05
17	40/II/777	1 Aug 40	Changes in parliamentary procedure	.04	.04	(.95)	-.05	.03
18	40/II/777	1 Aug 40	Changes in parliamentary procedure	.05	.06	(.91)	-.10	.04
19	40/II/778-79	1 Aug 40	Changes in parliamentary procedure	.16	.12	(.85)	-.06	-.08
20	40/II/780	1 Aug 40	Changes in parliamentary procedure	.12	.07	(.87)	-.02	-.00

Table C-19. 1940-41 *(continued)*

Roll-call no.	Yr./vol./p. in *Diario de Sesiones*	Date of vote	Issue	I	II	III	IV	V
						Factors		
21	40/III/134	16 Aug 40	Changes in parliamentary procedure	.09	.24	.05	-.05	.43
22	40/III/263	21 Aug 40	Changes in parliamentary procedure	.11	-.22	(.59)	.06	.09
23	40/III/946	6 Sept 40	Exonerating minister of war from land purchase scandal (El Palomar)	.37	.08	-.03	(.70)	.09
24	40/IV/321	18 Sept 40	Restitution of illegally collected taxes	-.11	-.05	-.08	.05	(-.68)
25	40/IV/389	19 Sept 40	Restitution of illegally collected taxes	.19	-.02	-.07	-.00	(.67)
26	40/IV/451-52	20 Sept 40	Permanent session till September 30	.06	.18	-.00	-.26	-.29
27	40/IV/452	20 Sept 40	Order of business	(-.56)	-.02	-.03	-.10	.21
28	40/IV/599-600	24 Sept 40	Order of business	-.42	-.11	-.09	.19	-.14
29	40/IV/658	25 Sept 40	Order of business	(-.81)	-.04	-.04	-.07	.01
30	40/IV/882	26-27 Sept 40	Investigation of concessions made to CHADE (electric power company)	.08	.18	-.06	.60	-.14
31	40/V/206-7	4 Dec 40	Subsidy for tourist hotels in Northwest	-.29	.07	-.23	.18	.15
32	40/V/578	8 Jan 41	Officership: president	(.83)	.32	.12	-.02	.01
33	40/V/579	8 Jan 41	Adjournment, instead of interpellation	(-.77)	-.08	.03	.03	-.11
34	40/V/622	9-10 Jan 41	Political situation in Santa Fe	(.80)	.18	.08	.00	.03
35	40/V/869-70	16 Jan 41	Recess; intervention in Santa Fe	(-.80)	-.36	-.15	-.00	-.03
36	40/VI/99	6 Feb 41	Intervention in Santa Fe	(-.65)	(-.54)	-.07	-.15	-.05
37	40/VI/152	12 Feb 41	Intervention in Santa Fe	(-.68)	-.49	-.00	-.17	-.17
38	40/VI/390	5 Mar 41	Order of business	(.93)	.08	.06	-.00	.05
39	40/VI/390-91	5 Mar 41	Order of business	(.93)	.06	.03	-.00	.04
40	40/VI/424	6 Mar 41	Order of business	(-.78)	(-.53)	-.00	-.19	-.08
41	40/VI/467	6 Mar 41	Intervention in Santa Fe	(.90)	.10	-.00	.01	-.03

42	40/VI/540	12 Mar 41	Consideration of budget bill for 1941	(-.74)	(-.52)	.06	-.22	-.05
43	40/VI/559	12 Mar 41	Role of Congress in declaring presidential succession	(.91)	.00	-.01	.11	.07
44	40/VI/848	3 Apr 41	Leave for Mauricio A. Questa	(-.65)	-.04	-.14	.06	-.15
45	40/VI/938	18 Apr 41	Emergency relief for Corrientes and Santa Fe	(.68)	.44	.09	.23	.20
46	40/VI/938	18 Apr 41	Emergency relief for Corrientes and Santa Fe	(.69)	.44	.10	.22	.21
47	40/VI/966	24 Apr 41	Emergency relief for Corrientes and Santa Fe	(-.64)	(-.51)	-.01	-.22	-.13
48	41/I/2	26 Apr 41	Officership: president	(.62)	(.71)	.04	.08	.06
49	41/I/3	26 Apr 41	Officership: vice-president	(.59)	(.68)	.08	.10	.03
50	41/I/3	26 Apr 41	Officership: vice-president	(.58)	(.71)	.05	.06	.03
51	41/I/370	6 June 41	Interpellation on prohibition of Nazi propaganda	(-.78)	-.05	-.02	-.02	.05
52	41/II/502-3	23 July 41	Power of Comisión Investigadora de Actividades Antiargentinas	-.16	(.66)	.09	.30	-.08
53	41/II/669	29 July 41	Restriction on independent labor (trabajo a domicilio)	.02	-.23	-.08	-.46	.01
54	41/III/837-38	3 Sept 41	Construction of building for Ministry of Agriculture in Rosario	.03	-.01	.10	-.32	-.14
55	41/IV/207	9 Sept 41	Order of business	(-.55)	-.03	-.22	-.15	.10
56	41/V/165-66	23 Sept 41	Consideration of resolution on contracts with electric companies	-.06	.03	.05	(-.56)	.43
57	41/V/270	24 Sept 41	Order of business	(.82)	.28	.06	.26	.05
58	41/V/271	24 Sept 41	Order of business	(.81)	.34	-.01	.29	.08
			% of total variance explained	35.6	12.7	8.3	4.9	3.5
			% of factor variance explained	54.9	19.5	12.8	7.5	5.3

Table C-20. Rotated Factor Matrix for Contested Roll Calls in 1942

Roll-call no.	Yr./vol./p. in *Diario* de *Sesiones*	Date of vote	Issue	Factors I	Factors II	Factors III
1	42/I/2	25 Apr 42	Officership: provisional president	(.96)	.13	.21
2	42/I/5	25 Apr 42	Officership: vice-president	.25	(.93)	-.06
3	42/I/5	25 Apr 42	Officership: 2nd vice-president	.25	(.93)	-.08
4	42/I/917	17 June 42	Dismissal of stenographers from secret session (on foreign affairs)	(-.93)	-.12	-.23
5	42/I/922-23	17 June 42	Dismissal of stenographers from secret session (on foreign affairs)	(-.90)	-.12	-.26
6	42/II/433	1 July 42	State of seige	(.88)	.15	.24
7	42/III/113	31 July 42	Constitutionality of presidential policies	(.72)	.06	.06
8	42/III/316-17	6 Aug 42	Hospital usage tax in Buenos Aires City	-.49	(-.74)	-.04
9	42/III/470	11 Aug 42	Investigation on purchase of sunflower seeds	(.64)	(-.59)	.04
10	42/III/701	14 Aug 42	Order of business; land tenancy regulations	-.42	(.51)	.08
11	42/IV/208	1 Sept 42	Inheritance tax (status of concubines)	.25	-.01	(.89)
12	42/IV/214	1 Sept 42	Inheritance tax (status of common-law spouses)	.39	-.10	(.81)
13	42/IV/295	2-3 Sept 42	Consideration of expulsion of foreigners	(.79)	.11	.07
14	42/V/44	15 Sept 42	Abolition of Junta Reguladora de Vinos	(-.85)	-.11	-.14
15	42/VI/84	29-30 Sept 42	Hemispheric solidarity: approving Pact of Rio de Janeiro	(.90)	.09	.29
16	42/VI/84	29-30 Sept 42	Hemispheric solidarity: approving Pact of Rio de Janeior	(.90)	.10	.29
17	42/VI/85	29-30 Sept 42	Rupture of diplomatic relations with Axis powers	(.94)	.11	.22
18	42/VI/233	30 Sept 42	Order of business	(-.74)	.03	-.29
			% of total variance explained	52.4	16.8	11.2
			% of factor variance explained	65.2	20.8	14.0

Table C-21. Rotated Factor Matrix for Contested Roll Calls in 1946-47

Roll-call no.	Yr./vol./p. in Diario de Sesiones	Date of vote	Issue	Factors I	II	III	IV	V
1	46/II/366	2-3 Aug 46	Presidential authority for setting price ceilings	-.46	-.22	-.43	-.32	-.05
2	46/III/274	22 Aug 46	Naming street for Hipólito Yrigoyen	.15	.13	.13	(.88)	-.03
3	46/III/275	22 Aug 46	Naming street for Hipólito Yrigoyen	.15	.15	.12	(.87)	.11
4	46/III/335-36	23 Aug 46	Information about bureaucratic restrictions on port of Rosario	(-.54)	-.31	-.32	-.19	-.14
5	46/III/460	28 Aug 46	Consideration of declaration in favor of constructing a hospital in Rosario	(.57)	.43	.23	.17	-.02
6	46/V/62	20 Sept 46	Information on acquisition of Compañía Unión Telefónica	.36	.34	.48	.09	.15
7	46/V/236-37	24 Sept 46	Consideration of bill to abolish Ley de Residencia	(.64)	.20	.39	-.09	.12
8	46/V/334-35	25 Sept 46	Solidarity with Guatemala in dispute with Great Britain	.48	.38	.43	.16	.12
9	46/V/447	26 Sept 46	Consideration of bill to abolish Ley de Residencia	(.75)	.24	.32	.19	.01
10	46/V/531	26 Sept 46	Exemptions from antitrust provisions	-.41	-.33	-.46	-.10	.17
11	46/V/761-62	27-28 Sept 46	Consideration of bill to abolish Ley de Residencia	(.52)	.07	.30	.23	.05
12	46/VI/69	1 Oct 46	Investigation of export-permit practices	.35	.27	(.52)	.02	-.39
13	46/VI/70	1 Oct 46	Investigation of export-permit practices	.35	.30	(.61)	.05	-.31
14	46/VI/73	1 Oct 46	Celebration of October 17	.49	.17	.31	.27	-.21
15	46/VI/223	3 Oct 46	Consideration of bill to abolish Ley de Residencia	(.61)	.21	.24	-.02	.13
16	46/VI/388	24 Oct 46	Consideration of resolutions	(-.64)	-.29	-.40	-.23	-.16
17	46/VI/418	24 Oct 46	Settlement of strike by packinghouse workers	(.55)	.09	.41	.19	.14
18	46/VI/492	30 Oct 46	Authority of parliamentary investigating committees	(.61)	.26	.38	.14	.15

Table C-21. 1946-47 (continued)

Roll-call no.	Yr./vol./p. in Diario de Sesiones	Date of vote	Issue	Factors				
				I	II	III	IV	V
19	46/VI/524	31 Oct 46	Investigation of alleged judicial abuses	(.62)	.25	.42	.18	-.00
20	46/VI/526	31 Oct 46	Consideration of possible violation of military secret	(-.66)	-.23	-.43	-.13	.06
21	46/VI/530	31 Oct 46	Investigation of export-permit practices	(.66)	.31	.48	.14	-.09
22	46/VI/562	6 Nov 46	Consideration of resolutions	.44	.35	(.56)	.16	.22
23	46/VI/562	6 Nov 46	Consideration of resolutions	.46	.29	(.58)	.16	.18
24	46/VI/644	7 Nov 46	Political agitation in packinghouse union	.15	.18	.11	.05	(.62)
25	46/VI/672	7 Nov 46	Governance of packinghouse union	.43	.33	(.75)	.18	.13
26	46/VI/672	7 Nov 46	Payment of compulsory wage increases	.45	.31	(.73)	.16	.13
27	46/VI/672-73	7 Nov 46	Payment of compulsory wage increases	.43	.33	(.75)	.18	.13
28	46/VI/673	7 Nov 46	Payment of wages during lockouts	.43	.33	(.75)	.18	.13
29	46/VI/673	7 Nov 46	Intervention in packinghouses	.43	.33	(.75)	.18	.13
30	46/VI/732	13 Nov 46	Delegation to presidential inauguration in Mexico	(-.68)	-.36	-.42	-.14	-.01
31	46/VI/801	15 Nov 46	Decoration for General Francisco Franco	(-.69)	-.21	-.42	-.08	-.03
32	46/VII/370	21 Nov 46	Consideration of ordinance on taxis in Buenos Aires City	(.69)	.17	.31	.15	.23
33	46/VII/372	21 Nov 46	Information on highway programs	(.60)	.29	.44	.10	.10
34	46/VII/376	21 Nov 46	Publication of protest by former federal judge	(-.52)	-.35	-.42	-.18	-.18
35	46/VII/573	28-29 Nov 46	Retroactive pay (from 1 July 1946) for railroad workers	(.66)	.40	.36	.09	.07
36	46/VII/702	29 Nov 46	Order of business	(-.69)	-.33	-.30	-.08	-.06
37	46/VIII/377	11 Dec 46	Public funds for Círculo de Aeronáutica	(.61)	.32	.34	.04	-.02
38	46/VIII/458-59	12 Dec 46	Subsidy for Asociación de Propietarios de Caminos	.41	.32	.31	.21	.19
39	46/X/252	6 Feb 47	Governance of universities	(-.57)	-.35	-.33	-.05	-.11

No.	Reference	Date	Description					
40	46/X/350	12 Feb 47	Governance of universities	(.68)	.30	.12	.10	.02
41	46/X/457-58	14 Feb 47	3-week congressional recess	.49	.32	.15	.21	.05
42	47/I/158	7 May 47	Consideration of bill to abolish Ley de Residencia	(.61)	.38	.37	.15	-.01
43	47/I/175-76	7 May 47	Fixed fees for solicitors	.33	(.50)	.23	.38	-.07
44	47/I/249	8-9 May 47	Salaries for judges in interior	.16	(.72)	.35	.12	.21
45	47/I/350	8-9 May 47	Government control over shares in Sociedad Mixta Siderurgia Argentina	.16	(.62)	.40	.11	.16
46	47/I/515-16	11 June 47	Homage to Basque labor strike	(-.67)	-.46	-.37	-.09	-.03
47	47/I/519-20	11 June 47	Shutting off polemic on Perón	(.64)	.46	.40	.07	.06
48	47/I/524	11 June 47	Shutting off polemic on Perón	(.58)	(.51)	.48	.14	.11
49	47/I/525-26	11 June 47	Investigation of charges on Perón's attack on deputy	(.61)	(.50)	.42	.14	.08
50	47/I/539	11 June 47	Abusive language in parliament	(.51)	(.64)	.33	.13	.08
51	47/I/539-40	11 June 47	Abusive language in parliament	(.59)	(.57)	.35	.18	.06
52	47/I/611	12 June 47	Political situation in Córdoba	.35	(.68)	.38	.10	.13
53	47/I/766	19 June 47	Publication of railroad workers' statement on cost of living	(.64)	.48	.21	.08	.20
54	47/I/767	19 June 47	Publication of railroad workers' statement on Ley de Residencia	(.66)	.49	.27	.08	.22
55	47/I/767-68	19 June 47	Publication of railroad workers' statement on Franco regime	(.65)	.46	.31	.08	.21
56	47/I/773	19 June 47	Information on government of Buenos Aires City	(.65)	.41	.36	-.02	.17
57	47/I/821	25-26 June 47	Homage to people of Paraguay	.47	(.54)	.28	.13	-.12
58	47/I/829	25-26 June 47	Homage to people of Paraguay	(-.71)	-.48	-.26	-.06	.03
59	47/I/834	25-26 June 47	Order of business; debate on foreign policy	(.65)	.44	.25	.08	.00
60	47/II/326	3 July 47	Order of business; commerce in grain	(.57)	(.53)	.34	.09	.13
61	47/II/467	16 July 47	Order of business; violation of parliamentary privilege	(.56)	.48	.42	.17	.14
62	47/II/545	17 July 47	Order of business; regulation of political parties	(.58)	.36	.40	.17	.02
63	47/II/661	23-24 July 47	Consideration of tenant protection (or control of universities)	.41	(.70)	.23	.21	-.06

Table C-21. 1946-47 (continued)

Roll-call no.	Yr./vol./p. in Diario de Sesiones	Date of vote	Issue	Factors				
				I	II	III	IV	V
64	47/III/133	7-8 Aug 47	Information on intervention in universities	(.65)	.47	.26	.05	.02
65	47/III/134	7-8 Aug 47	Information on intervention in universities	(.71)	(.50)	.26	.04	-.04
66	47/III/285	13 Aug 47	Leave of absence for Joaquín Díaz de Vivar	(-.68)	-.33	-.23	-.16	.08
67	47/III/439	20-21 Aug 47	Leave of absence for Joaquín Díaz de Vivar	(-.62)	(-.54)	-.39	-.08	.05
68	47/III/462	20-21 Aug 47	Policy on public land in southern territories	(.57)	.43	.37	.06	-.07
69	47/III/470	20-21 Aug 47	Consideration of interpellation on agrarian policy	(.63)	.47	.31	.05	-.05
70	47/III/534	21 Aug 47	Pensions for civil service	-.21	-.26	(-.56)	.03	.22
71	47/III/537	21 Aug 47	Pensions for civil service	-.27	-.27	-.46	.03	-.01
72	47/III/549	21 Aug 47	Pensions for civil service	.44	.43	(.51)	.14	-.07
73	47/III/575	22 Aug 47	Pensions for civil service	(.51)	.23	.48	-.12	.04
74	47/III/597	22 Aug 47	Pensions for civil service	.44	.44	.44	.10	-.09
75	47/IV/313	10-11 Sept 47	Order of business; Ley de Residencia	(.65)	.38	.36	.11	-.00
76	47/IV/434	12 Sept 47	Order of business; Ley de Residencia	(.59)	.37	.34	.01	-.13
77	47/IV/436	12 Sept 47	Order of business; pensions	(-.54)	-.37	-.37	-.04	.21

No.	ID	Date	Description					
78	47/IV/797	24 Sept 47	Consideration of road and sewer construction	(-.65)	-.40	-.34	-.14	.05
79	47/V/287	25 Sept 47	Compatibility of professorships for duputies	(.52)	(.65)	.25	.12	-.09
80	47/V/290-91	25 Sept 47	Senate revision in bill on governance of universities	.36	(.80)	.17	.14	-.06
81	47/V/292	25 Sept 47	Senate revision in bill on governance of universities	.37	(.78)	.11	.18	-.04
82	47/V/600	26 Sept 47	Consideration of agrarian problems, especially land tenancy	-.09	-.37	-.14	.19	-.04
83	47/V/605	26 Sept 47	Order of business	(.60)	.38	.32	.13	-.16
84	47/VI/38	28-29 Sept 47	Congressional relationship to military	(.62)	(.57)	.22	.09	.05
85	47/VI/51	28-29 Sept 47	Autonomy of congressional committees	(.66)	(.51)	.30	.07	-.07
86	47/VI/92	28-29 Sept 47	Order of business	.34	(.74)	.34	.06	.12
87	47/VI/92	28-29 Sept 47	Order of business	.33	(.74)	.37	.12	.08
88	47/VI/95	28-29 Sept 47	Order of business; budget for 1948	(.65)	.48	.32	.13	-.00
89	47/VI/582	28-29 Sept 47	Compensation for school principals	.49	.17	.21	.19	-.19
90	47/VI/587	28-29 Sept 47	Budget bill for 1948	(-.50)	(-.60)	-.31	-.22	-.01
			% of total variance explained	29.0	18.0	15.3	3.7	2.0
			% of factor variance explained	42.7	26.4	22.4	5.4	3.0

Table C-22. Rotated Factor Matrix for Contested Roll Calls in 1948-49

Roll-call no.	Yr./vol./p. in Diario de Sesiones	Date of vote	Issue	Factors				
				I	II	III	IV	V
1	48/I/396	19 May 48	Order of business; bill on rural rents	(-.56)	.45	.29	-.33	.32
2	48/I/407	19 May 48	Interpellation of minister of foreign relations	(-.61)	.38	.30	-.32	.33
3	48/I/474-75	20 May 48	Postponement of debate on recognition of Israel	(.61)	-.40	-.24	.32	-.31
4	48/I/509	2 June 48	Publication of Socialist statement on economic policy	-.49	.49	.29	-.36	.34
5	48/I/582-83	2 June 48	Consideration of female suffrage	(.53)	-.38	-.34	.34	-.37
6	48/I/597	2 June 48	Support for minister of foreign relations	(.53)	-.49	-.32	.36	-.27
7	48/I/734	10 June 48	Role of Congress; purchase of British-owned railroads	(-.56)	.39	.40	-.35	.27
8	48/I/739	10 June 48	Statement by Virgilio Filippo	(.56)	-.38	-.39	.28	-.26
9	48/II/1131	23 June 48	Adjournment; or Perón's criticism of political parties	(-.51)	.44	.33	-.37	.33
10	48/II/1357	24-25 June 48	Budget for Ministry of Foreign Affairs	(-.50)	.44	.36	-.29	.32
11	48/II/1440	24-25 June 48	Subsidy to sporting clubs	.21	(-.64)	-.19	.20	-.23
12	48/II/1553	30 June 48	Alleged unethical conduct by opposition deputy	.46	-.47	-.43	.40	-.24
13	48/II/1554	30 June 48	Alleged unethical conduct by opposition deputy	.47	-.47	-.44	.39	-.24
14	48/III/1696	14 July 48	Censorship of speech in parliament	(.53)	-.40	-.31	.34	-.43
15	48/III/1877	16 July 48	Regulation of tenancy evictions	-.15	.41	.30	-.23	(.62)
16	48/III/1879	16 July 48	Regulation of tenancy evictions	-.32	.45	.31	-.37	(.52)
17	48/III/1881	16 July 48	Regulation of tenancy evictions	.36	-.23	-.19	.27	(-.62)
18	48/III/1882	16 July 48	Regulation of tenancy evictions	-.28	.45	.29	-.37	(.52)
19	48/III/2046	22 July 48	Order of business; pensions for laborers	-.47	.49	.28	-.29	.37
20	48/III/2055	22 July 48	Alleged unethical conduct by opposition deputy	.27	(-.53)	-.35	.34	-.24

No.	Code	Date	Description					
21	48/IV/2778	18 Aug 48	Publication of statement by Socialist party	-.47	.40	.38	-.32	.26
22	48/IV/3081-82	25 Aug 48	Consideration of schoolteacher law	-.44	.44	(.51)	-.25	.30
23	48/IV/3106	26 Aug 48	Rights and role of opposition parties	(.50)	-.39	(-.50)	.26	-.33
24	48/IV/3106	26 Aug 48	Rights and role of opposition parties	(-.53)	.40	.47	-.28	.33
25	48/IV/3168	27 Aug 48	Order of business; subsidy for hospitals in Salta	-.46	.36	.42	-.10	.24
26	48/IV/3172	27 Aug 48	Salaries for bank employees	(-.51)	.44	.47	-.14	.23
27	48/IV/3240	1 Sept 48	Reparations for earthquake in Salta	.47	-.33	-.49	.35	-.17
28	48/IV/3338	2-3 Sept 48	Interpellation of minister of agriculture	-.42	.28	.44	-.34	.33
29	48/V/3632	15 Sept 48	Order of business; information on Instituto Argentino de Promoción del Intercambio (IAPI)	-.42	.26	.38	-.43	.37
30	48/V/3639	15 Sept 48	Order of business; high cost of meat	-.48	.25	.42	-.41	.24
31	48/V/3678	16-17 Sept 48	Funds for creation of new embassies	.42	-.32	-.33	.36	-.35
32	48/V/3679	16-17 Sept 48	Order of business	.41	-.37	-.26	.38	-.36
33	48/V/3867	22-23 Sept 48	Impropriety of opposition's behavior	(.52)	-.39	-.42	.36	-.35
34	48/V/3887	22-23 Sept 48	Social security	-.46	(.53)	.26	-.34	.32
35	48/V/3888	22-23 Sept 48	Closure of debate	.42	(-.51)	-.29	.39	-.31
36	48/V/3940	23-24 Sept 48	Order of business	-.35	.31	.32	(-.50)	.29
37	48/V/3995	23-24 Sept 48	Approval of political activity by military soldiers	-.34	(.52)	.29	-.39	.22
38	48/V/4145-46	25-26 Sept 48	Salaries for journalists	-.20	.15	.35	(-.64)	.31
39	48/V/4175	25-26 Sept 48	Salaries for schoolteachers	.27	-.16	-.40	(.66)	-.06
40	48/V/4183	25-26 Sept 48	Salaries for schoolteachers	-.21	.23	.17	(-.75)	.23
41	48/V/4187	25-26 Sept 48	Salaries for schoolteachers	.31	-.27	-.27	(.73)	-.18
42	48/VI/4528	27-28 Sept 48	Old-age pensions	-.42	.22	(.54)	-.29	.12
43	48/VI/4531	27-28 Sept 48	Old-age pensions	.40	-.21	(-.65)	.31	-.24
44	48/VI/4532	27-28 Sept 48	Old-age pensions	-.43	.27	(.62)	-.26	.22
45	48/VI/4641	27-28 Sept 48	Order of business	-.27	.46	.42	-.36	.40
46	48/VI/4641	27-28 Sept 48	Order of business	.22	-.48	-.40	.34	-.40
47	48/VI/4665	29-30 Sept 48	State aid to private hospitals	-.17	.20	(.58)	-.32	.42
48	48/VI/4665	29-30 Sept 48	State aid to private hospitals	-.22	.25	(.68)	-.29	.25

Table C-22. 1948-49 (continued)

Roll-call no.	Yr./vol./p. in Diario de Sesiones	Date of vote	Issue	Factors I	II	III	IV	V
49	48/VI/4678	29-30 Sept 48	Interpellation on purchase of British-owned railroads	-.29	.47	(.50)	-.20	.24
50	48/VI/4717-18	29-30 Sept 48	Order of business	-.31	.37	(.53)	-.31	.29
51	48/VI/5215	30 Sept 48	Order of business	-.34	.38	.41	-.26	.37
52	48/VI/5216	30 Sept 48	Order of business	.36	-.41	-.44	.32	-.25
53	48/VI/5231	30 Sept 48	Order of business	-.28	(.52)	.41	-.20	.30
54	49/I/224	13 May 49	Import permits for materials needed to construct low-cost housing	-.40	.40	.04	-.37	.44
55	49/I/266	18 May 49	Leave of absence for Mauricio L. Yadarola	-.38	.19	.08	-.39	.37
56	49/I/269	18 May 49	Postponement of homage to rebellious laborers in Salta	(.61)	-.26	-.20	.38	-.31
57	49/I/279	18 May 49	Consideration of crisis in cattle industry	(.55)	-.33	-.23	.30	-.34
58	49/I/428-29	20 May 49	Lease of public land for municipal park	(.60)	-.23	-.15	.32	-.21
59	49/I/488	1 June 49	Leave of absence for Mauricio L. Yadarola	(-.56)	.35	.26	-.43	.34
60	49/I/745	8 June 49	Governance of Universidad Nacional de la Plata	(.57)	-.30	-.39	.23	-.32
61	49/I/831	15 June 49	Consideration of alleged defamation by parliament in Uruguay	(.67)	-.23	-.29	.30	-.31
62	49/I/848	15 June 49	Alleged defamation by parliament in Uruguay	(.71)	-.11	-.37	.29	-.27
63	49/I/851	15 June 49	Alleged defamation by parliament in Uruguay	(-.72)	.17	.38	-.30	.31
64	49/I/852	15 June 49	Alleged defamation by parliament in Uruguay	(-.72)	.17	.38	-.30	.31
65	49/I/854	15 June 49	Alleged defamation by parliament in Uruguay	(.60)	-.15	-.39	.34	-.37
66	49/I/901	22 June 49	Usurpation of power by Executive branch	(-.56)	.26	.37	-.34	.34
67	49/II/1236-37	30 June 49	Closing debate on policies of IAPI	(.58)	-.33	-.31	.33	-.36
68	49/II/1635	14 July 49	Authorization for sale of public real estate	(.59)	-.27	-.27	.15	(-.59)
69	49/II/1635-36	14 July 49	Authorization for sale of public real estate	(.58)	-.27	-.28	.13	(-.58)
70	49/II/1641-42	14 July 49	Authorization for sale of public real estate	(-.53)	.20	-.35	-.14	(.61)
71	49/II/1643	14 July 49	Authorization for sale of public real estate	(-.51)	.19	.33	-.19	(.66)

72	49/II/1644	14 July 49	Authorization for sale of public real estate	-.48	.23	.33	-.22	(.65)
73	49/II/1649	14 July 49	Authorization for sale of public real estate	(-.55)	.32	.26	-.25	(.50)
74	49/III/1958-59	27 July 49	Perón's verbal attack on opposition	(-.60)	.44	.29	-.27	.25
75	49/III/2031	28 July 49	Information on funding for electoral campaigns	(.58)	-.47	-.35	.16	-.31
76	49/III/2034-35	28 July 49	Acceptance of resignation by Ricardo Balbín from investigating committee	(-.56)	.43	.30	-.23	.29
77	49/III/2071	28 July 49	Athletic subsidy for youth	(.54)	(-.50)	-.34	.20	-.27
78	49/IV/3062	31 Aug 49	Investigation of personal fortunes of deputies	.48	-.35	-.33	.23	-.30
79	49/V/3425	15-16 Sept 49	Consideration of bill on governance and role of Banco Central	(-.57)	.35	.21	-.36	.36
80	49/V/3557-58	15-16 Sept 49	Governance and role of Banco Central	.54	-.33	-.26	.37	-.22
81	49/V/3579	15-16 Sept 49	Deposit guarantees through Banco Central	.40	-.30	-.23	(-.53)	-.24
82	49/V/4106	27 Sept 49	Alteration in law on job-related accidents	(-.61)	.43	.18	-.21	.18
83	49/V/4110	27 Sept 49	Law for bank employees	(-.64)	.42	.19	-.23	.11
84	49/V/4178	28-29 Sept 49	State control of cinema	(.52)	-.22	-.38	.29	-.31
85	49/V/4182	28-29 Sept 49	State control of cinema	(-.54)	.21	.30	-.27	.39
86	49/V/4186	28-29 Sept 49	State control of cinema	(.56)	-.35	-.39	.31	-.26
87	49/V/4190	28-29 Sept 49	Consideration of bill on regulation of political parties	.49	-.44	-.39	.39	-.27
88	49/V/4226	28-29 Sept 49	Regulation of political parties	.40	-.48	-.27	(.51)	-.16
89	49/V/4237	28-29 Sept 49	Regulation of political parties	.46	-.45	-.18	(.53)	-.08
90	49/VI/4256-57	29 Sept 49	Consideration of proposal to strip Ricardo Balbín of parliamentary immunities	(.52)	-.40	-.30	.38	-.37
			% of total variance explained	23.2	13.7	13.1	12.1	11.7
			% of factor variance explained	31.5	18.6	17.7	16.3	15.9

Table C-23. Rotated Factor Matrix for Contested Roll Calls in 1950-51

Roll-call no.	Yr./vol./p. in *Diario de Sesiones*	Date of vote	Issue	Factor I
1	50/I/627	22 June 50	Suspending Mauricio L. Yadarola from Chamber of Deputies	(.87)
2	50/I/684-85	28 June 50	Consideration of inter-American security pact	(.80)
3	50/I/848	5 July 50	Support for president of Chamber	(.82)
4	50/II/995	12 July 50	Homage to people of Colombia	(.77)
5	50/III/2229	7-8 Sept 50	Consideration of bill on treason	(.86)
6	50/III/2473	14-15 Sept 50	Legal role of notaries (*escribanos*)	(-.65)
7	50/IV/3351	27 Sept 50	Fundación Eva Perón	(.86)
8	50/IV/3723	30 Sept 50	Consejo Nacional de Pesca	(-.81)
			% of total variance explained	65.0
			% of factor variance explained	100.0

Table C-24. Rotated Factor Matrix for Contested Roll Calls in 1952-54

Roll-call no.	Yr./vol./p. in *Diario de Sesiones*	Date of vote	Issue	Factor I
1	52/II/934	10 Sept 52	Contribution to Fundación Eva Perón	(.83)
2	52/II/1137	23 Sept 52	Creation of Instituto Nacional de Carnes	(.84)
3	52/III/1567	28-29 Sept 52	Budget for Distrito Federal	(.82)
4	52/III/2327	11-12 Mar 53	Solidarity with Chile	(.84)
5	53/II/1136	13 Aug 53	Regulations on foreign investment	(.85)
6	53/II/1260	26 Aug 53	Contribution to Fundación Eva Perón	(.80)
7	53/II/1649	17-18 Sept 53	Social security regulations	(.81)
8	53/III/1866	24-25 Sept 53	Control of radio transmissions	(.76)
9	53/IV/2784-85	18 Dec 53	Governance of universities	(.84)
10	54/II/1067	29 July 54	Expropriation of Bemberg holdings	(.72)
11	54/II/1219-20	11 Aug 54	Consideration of subsidy to sporting club	(.80)
12	54/II/1231	11 Aug 54	Subsidy to sporting club	(.80)
13	54/III/1694	16-17 Sept 54	Violation of parliamentary privilege	(.76)
14	54/III/2114-15	29-30 Sept 54	Legal rights of illegitimate children	(.78)
			% of total variance explained	64.7
			% of factor variance explained	100.0

Bibliography

The major primary source for this study has been, of course, the *Diario de Sesiones* of the Cámara de Diputados de la Nación for 1904 through 1955, approximately 250 volumes in all (the exact number varies from collection to collection). It was by leafing through these tomes that I located the 1,712 roll-call votes which have been so central to my investigation; the transcripted debates also yield a fascinating picture of the substance and tenor of relationships among the national elites in Argentina.

Biographical information on the 1,571 deputies who served during those years has been difficult but not impossible to find. As explained in Appendix A, I determined membership in social clubs by examining the *Nómina de socios* of the Sociedad Rural Argentina (Buenos Aires, 1897, 1932, 1939, 1943, 1948, 1954), plus the roster published in the *Anales de la Sociedad Rural Argentina*, 52 (February 1918), 116-34; and the *Nómina de los socios* of the Jockey Club (Buenos Aires, 1902-1960, especially 1902, 1913, 1925, 1938, 1950, 1960). Data on political party affiliation for 1912 through 1946 have been found in Ministerio del Interior, *Las fuerzas armadas restituyen el imperio de la soberanía popular*, 2 vols. (Buenos Aires, 1946). Professor Joseph Tulchin kindly gave me a list of party affiliations for deputies serving between 1904 and 1910; and staff members at the División de Archivo, Museo, y Publicaciones del Congreso Nacional, in Buenos Aires, furnished a similar list for the period from 1946 through 1955. Comprehensive material on parliamentary tenure can be located in Cámara de Diputados, *El parlamento argentino, 1854-1951*, 2nd ed. (Buenos Aires, 1951). For information on date of birth—plus education, occupation, and other variables not used here—I have consulted a (woefully incomplete) biographical *fichero* at the División de Archivo, Museo, y Publicaciones, and a variety of published works, the most helpful being Marcelo Echevarrieta, *Argentina, sus hombres* (Buenos Aires, 1934); Guillermo Kraft Ltda., *Quien es quien en la Argentina* (Buenos Aires, 1939, 1941, 1943, 1947, 1950); R. Piccirilli, R. Romay, and L. Gianello, *Diccionario histórico argentino*, 6 vols. (Buenos Aires, 1953-54); Diego Abad de Santillán, *Gran enciclopedia argentina*, 8 vols. (Buenos Aires.

199

1956-63); Sociedad Inteligencia Sudamericana, *Hombres del día 1917, el diccionario argentino* (Buenos Aires, 1917); and Enrique Udaondo, *Diccionario biográfico argentino* (Buenos Aires, 1938).

Aside from gathering these hard data I have naturally consulted many other sources. The following list is highly selective, noting only those works (apart from those mentioned above) which have been cited in this study.

Agor, Weston H. *The Chilean Senate: Internal Distribution of Influence.* Austin, Tex., 1971.

————, ed. *Latin American Legislatures: Their Role and Influence.* New York, 1971.

Alexander, Thomas B. *Sectional Stress and Party Strength: A Study of Roll-Call Voting Patterns in the United States House of Representatives, 1836-1860.* Nashville, Tenn., 1967.

Alsina, Juan A. *La inmigración en el primer siglo de la independencia.* Buenos Aires, 1910.

Anderson, Lee F., et al. *Legislative Roll-Call Analysis.* Evanston, Ill., 1966.

Argentine Republic. Comisión del Censo Nacional. *Tercer censo nacional, levantado el 1º de junio de 1914*, 10 vols. Buenos Aires, 1917-19.

————. Dirección General de Estadística. *Anuario de la Dirección General de Estadística correspondiente al año 1912.* Buenos Aires, 1914.

————. Dirección General de Estadística. *Informes* nos. 11, 24, 33, 34, 40. Buenos Aires, 1924-33.

————. Dirección Nacional de Investigaciones, Estadística y Censos. *Síntesis estadística mensual de la República Argentina*, 1, no. 1 (January 1947).

————. División de Estadística, Departamento Nacional del Trabajo. *Estadística de las huelgas.* Buenos Aires, 1940.

Aydelotte, William O., ed. *The Dimensions of Parliamentary History.* Princeton, N.J., forthcoming.

Baily, Samuel L. *Labor, Nationalism, and Politics in Argentina.* New Brunswick, N.J., 1967.

Binder, Leonard, et al. *Crises and Sequences in Political Development.* Princeton, N.J., 1971.

Blanksten, George I. *Perón's Argentina.* Chicago, 1953.

Bosch, Mariano. *Historia del Partido Radical: la U.C.R., 1891-1930.* Buenos Aires, 1931.

Burgin, Miron. *The Economic Aspects of Argentine Federalism, 1820-1852.* Cambridge, Mass., 1946.

Cantón, Darío. *Elecciones y partidos políticos en la Argentina. Historia, interpretación y balance: 1910-1966.* Buenos Aires, 1973.

————. *Materiales para el estudio de la sociología política en la Argentina*, 2 vols. Buenos Aires, 1968.

————. *El parlamento argentino en épocas de cambio: 1889, 1916 y 1946.* Buenos Aires, 1966.

————. *La política de los militares argentinos, 1900-1971.* Buenos Aires, 1971.

————. "Universal Suffrage as an Agent of Mobilization." Paper presented at

Sixth World Congress of Sociology, Evian, France, September 1966.

Cantón, Darío, José L. Moreno, and Alberto Ciria. *Argentina: la democracia constitucional y su crisis.* Buenos Aires, 1972.

Ciria, Alberto. *Partidos y poder en la Argentina moderna (1930-1946).* Buenos Aires, 1964.

——, et al. *New Perspectives on Modern Argentina.* Bloomington, Ind., 1972.

Ciria, Alberto, and Horacio Sanguinetti. *Los reformistas.* Buenos Aires, 1968.

Coca, Joaquín. *El Contubernio: memorias de un diputado obrero.* Buenos Aires, 1961.

Columba, Ramón. *El congreso que yo he visto,* 3 vols. Buenos Aires, 1949.

Cornblit, Oscar. "El fracaso del Conservadorismo en la Argentina." Trabajo Interno no. 14, Centro de Investigaciones Sociales, Instituto Torcuato di Tella. Mimeographed. Buenos Aires, 1973.

Dahl, Robert A. *Polyarchy: Participation and Opposition.* New Haven and London, 1971.

——. *Who Governs? Democracy and Power in an American City.* New Haven and London, 1961.

Del Mazo, Gabriel. *El Radicalismo: ensayo sobre su historia y doctrina,* 3 vols. Buenos Aires, 1957.

Di Tella, Guido, and Manuel Zymelman. *Las etapas del desarrollo económico argentino.* Buenos Aires, 1967.

Di Tella, Torcuato, Gino Germani, and Jorge Graciarena, eds. *Argentina, sociedad de masas.* Buenos Aires, 1965.

Díaz Alejandro, Carlos F. *Essays on the Economic History of the Argentine Republic.* New Haven and London, 1970.

Dollar, Charles M., and Richard J. Jensen. *Historian's Guide to Statistics.* New York, 1971.

Dorfman, Adolfo. *Evolución industrial argentina.* Buenos Aires, 1942.

Economic Commission for Latin America (United Nations). "El desarrollo económico de la Argentina." Mimeographed. Santiago de Chile, 1958.

——. *El desarrollo económico de la Argentina,* 3 vols. Mexico, 1959.

Editorial Sur. *Argentina 1930-1960.* Buenos Aires, 1961.

Fennell, Lee C. "Class and Region in Argentina: A Study of Political Cleavage, 1916-1966." Ph.D. dissertation, University of Florida, 1970.

——. "Reasons for Roll Calls: An Exploratory Analysis with Argentine Data." *American Journal of Political Science,* 18, no. 2 (May 1974), 359-403.

Ferns, H. S. *Britain and Argentina in the Nineteenth Century.* London, 1960.

Ferrer, Aldo. *The Argentine Economy,* trans. Marjory M. Urquidi. Berkeley and Los Angeles, 1967.

Galletti, Alfredo. *La realidad argentina en el siglo XX: la política y los partidos.* Mexico and Buenos Aires, 1961.

Gallo, Ezequiel, and Roberto Cortés Conde. *Argentina: la república conservadora.* Buenos Aires, 1972.

Germani, Gino. *Estructura social de la Argentina: análisis estadístico*. Buenos Aires, 1955.

_____. *Política y sociedad en una época de transición: de la sociedad tradicional a la sociedad de masas*. Buenos Aires, 1963.

_____. "El surgimiento del peronismo: el rol de los obreros y de los migrantes internos." *Desarrollo Económico*, 13, no. 51 (October-December 1973), 435-88.

Goldwert, Marvin. *Democracy, Militarism, and Nationalism in Argentina, 1930-1966: An Interpretation*. Austin, Tex., 1972.

_____. "The Rise of Modern Militarism in Argentina." *Hispanic American Historical Review*, 48, no. 2 (May 1968), 189-205.

Gómez, Rosendo A. "Intervention in Argentina, 1860-1930." *Inter-American Economic Affairs*, 1, no. 3 (December 1947), 55-73.

Graham, Richard, and Peter H. Smith, eds. *New Approaches to Latin American History*. Austin, Tex., 1974.

Halperín Donghi, Tulio. *Argentina: la democracia de masas*. Buenos Aires, 1972.

Hobhouse, L. T. "Aristocracy." *Encyclopedia of the Social Sciences* (New York, 1937), I, 183-90.

Huntington, Samuel P. *Political Order in Changing Societies*. New Haven and London, 1968.

Imaz, José Luis de. *La clase alta de Buenos Aires*. Buenos Aires, 1962.

_____. *Los que mandan*. Buenos Aires, 1964.

Johnson, John J. *Political Change in Latin America: The Emergence of the Middle Sectors*. Stanford, Cal., 1958.

Kenworthy, Eldon. "The Function of the Little-Known Case in Theory Formation or What Peronism Wasn't." *Comparative Politics*, 6, no. 1 (October 1973), 17-45.

Kirkpatrick, Jeane. *Leader and Vanguard in Mass Society: A Study of Peronist Argentina*. Cambridge, Mass., and London, 1971.

Legón, Faustino, and Samuel W. Medrano. *Las constituciones de la República Argentina*. Madrid, 1953.

Lieuwen, Edwin. *Generals vs. Presidents: Neomilitarism in Latin America*. New York, 1964.

Lipset, Seymour Martin. *Political Man: The Social Bases of Politics*. Garden City, N.Y., 1963.

Linz, Juan J. "An Authoritarian Regime: Spain." In Erik Allardt and Stein Rokkan, eds., *Mass Politics: Studies in Political Sociology* (New York, 1970), pp. 251-83 and 374-81.

Little, Walter. "Electoral Aspects of Peronism, 1946-1954." *Journal of Inter-American Studies and World Affairs*, 15, no. 3 (August 1973), 267-84.

_____. "Party and State in Peronist Argentina, 1945-1955." *Hispanic American Historical Review*, 53, no. 4 (November 1973), 644-62.

_____. "La tendencia peronista en el sindicalismo argentino: el caso de los obreros de la Carne." *Aportes*, 19 (January 1971), 107-24.

Luna, Félix. *Yrigoyen.* Buenos Aires, 1964.

MacRae, Duncan, Jr. *Issues and Parties in Legislative Voting: Methods of Statistical Analysis.* New York, 1970.

_____. *Parliament, Parties, and Society in France, 1946-1958.* New York and London, 1967.

Marotta, Sebastián. *El movimiento sindical argentino,* 2 vols. Buenos Aires, 1961.

McGann, Thomas F. *Argentina, the United States, and the Inter-American System, 1880-1914.* Cambridge, Mass., 1957.

Melo, Carlos R. *Los partidos políticos argentinos,* 3rd ed. Córdoba, 1964.

Merkx, Gilbert W. "Recessions and Rebellions in Argentina, 1870-1970." *Hispanic American Historical Review,* 53, no. 2 (May 1973), 285-95.

Murmis, Miguel, and Juan Carlos Portantiero. *Estudios sobre los orígenes del peronismo,* vol. I. Buenos Aires, 1971.

Newton, Jorge. *Historia de la Sociedad Rural Argentina.* Buenos Aires, 1966.

Newton, Jorge, and Lily de Newton. *Historia del Jockey Club de Buenos Aires.* Buenos Aires, 1966.

Oddone, Jacinto. *La burguesía terrateniente argentina,* 2nd ed. Buenos Aires, 1936.

O'Donnell, Guillermo A. *Modernization and Bureaucratic-Authoritarianism: Studies in South American Politics.* Berkeley, Cal., 1973.

Payne, James L. "The Oligarchy Muddle." *World Politics,* 20, no. 3 (April 1968), 439-53.

[Perón, Juan]. *Perón expone su doctrina.* Buenos Aires, 1947.

Portnoy, Leopoldo. *La realidad argentina en el siglo XX: análisis crítico de la economía.* Mexico and Buenos Aires, 1961.

Potash, Robert A. *The Army and Politics in Argentina, 1928-1945.* Stanford, Cal., 1969.

Ramos, Jorge Abelardo. *Revolución y contrarrevolución en la Argentina: las masas en nuestra historia.* Buenos Aires, 1957.

Remorino, Jerónimo, et al. *Anales de legislación argentina, 1852-1954,* 5 vols. Buenos Aires, 1953-57.

Rock, David, "Machine Politics in Buenos Aires and the Argentine Radical Party, 1912-1930." *Journal of Latin American Studies,* 4, no. 2 (November 1972), 233-56.

Rummel, R. J. *Applied Factor Analysis.* Evanston, Ill., 1970.

Sarobe, José María. *Memorias sobre la revolución del 6 de septiembre de 1930.* Buenos Aires, 1957.

Schoultz, Lars. "A Diachronic Analysis of Peronist Electoral Behavior." Ph.D. dissertation, University of North Carolina, 1973.

Scobie, James R. *Argentina: A City and a Nation,* 2nd ed. New York, 1971.

_____. "Buenos Aires as a Commercial-Bureaucratic City, 1880-1910: Characteristics of a City's Orientation." *American Historical Review,* 77, no. 4 (October 1972), 1035-73.

_____. *Revolution on the Pampas: A Social History of Argentine Wheat, 1860-1910.* Austin, Tex., 1964.

Sheldon, Eleanor Bernert, and Wilbert E. Moore, eds. *Indicators of Social Change: Concepts and Measurements*. New York, 1968.

Siegel, Sidney. *Nonparametric Statistics for the Behavioral Sciences*. New York, 1956.

Silvert, Kalman H., ed. *Expectant Peoples: Nationalism and Development*. New York, 1963.

Skidmore, Thomas E. "The Populist Politician as Inflation-Fighter: The Stabilization Policies of Juan Perón, 1943-1955." Unpublished manuscript.

Smelser, Neil J., and Seymour Martin Lipset, eds. *Social Structure and Mobility in Economic Development*. Chicago, 1966.

Smith, Peter H. "The Breakdown of Democracy in Argentina, 1916-1930." Paper presented at the Seventh World Congress of Sociology, Varna, Bulgaria, September 1970.

_____. *Politics and Beef in Argentina: Patterns of Conflict and Change*. New York and London, 1969.

_____. "The Social Base of Peronism." *Hispanic American Historical Review*, 52, no. 1 (February 1972), 55-73.

_____. "Social Mobilization, Political Participation, and the Rise of Juan Perón." *Political Science Quarterly*, 84, no. 1 (March 1969), 30-49.

Snow, Peter G. *Political Forces in Argentina*. Boston, 1971.

[Sociedad Rural Argentina]. *Anuario de la Sociedad Rural Argentina*. Buenos Aires, 1928.

Solberg, Carl. "Decline into Peonage: The Fate of Argentina's Gaucho Population, 1860-1930." Unpublished manuscript.

_____. *Immigration and Nationalism: Argentina and Chile, 1890-1914*. Austin, Tex., 1970.

_____. "Rural Unrest and Agrarian Policy in Argentina, 1912-1930." *Journal of Inter-American Studies and World Affairs*, 13, no. 1 (January 1971), 18-52.

_____. "The Tariff and Politics in Argentina, 1916-1930." *Hispanic American Historical Review*, 53, no. 2 (May 1973), 260-84.

Sonquist, John A., and James N. Morgan. *The Detection of Interaction Effects: A Report on a Computer Program for the Selection of Optimal Combinations of Explanatory Variables*. Ann Arbor, Mich., 1964.

Spalding, Hobart, ed. *La clase trabajadora argentina (documentos para su historia – 1890/1912)*. Buenos Aires, 1970.

_____. "Education in Argentina, 1890-1914: The Limits of Oligarchical Reform." *Journal of Interdisciplinary History*, 3, no. 1 (Summer 1972), 31-61.

Stone, Lawrence. *The Crisis of the Aristocracy, 1558-1641*. London and New York, 1965.

Strout, Richard Robert. *The Recruitment of Candidates in Mendoza Province, Argentina*. Chapel Hill, N.C., 1968.

[Uriburu, José Félix]. *La palabra del General Uriburu*, 2nd ed. Buenos Aires, 1933.

Vollmer, Howard M., and Donald L. Mills, eds. *Professionalization*. Engle-wood Cliffs, N.J., 1967.

Waldmann, Peter. "Las cuatro fases del gobierno peronista." *Aportes*, 19 (January 1971), 94-106.

Walter, Richard J. *Student Politics in Argentina: The University Reform and Its Effects, 1918-1964*. New York and London, 1968.

Weisberg, Herbert F. "Scaling Models for Legislative Roll-Call Analysis." *American Political Science Review*, 66, no. 4 (December 1972), 1306-15.

Wilensky, Harold L. "The Professionalization of Everyone?" *American Journal of Sociology*, 70, no. 2 (September 1964), 137-58.

Zuvekas, Clarence, Jr. "Economic Growth and Income Distribution in Post-war Argentina." *Inter-American Economic Affairs*, 20 no. 3 (Winter 1966), 19-38.

Index

Specific items in figures and tables are not included in this index; for guidance consult the List of Figures and the List of Tables on pages ix-x and xi-xii.

207

COMPOSED BY FOCUS/TYPOGRAPHERS, ST. LOUIS, MISSOURI
MANUFACTURED BY CUSHING-MALLOY, INC., ANN ARBOR, MICHIGAN
TEXT IS SET IN PRESS ROMAN, DISPLAY LINES IN TIMES ROMAN

Library of Congress Cataloging in Publication Data

Smith, Peter H
Argentina and the failure of democracy.

Bibliography: p. 199-205
1. Argentine Republic—Politics and government.
I. Title.

F2848.S64   320.9'82'06   74-5907
ISBN 0-299-06600-2